P9-DHT-326

THE WELL HOUSE

A STORY OF WAR, PEACE, LOVE AND FOREVER

By

Mark Van Voorhis
&
Ed Kugler

1663 Liberty Drive, Suite 200
Bloomington, Indiana 47403
(800) 839-8640
www.AuthorHouse.com

This book is a work of fiction. Places, events, and situations in this story are purely fictional and any resemblance to actual persons, living or dead, is coincidental.

First published by AuthorHouse 12/21/04

ISBN: 1-4208-0957-1 (e)
ISBN: 1-4208-0958-X (sc)
ISBN: 1-4208-0959-8 (dj)

Library of Congress Control Number: 2004098861

Printed in the United States of America
Bloomington, Indiana

This book is printed on acid-free paper.

Dedication

We dedicate this book to the men and women of our Armed Forces. We thank them past and present for their dedication, sacrifice and honor. You give us hope that our constitutional freedoms will always be preserved.

Acknowledgements

I would like to thank my wife Gloria and daughters Cortney Vance, Whitney and Shawna Kugler … your help has been invaluable and your inspiration essential.

Ed Kugler

I would like to thank my wife Joannie and our children, Vanessa, Megan, Dabney, Caleb, Kristin and Josh for their support during this wonderful journey. I am deeply grateful to archivist Kathleen D. Connors for her historical research, illustrations and poetry. She gave Maggie's letters the breath of life.

Mark Van Voorhis

Author's Notes
The Rose Well House

This open structure in the heart of the IU campus was a gift from Theodore F. Rose in 1908 and covers the original well for IU. It is listed on the National Register for Historical Landmarks.

Tradition holds that a female student is not officially a co-ed until she has been kissed beneath its dome at midnight.

Where am I? What am I? Am I in hell? I hurt. Oh, I hurt. Am I alive? I must be. I can't see. I can't move. Maggie? Where's Maggie?

Riggs's mind raced … wildly out of control. Anxiety smothered his soul while streams of blood dripped from his eyebrows. *What is it?* A vicious battle raged in his mind as he fought for air and anything that made sense. *What am I feeling, anything, anything but pain? I have to move. I have to get out of here ... wherever here is.*

Riggs dug deep, prying inside what was once his soul. The young Marine frantically searched for even an ounce of the strength and endurance he once used to dominate the courts of old Hope High. Right now he needed each ounce of courage that struggled to survive in every dark space of his near dead body.

As he pushed down, his hands sunk, swallowed in cold slime. His arms shook violently as he fought to rise from the dead. He was suffocating, as if death itself was a cold, dark blanket that sucked the life from his every breath. *I've gotta' get up. I've gotta' go! I can't die! I won't die here, far from Maggie, in a war I don't understand.*

He twisted his neck in a vain effort to live. Pain streaked through his body like a hot bullet. With one eye open, Riggs peered into an ugliness disguised as morning. *Light. I can see light but nothing else. Oh my God! The wretched smell of rotting bodies. Where am I? Where is Maggie? Maggie?*

Riggs was at the ass end of a bitter lesson disguised as a new day in Vietnam. *My God! My God! My God! I woke up in hell?* PFC Clayton Wesley Riggs, USMC, farm boy from Hope, Indiana, never imagined a day quite like this.

I'm going to die. I can't. I won't die ten thousand miles from the sweet smell and warm smile of Maggie O'Reilly. She loves me.

Riggs was buried inside a mass of humanity, heavy lifeless pieces that just hours ago were fellow Marines but now covered him with death and the smell of a thousand rotten eggs. As he poked his head free of the stifling mass, he was a lone rose coming to life in a parched desert. The kid from Hope looked around, soaked in misery and dripping in devastation, and began to quietly sob.

Suddenly, ignited by a strange presence, he knew he wasn't alone. Riggs's body quivered as the cold barrel of an AK-47 pressed hard against the side of his head. *This is it ... this is the end.* Closing his eyes, Riggs waited for the earth-shattering boom of the AK.

Goodbye Maggie, I love you ... Forever.

1

November 13, 1982
Washington D.C.

Dear Beverly,

This morning I awoke from a dream that had spun me yet again into that ethereal space where minds and souls meet across an ancient plateau. My spiritual senses experienced images I knew were real.

I can guess what you are thinking—here I am writing another rambling letter to Big Sis who already understands me thoroughly, when I should be writing to Poor Mother about why I have abandoned my "last chance at happiness" by not marrying Richard. Here I am going off again about Clayton, the-one-that-got-away, the one who first and forever shared my heart.

But something has happened—it all connects; I think I'm figuring it out. So now I need to write it all down to sort it out in my mind, and send it on to my Eternal audience of one—that's you, Beverly.

You can see from the stationery that I am staying at the Watergate Hotel! I booked it so I could revel in the great history, talk to the walls and hope they talk back. So far I've not heard a word.

The Tribune sent me to D.C for today's dedication of The Wall, the new Vietnam memorial designed by some undergrad, and a Chinese-American woman named Lin who won the competition—good for her!

I arrived yesterday just in time to miss the height of the Veteran's Day hoopla (this has been going on all week) and decided to take a peek at the artwork before the ceremony made the crowds impossible.

It's a real knock out, Beverly, stunning almost beyond words, with an impact nearing the ape-meets-

obelisk scene in the movie 2001 with that fabulous music and cosmic sense of wonder and awe. You get this "nothing-will-ever-be-the-same" feeling standing in front of it, at least when you think about the consequences of Vietnam.

It's a vast 500-foot long V-shaped wall of glossy black granite with over 58,000 names of Americans lost in the war engraved forever in stone. And there I was, like everyone else, searching for that one name that would certainly be there--that one name that drew you in and scared you at the same time.

I'm struggling to capture it, the deep sense of sadness and shock, beauty and closure, memory and love that everyone seemed to be feeling as a shared family. All of this was mixed together with the dead and the living.

Of course he was there: Clayton Wesley Riggs. I read his name like Braille with my touch, eyes closed, as if I were reaching out to him. This was not a monument of cold marble in front of me but the warm man lost but somehow found in this new public plane, this long black scroll hardened into history. It was chilling—and unforgettable.

But in my early morning dream I returned to those names again, moving closer and closer, wearing a bright red dress and black lacy widow's veil of sorts, gliding toward this vivid and glowing dark aura, this unspeakably wide tombstone, to find Clay's name amongst the others.

But just as I touched its surface to trace the letters, I knew his name was not there with a certainty as sure as any waking state. It wasn't. Not only was his name missing, my hand passed right through the surface of the granite like it was a dark pool of water, and then I moved through it to a bright morning jungle riverside scene that must be the countryside of Vietnam. There were sounds of strange birds and insects and a woman *in a broad-rimmed straw hat gliding in a small boat down a river that snaked through the trees.*

As I came out of the dream, my bones told me, "even if he is among the missing in action, assumed dead, with no word for fifteen years, all hope abandoned by family and friends, that this friend, (his bestest friend ever he called me) is not totally convinced of his death."

We all know Grandmother had the "second sight" and we all used to joke about how that was the only inheritance I would get from her. Yet, when I have a vision like this I feel it is true. Thanks Grandmother!

So when I faced the real black obsidian wall of names it reminded me of the space across a vast expanse like a lake or desert where Clayton and I still meet in my imagination. It's a place where both men and women can see the face of God, touch His hem, and know that God's love is truth and truth is God's love. It goes on forever and nothing can separate those who face themselves across that field. If Clay is only alive in one place where we have no solid form, but exists as a spirit body with feelings and emotions, then he is still alive in any case.

My love has kept him alive, and he still comes to me in this field. Though I cannot touch his hand he smiles at me and we have no need for words. Can you imagine Beverly, me with no need for words? That is a miracle in its own right...

Just before sitting down to write you this morning, I was thinking that with all I've been through with this man, what evidence was there on the face of the earth of our friendship? It's like we are water sculptors, whose designs disappear as soon as they are created.

Sure the column I write will bear his name and the reader can see that we were friends—even strangers will know we were close and that I mourned his loss, but these words in the column are written for those I will never meet.

And here's a strange coincidence: two days ago while I was going through my files on the war to refresh my facts and reorient myself to those turbulent years, I came upon my drafts of the twelve letters, my Christmas gift to Clayton while he was on the frontline and I realized I started writing fifteen years ago today—the day of the Wall's dedication!

I remember it well, the 13th of November 1967, because I began composing the dozen letters for Clayton, to be read one-a-day starting on December 13, with the last one on Christmas Eve. I began the letters before going home for Thanksgiving, and perhaps you remember what a state I was in, trying to trace the line that connected him in the battlefield to me safe at home with my family. We were getting ready to feed 'til we dropped, and mother was upset because she knew I was thinking about him and his friends facing death and fighting in that strange land for some vague cause no one understood.

I know it was the worst Thanksgiving for our family. Ever! And I may have ruined it, and to think a mere nine months later, like the birth of some horrid creature, we had the Democratic National Convention within miles of our own home! More unforgettable sadness; why should we forget? That's what "The Wall" is about, giving us a place to bring our memories and mourning to the surface. It is terribly beautiful—and sad – yet necessary.

Another thing: just as surely as Clayton's name was not there in my dream, I know that those twelve letters I sent him were delivered to him. I could almost feel him opening one each day, peeling away the veils that covered my feelings, until the last letter on Christmas Eve gave them all away, feelings I imagined might or might not be a secret to him.

I came to this realization, just this morning after my dream, when I tried to trace its meaning. It wasn't just the last letter that gave away my secret... it was that each letter gave away some important part of me, and if you placed them all together, I would be there in full.

The first gave him my vision as an artist, my image of him at the Well House on the Bloomington campus—do you remember that portrait I was so proud of? This was the beginning. The second offered my view from the "tower" at the Union Building. As a writer for the Daily Student I could not escape being a critic of war, having lies perpetrated on innocent men and women who were willing to die in some faraway land for this elusive American dream of freedom.

Then it was my memory of places and the whole range of feelings from affection to surprise to anger all mixed in with things we had done while mere kids at Indiana University-- all this together with the silly pictures and poems and ribbons thrown in and lipstick kisses on perfumed pages. By the last letter I had given away the layers of my mind and body to reveal my heart and in the end, there was nothing left to give.

From that Christmas on, I knew that he knew, because the winds on that plane where we met were rushing and encircling us like a golden belt, holding us tight and expanding at the same time. It was reminiscent of that gorgeous Ewan McCall song where he, "twists the sweet river Thames into a bracelet for his love's wrist, a gift of jewels all the same." That was me, Beverly.

Don't you see? That is why I cannot marry the lovely and oh-so-adoring Richard, as good a man as he is; I had already given my heart to Clayton long ago. I knew while looking into my fiancé's blue eyes, the man I was supposed to love and cherish forever, they were Clayton's brown eyes I longed to see. And in some way those eyes still look at me; their gaze has never left me. No one should start a partnership feeling like this, poised in uncertainty on the invisible corner of a triangle that haunts and burns in a slow flame never to be extinguished.

So maybe you and Mother are right—I threw my private life away chasing after a dream of a knight in shining armor, to whom no one can ever compare... especially since he was dead and would not grow old or boring, fat or indifferent, glued to the tube or drinking with friends, ignoring wife and children, or even being narrow-minded and mean or all the things you say happen in marriage. Wait-a-minute—shall I blame you for turning me away from this hallowed institution?

You may be right, but I will only say this to you, since I cannot write this in my column or say it to Mother or Richard or anyone else: I know he's out there Beverly. I know he's watching me and waiting for me to find him, even if it is only his spirit.

I feel like Jane Eyre at the crossroads of her life, when she too considered marriage to a man who was not The One, but was drawn back by the spirit of Rochester to the place, his home, where they had fallen in love. Someday I too will go back. I will go back to the Well House standing on the edge of the small patch of woods that will never be replaced with limestone and cement.

I need to get dressed for the dedication; and yes, I will wear my red dress but without black veil or black anything. I will not concede to this tradition of basking your limbs in the color of death. (How many will be wearing the white of Vietnamese mourners? Where is their monument?)

I prefer the color of living blood, even if it is spilt over the length of 500 feet and farther into the river waters of that jungle where he was lost. I will write about the event and the black obelisk that does and does not hold Clayton's name. I'll let you know how it goes.

P.S. Don't tell Mother I am here—she thinks I am still obsessed with the Vietnam experience, always chasing ghosts (but you don't think that, do you Beverly?) She can read about it when it's out.

P.P.S. Hello to Ben and the kids. I'll bring back some cool souvenirs.

Love,

Maggie

2

December 10, 1967
In the air – heading to Vietnam

It was only the fourth plane Clayton Riggs had ever been on in his life. He flew the first time from Indianapolis to Charleston for the ride to Parris Island. Then he flew from Charleston back to Indianapolis for leave, then from Indy to LAX and now he was one of a few hundred, a full 707 load of fresh recruits winging their way on a Continental charter bound for some place called Da Nang, South Vietnam.

The sign read "10,000 miles that way" with an arrow pointing west. No one knew if it was 10,000 miles to Vietnam, but they did know the ride would be eighteen hours non-stop.

The thought of eighteen hours in a cramped airline seat was too much for anyone, especially Clayton Wesley Riggs. A seasoned flier of four whole flights, he still wasn't comfortable up in the air. He wasn't sure he'd ever be comfortable after this flight.

He was asleep, fast asleep, mostly to escape the wild antics, raucous laughter and party atmosphere that filled the cabin to overflowing. He fell asleep remembering his last promise to Mom, that he wouldn't come home talking like a Marine, even if the Riggs family genes were chock full of Marine green. Mom knew too well what Marine language really was and she wasn't going to stand for it.

It was near the eleventh hour mark of the trip when Riggs woke up for a second time. The noise remained on high and he was sure he'd die from the splitting headache he now endured along with an upset stomach.

He sat up from sleeping against the window. His neck was cramped, his back hurt and he was dead tired. He felt worse than he did after a day hauling in three loads of green hay on a blazing hot Indiana afternoon dripping in humidity that made you fight for every breath. He sat cramped in a window seat, needing to use the Head so bad he was about to hold himself like the little boy who used to sheepishly walk the halls back at Hope Elementary.

The guy in the middle seat was up trying to put the moves on one of the stewardesses, along with a planeload of other young Marines with some variation of the same line.

How could they be so foolish?

Riggs excused himself and climbed over a young Marine sitting in the aisle seat. He weaved his way up the aisle to the miniature head, still barely comfortable calling the bathroom a "head" as it made no sense to the simple young farmer following in his family's footsteps. His Mom thought it was something dirty the first time he said it at home. In all the years living with Homer she'd never picked up the term, a term he probably knew far better than to use around her.

Finishing his business, he clawed his way out of the tiny room that was getting its share of work with this crowd. He felt better just being up and stretching his sore muscles. As he forced his way back down the aisle, it reminded him of the crowds he often fought on a busy day at the Indiana State Fair. The fair was wall-to-wall people having fun all day long and into the night.

These "leathernecks" might be having fun now ... but how many are coming home to tell their tales?

Riggs couldn't help but think of the painful reality. It was inevitable. Some of these guys weren't coming home and he might be one of them.

The mere thought of not coming home took its toll. Back in his seat, Riggs closed his eyes and decided to "trip out" and go back home, his home sweet home in Hope, Indiana. He thought of Maggie and how she'd surprised him at the airport as he left on this trip "across the pond" as Grandpa was fond of saying. He felt great just thinking of Maggie and all the times they shared.

The Marines and Vietnam just a few short months ago were no more than another news item taking up space in the local weekly paper, The Hope Star Journal. Now he found himself sitting on a jet streaking off into the night sky and in-to what … he wasn't quite sure.

Riggs turned, gazing through the tiny window of the 707, wanting to reach out and touch the puffs of white, the clouds that blanketed the darkening sky while inside, another load of raw meat, mere teenagers, were happily jetting off to a destiny only God knew. Clayton Wesley Riggs wasn't sure what he knew right now. He left everything he knew back at the airport in Indianapolis.

Maybe this thirteen- month tour will go as fast as the last thirteen months have. Yea, maybe everything will be fine. Maybe.

His mind churned like water boiling in the spring rapids, swirling, sinking him deeper and deeper into his own little world. It was a world that seemed to be moving 500 miles per hour. The clouds were turning a hint of orange on the top edges, as the sun dropped in the western sky. The beautiful glow was a testimony of the approaching night and a blessing Maggie often reminded him came from God.

I can't believe it's been over a year since Maggie and I met. I really can't. It's like yesterday. It's like I've always known her.

The loud laughter and belligerent clowning around dominated the cabin. The noise and verbal madness made it impossible to stay in dreamland for long. Riggs, always the quiet thinker, was more focused than anyone on the plane and remembered his basketball coach telling him to lighten up. But Clayton Riggs didn't lighten up and wouldn't be denied his private dreamland express right now. He sat back and closed his eyes.

I really can't believe Maggie O'Reilly ever gave me a second look. I can't imagine the summer we've had. I was never unhappy growing up at home but until I met Maggie I didn't know what being truly happy meant. I didn't know joy or maybe I didn't even know fun because I didn't know Maggie then.

There were five, maybe six more hours left in the air before the big bird full of vibrant young men would land in Vietnam. Riggs relaxed in spite of the annoying commotion he was growing to hate more with each passing hour. He longed to have a moment of silence, just one more minute dreaming of his new best friend.

I can't believe she drove up and met us at the airport. What a surprise it was to turn around and see her standing behind Mom. I don't know if Dad or I was more surprised. Sometimes Dad is really out of it and this was one of those times for sure. He doesn't like Maggie and he didn't hide it either.

Clayton's dad, Homer Riggs, had no use for anyone that opposed the war against communism, and Maggie's family fell into that category. It didn't take Homer long to pick up on the fact that the O'Reilly family were pacifists and against the Vietnam War. That was like lighting a match inside an empty gas can. Homer saw more than red. He saw people he didn't want to know, much less be around, especially as his only son went off to war.

Clayton had split his time last summer between the farm and his newly discovered girl friend, Maggie O'Reilly. He was careful to point out she was just a "friend," not really a "girlfriend." That was something Daddy Riggs didn't get at all. He didn't "get" a lot of things and it all added up to a tough summer for him as well as Momma Riggs. It became a lot tougher when he had to send his only son off to war, a war he wasn't sure he believed in but one his upbringing required he support.

If Dad would just get to know her as I do, I know he'd feel the same way I do about her. I just know he would. She is a beautiful person. I know he'd love her as I do. Do I love her? Do I?

If looks could send you home in a hurry, Homer would have sent Maggie packing with one glance when she showed up at the Indianapolis International Airport for the Riggs's farewell. It was supposed to be a private affair and no "girlfriend" was going to take away from his son's farewell. She wasn't invited and shouldn't be crashing the party and messing things up.

But steal the show she did.

Her strawberry blonde hair was so beautiful. It was a perfect match with her pure, kind, almost saintly personality. She always dressed so neat and ... well, cute. Her smiles... oh man ... what I wouldn't give to see that smile right now.

There was a riot going on near the plane's galley. It wasn't really a riot but it sure sounded like one. One of the many guys from the east coast stood tall above the rest. As far as Riggs was concerned the east coast crowd was worse than the rest, that's for sure.

"Where's that pig farmer? Souie, Souie, Souie!" It was a guy everyone was calling Glubo. He was a loudmouth Italian from somewhere back east like Pittsburg or Philly. Riggs was learning the city guys were the ones making all the noise and causing all the problems.

"Where the hell is that pig farmer?" Glubo looked Riggs's way as he blasted off with one smart remark after another.

I can't believe it. I trust one guy, tell him something about myself and now everyone on the plane knows, worst of all, this guy.

Glubo made his way down the aisle looking side-to-side, searching for the pig farmer. About two rows in front of Riggs, he locked on like his radar just kicked in.

"There he is!" he announced with all the authority of a hijacker with the "kahunas" to take over a plane full of U.S. Marines.

It was clear this guy was the source of most of the noise that prevented Riggs from winging his way to Nam with nothing but Maggie on his mind. The last thing he wanted was this bullhorn honing in and making a scene.

Glubo had had more than a few laughs at the expense of the kid from Hope and his pigs back home. He moved on down the aisle in search of a "Georgia Cracker." Whatever and whoever that was, Riggs didn't know.

I don't mind the Marine Corps but I do mind people like that. I don't like people making fun of other people or interrupting me right now. I just want to be left alone to dream of what I miss the most.

Riggs wanted nothing more but to "trip out" and go back outside the window and imagine he was riding the now dark clouds of cotton disappearing in the young night sky. He really wanted to be back in Indiana with his family and with Maggie, his good friend, his best friend and the one who made him feel better than he'd ever felt before in his entire life.

Oh Maggie ... at least now, after surprising me at the airport, I know we're friends again. She shocked me so much by kissing me on the cheek as I walked away ... in front of my parents too. I couldn't believe it and Dad would never understand we were just friends after all. But I can still feel her soft, warm lips on my cheek. I hope I can always remember them.

Riggs wondered if they could ever be more than good friends. Maybe they could; she came to the airport to see him off. But he still lived with the little shadow of self-doubt that followed him around reminding him he was from a farm in Hope, Indiana, and she was from the gold coast of Chicago's north side. Just being friends was a big accomplishment and one he'd have to be happy with, at least for now.

I'm so happy she came to see me. After surprising her like I did at school this fall with the news of my joining the Corps, I just knew I'd never see her again. I'll never forget the look of pain on her face when I told her I was not going back to school but was leaving for Parris Island and the Marines. I could see I broke her heart; it was written all over her beautiful face.

It never seemed that Maggie was as serious about the anti-war thing as her parents were. She was active in the movement on campus at IU but didn't seem as serious as some of her friends. Riggs never let it get to him; he felt it was okay to have differences and still be friends. He'd been raised in a family who fought for freedom and freedom was the right to do what you wanted.

I hurt her like I don't ever want to hurt anyone again. I think I'm a Christian; at least Mom wants me to be and I trust her. I don't know about religion and church but I do try to be a good person. I hate how I made her feel; it was like I violated her in some deep, emotional way. I can hardly live with myself for the hurt I caused. I will never forget the look on her face.

It was soon dark, the cabin lights were down and for the first time … things were quiet. Riggs looked around and realized that the majority of the Marines were worn out, fast asleep. He didn't even hear Glubo roaring above the crowd.

He turned to look out and his window was black; there were no clouds to peer at, and no white fluffy cushions to imagine bouncing across like the Shoaf kids bouncing on their trampoline in the yard across the meadow. They were his long-time neighbors that he wouldn't see or hear from for thirteen long months.

I had to make the decision I did... I had to join the Marines. Yet I never really thought I would. Dad was in the Corps and talked about duty, honor and country my whole life, but to me they were just words. And the whole God, country and Corps thing ... well I just couldn't imagine me doing it.

Sundays? I remember them well. It was chicken, gravy, homemade mashed potatoes and noodles and family time. Our table was the site of stories of the wars of our family. There were stories every Sunday of Uncle Ben, Chesty Puller and the Frozen Chosin in Korea. Then it was time for Grandpa Riggs and his stories of World War I, whatever that was. But they were exciting times for me.

Growing up in the Midwest, on a farm in Indiana, with a family of Marines was enough to make you bleed red, white and blue. Riggs new the drill from early in life and wanted to march tall and be a Marine like all the stories he'd heard all his life. He often wondered if he really knew what that meant.

He was gung ho like the family expected until he met Maggie O'Reilly. He was hypnotized by how she made him feel with a mere glance. He couldn't believe her warmth, tenderness and kindness. Most of all, she made him realize he wanted to be a better person. He liked how he felt when she was near.

I just knew I blew it. I knew when I told her I'd decided to join the Marines; she'd never speak to me again. Wow! I just knew I was right too. She would never speak to me, the "farm boy," again.

Speeding along in the black of night, Riggs new he was lucky, lucky to have Maggie O'Reilly as a good friend. He didn't know why he had her, but he was sure glad he did.

Those days in boot camp were the toughest days of my life. Parris Island was tough. It was tough in training and tougher because Maggie didn't write ... not once. It was twelve long weeks and I knew it was over. A special friendship gone because of a choice I made--a choice I felt I had to make and yet one I regretted.

Night wore on like a bad sock on a long march. The 707 chock full of fresh "meat" streaking towards a place Riggs barely knew existed until just a short time ago. He wondered what it would be like, being a Marine and all, like his Dad and Grandpa. Would it be hot? Would he see people die? Even imagining horror couldn't stop him from thinking about Maggie O'Reilly.

I am one lucky guy. Most of these guys have no idea what it would mean to have a friend like her. All they talk about and all they think about is how to get their "girl" in bed. Maggie isn't that kind of girl. I don't even think of her in "that way" really. I just know how she makes me feel better than I've ever felt. I want more of that, with her. I know I can be more than a pig farmer. I know I can.

The black night streaked along as fast as the jet they were riding. It whisked Riggs away as he recalled his relationship with that special person. He traced every step of how they met, where they went, what they did, and how they talked for hours long into the night. He could even remember their words and phrases as if they had just been spoken.

He couldn't help but think how different they really were, almost from two different worlds. He was a full-fledged farm boy from the Midwest. She was a rich girl from Chicago; only she didn't act like a rich girl.

She was made for college from the get-go while education for him was a long shot at best. He was driven by a desire to have something-- he wasn't sure what--but something better than what he perceived his family had. He wanted more, and he felt it was somehow possible with Maggie.

Riggs wasn't ashamed of his family but he didn't want to be a pig farmer his whole life like his Dad. He loved his Dad and especially his Mom; she was always there for him. He didn't always understand his Dad and the whole Marine thing but he knew from early on he was destined to one day live out the dream they had for him. It was a dream that came with being a Riggs.

I knew I had to go in the "Corps." I knew it since I was little but I didn't know it would take me away from a life I was beginning to enjoy. Of course I didn't know I would meet someone that made me feel so much more than I'd ever felt...someone who made me feel alive...someone who made me see I could be more than a farmer.

From the time Maggie and Clayton met at the Well House on the campus of Indiana University at Bloomington, he felt like he'd been sprinkled with pixie dust. He was smitten like a little boy on his birthday that'd just received his first puppy.

The differences always worried him. Just how long would she put up with someone like him? A pig farmer and a golden girl, a match even he couldn't imagine working out. What made it worse were the other differences, the family differences that made any ideas about something more than being best friends impossible to even dream about.

It was a choice I just had to make. Dad has been so upset with the protests and the Vietnam War. How could I do anything but join the United States Marine Corps? It was something I had to do. In spite of how Maggie felt about the whole thing, I had to do it. I hope some day she'll understand. She came to the airport; maybe she at least accepts me for what I am. I sure hope she writes me like she said she would at the airport.

The O'Reilly and Riggs families couldn't be more different. Maggie grew up with wealth, with parents who graduated from college. They graduated from Berkeley no less! The Riggs family was three-generations of farmers and two generations of Marines. Grandpa Riggs fought in The War to End All Wars; World War I; his younger brother, Dad's Uncle Ben, died fighting with Chesty Puller in Korea; while Clayton's Dad fought in the islands during World War II and survived to carry on a burning desire to serve the country he loved.

The O'Reilly kids got their beliefs as honestly as the Riggs. Maggie was against Vietnam and any war anywhere. Her strong and spirited commitment made Riggs struggle to spend time with her in and around the campus protests. He wanted to understand her actions but knew he came from a family that saw life differently.

She was always going away to Chicago on weekends to participate in anti-war activities. He even snuck away one time just to be with her. She seemed to like that a lot. He went with her to one protest but he knew that was one truth that could never be discussed inside the four walls of the Riggs home.

What might have been? What if I hadn't joined the Marines? What if I had stayed in school? I guess I would have been drafted and I couldn't bring myself to end up in the Army. But I may play these "what ifs" my whole life. If only I hadn't surprised her and not come back to school and ...

Morning was showing signs of life as the sun came up outside the Boeing 707 charter. Inside, the plane was coming to life too. Riggs had come to the realization that his life was going to be very different. Yes, life for Riggs was going to be very, very different and he wasn't quite sure what that meant.

Man, the white beaches, the sand ... there's green vegetation everywhere ... it looks beautiful ... how could it be as bad as they say? Vietnam looks like a gorgeous place.

I wish Maggie could see this ... I wish I could walk that beach with her. I wish I could talk to her and tell her why I joined the Corps and why I didn't go back to school with her. Most of all I wish I could tell her how much I appreciated her meeting me at the airport when I left. I wish ...

"This is your Captain speaking," the pilot brought everyone to reality with a blaring interruption explaining they were about to land. It was a plane full of kids about to drop from the sky into hostile territory known to them only as Vietnam.

"Fasten your seat belts and be ready to debark quickly."

Wow ... it doesn't look that bad. Maybe it won't be like they say. Maybe all this will go away and Washington will make peace. Maybe the protestors are right and this will come to an end. Maybe.

"Gentlemen … I wish you all the best. Godspeed and good luck my young friends."

Now that's a scary way to bring in new troops. Does he know something we don't? I ... well I'm sure he does.

The plane straightened out from a steep left bank and headed down to the Tarmac of the Da Nang Marine Air Base. The tires screeched and with a windy bump and roll … Clayton Wesley Riggs had touched down along with several dozen other United States Marines.

"Welcome to the Republic of South Vietnam, Gentlemen."

3

December11, 1967
Da Nang, Vietnam & On to the front.

Da Nang was a big surprise to everyone, but then no one knew what to expect, least of all Clayton Riggs. It was hot. Hot, muggy and mind melting. Sweat poured from the new men like a pot of potatoes boiling over on Momma's stove way back home. The air stood thick and hung like a wet rug.

Welcome to Vietnam. Man this is terrible.

It was hot. Hot and filthy, filthy beyond anything Riggs had ever imagined, and being a pig farmer, he could imagine more filth than most. There was mud everywhere. It was an ugly place with an uglier air about it.

There wasn't time to worry about the hot air or the dirt or the explosions echoing from the surrounding hills. There was only time to listen up Marine Corps style.

"Get your gear and grab your rear and move it out!" the sergeant in charge bellowed through the thick air, bringing the Marines to the reality they were still in the Corps.

I can't believe I have to live like this for thirteen whole months. I just can't believe it. I can't believe I'm really here.

"You've all been organized in companies to get your young asses here," the sergeant continued his tirade aimed at the fresh troops straggling past his newly acquired post.

"Fall in with your unit," he screamed.

I'm already dripping wet with sweat and its only 0900. I wonder if I can do it. I can't believe they call that stuff we just had food. I don't know how to deal with this heat. I don't know how to deal with anything about this place. I don't know what I'm going to do for sure.

Riggs struggled to come to grips with the result of his choices. He could be back at IU enjoying life like all the protestors. He could be back with Maggie; repairing the friendship he left standing at the airport. He could be anywhere but here. But he wasn't … he was a United States Marine and he was in Nam.

He and all the Marines surrounding him were replacements. Fresh from the states, they were good to go. They'd fill the gaps and replace the dead, the dying and those lucky enough to rotate home in one piece. Riggs was in for the hunt, the hunt taking place across Vietnam. In Marine territory, Riggs was headed with the others to an area known as I Corp where he would spend the next thirteen months.

Riggs looked around and couldn't believe his tired eyes.

Oh no ... Glubo's in my unit. I have to put up with him? I can't believe it. He can't go wherever I'm going. I can't take him.

The sergeant standing in front and yelling orders to the shipload of Marines looked eerily like a dirty version of Hogan's Heroes. Riggs stared in utter disbelief. What happened to the spit and polish of the United States Marine Corps? He knew he wasn't going to be walking around looking like that. That wasn't the outfit he joined, that's for sure. He joined for the discipline and order.

The sergeant kept things moving and didn't waste any time in barking out orders.

"Smith, James" …

"Yessir!" …

"Over here Marine, you're going to 1-7 in Chu Lai.

Malsom, Rodney … you're going to 2-3 over at Marble Mountain."

Forty-five minutes went by and the growing heat of their first day in Nam was taking a toll. Riggs couldn't imagine being out fighting in heat that barely allowed you to breath. Life was different already and the raw recruits were fast realizing this was worse than they'd ever known or could even imagine.

Where on earth am I going? Why haven't they called my name? There must be only ten or twelve of us left.

"Romero, Frank … you're going up north where the shit's as thick as your accent."

Oh man it's Glubo and they're getting him out of here thank goodness. Now where in the heck am I going?

"Hey Mafia Man, go over there!" the grizzled sergeant growled at Glubo as he pointed to a 6-by parked with engine running and driver at the ready. "Stand over there; a few of you are heading up north to the DMZ. You'll need a hitch to the airfield for your lift up to Phu Bai."

Good riddance. He didn't see me and he's heading north. I won't have to endure his insulting "city humor" anymore. Thank God.

The Marines' exercise in frustration droned on for another 30 minutes until Riggs was one of five Marines left. Then the tired and irritated sergeant barked out, "Riggs, Claaaayton. What the hell is that?"

"Here sir!" Riggs awkwardly grunted to the dissatisfaction of his tormentor as he awkwardly stepped forward.

"What the hell is a Claaayton Riggs?" he squeaked, exaggerating the a's in Clayton.

"Clayton Riggs is, well, me sir," Riggs replied, confused and concerned where this was headed, all the time hoping upon hope that Glubo didn't hear the exchange of ignorance aimed at the pig farmer. Riggs stood frozen in the searing heat, embarrassed, confused and without a clue. He felt like he was in Parris Island all over again. His worst nightmare came screaming from a distance.

"Sarge, Claaaaaayton there is a pig farmer."

It was Glubo.

Riggs temperature shot up like the hair on the back of his neck. There were few people he didn't like but he reeeeally didn't like him. He was surprised how much he didn't like Glubo.

The sergeant, with several days' growth on his face and a scowl that would make a Halloween ghoul look good, came strutting over to Riggs. He stood bolt upright, front and center, staring Riggs straight in the eyes.

I thought this crap was over after boot camp. Why are they picking on me here in a combat zone? I thought it would be different.

They were eyeball to eyeball when the sergeant's face broke into a grin as wide as his face when he said …

"Well put'er there fella," he said with a light chuckle. "My grandpa was a pig farmer too."

He reached his grimy hand out and shook Riggs's hand hard. He grabbed the surprised farmer by the shoulder and wished him well with a hard pat on the back.

This is an insane asylum. I'm not sure what's going on and don't know if I ever will. What am I doing here in this mess?

"Riggs, go over there with the wop. Get ready for your flight up north. You're going to Con Thien."

Where the hell is that? What the hell is it?

The sergeant yelled over his shoulder, "Riggs … you're going to 2nd Battalion 4th Marines … they're in the DMZ at Con Thien. Take care of yourself Marine."

Take care of yourself? You didn't say that to anybody else. Or did you? I don't think so. What did he mean? Why did he say that to me? Maybe he said it to everyone. I don't know. It's scary here.

His mind raced like his heroes at the Indy 500, his favorite pastime back home. The unknown always terrified Riggs but the known here in Vietnam wasn't looking too good either. He didn't care for a lot of people but people like Glubo were from a different planet than Clayton Wesley Riggs. He wasn't about to let himself become like them.

Two odd members of a new team, Glubo and Riggs tossed their gear into the back of the already moving 6 – by, as the driver roared off leaving them hanging over the side. Riggs rolled into the moving truck and onto his back at the first corner.

This guy is flyin' low!

It was a short ride to the Da Nang chopper pad but it seemed like the longest ride ever. The pair of mismatched Marines bounced up, down and all over the back of the truck as Glubo gave it to Riggs like he did everyone back home in Pittsburg.

"Riggs, you better lighten up my man or you won't make it in this town."

Glubo was already the authority … after twelve hours in country this guy knew it all.

I'm just going to ignore him. I know I'm not going to the same outfit as him. I couldn't. I can't stand his mouth. I couldn't stand being with him for a year that's for sure.

The 6-by came to a stop in a cloud of brown dust that swirled around like a swarm of angry bees. Riggs was already dirtier than he'd ever been in his life and he tasted the grainy grit of dirt whenever he swallowed. The driver hadn't said a word and never would. He just stopped, motioned over to a makeshift hangar where an old UH-34 chopper sat and walked off. The odd couple grabbed their sea bags, jumped down and started for the chopper.

God I want away from this guy. I want away from this Godforsaken place and I want something to eat. It's gotta' be afternoon. When are we going to eat? Who are those guys?

As they walked towards the old vintage chopper they noticed two guys sitting in the doorway. One had an M-60 machine gun hanging over his head. Glubo walked up and announced that the two of them were there for a ride to Phu Bai.

How did he know that's what to do? He acts like he owns the place that's for sure.

"Well … you came to the right place."

They both were young and wore sunglasses and carried an attitude the size of Texas. Riggs realized they were pilots … officers!

"Sorry sir," Riggs said smartly, saluting the two pilots, both lieutenants in the Marine Corps.

They both jumped up as if grown together like Siamese twins and began screaming at the same time.

"What the hell is wrong with you Marine? You don't salute in a combat zone. You're gonna' get our young asses killed. "

After chastising Riggs for longer than he liked, both lieutenants strutted off to fire up their chopper. They were going to give them a lift to Phu Bai. Riggs sat down by the wheel of the chopper, licking his wounds from another encounter with "a someone" more powerful than he.

Why do I feel this way? Why do I just ask for somebody to crap on me? Why don't I have the confidence I do with Maggie around? I don't get it.

For a short while Riggs forgot about his aching stomach and splitting headache. He sat back and might have even dozed off for a while leaning his head against the skin of the chopper next to the wheel.

"Hey pig farmer." It was Glubo returning from somewhere, Riggs didn't know. "Here … catch." He had been on a "recon mission" as he called it, and returned with some c-rations. He brought enough for Riggs and himself.

"Here … choose your poison," he said.

As he did he tossed a can of Ham and Moms Riggs's way. He hadn't been in country long but he knew that Ham and Moms were horrible. He also knew he wasn't going to tell Glubo he didn't appreciate what he'd done. He didn't need to give him any more reason to hate him.

"I'm tellin' ya' Riggsy … lighten up and get ready for the ride of your life."

While Riggs gritted his teeth and gutted down his cold meal of ham and lima beans, Glubo expounded on what awaited them in the DMZ.

"Riggsy…"

Clayton hated it when people called him that.

"I tell you, it's wild."

As it turned out this was Glubo's second tour of duty in Nam. He'd been wounded once in early 1966 and was sent home to recuperate. He hated life in the states, the protests and the bureaucracy in the stateside Marine Corps. He gave up and volunteered for another tour of duty in Nam.

"I want to be here Riggsy. Life is exciting."

Exciting? This is a despicable place. It's hot, filthy and I'm starved and you like it. I can't believe this guy.

Riggs thought about a lot of things but he wasn't going to say them and challenge Glubo. There was something different about him. Riggs was surprised that he'd brought him the c-rations and appreciated them even if they were terrible.

"Riggsy, I tell you man, lighten up, lay back and have some fun. Life is short so go with the flow my man."

Glubo chimed in with an almost caring attitude that surprised him beyond belief. He couldn't believe he was talking to him like he was and wasn't sure what he wanted.

"How is it … the combat I mean?"

"How is it?" Glubo asked with an air of disbelief. "It's a shit sandwich, that's what it is. But man is it a rush! Wow! I mean you can really get off on it when the bullets fly."

A rush? Exciting? Fun? Get off on it? Come on!

Riggs's mind was a bowl of scrambled eggs. Thoughts he'd never thought before about things he couldn't imagine were interrupted by the two UH-34 pilots who sauntered up with another Marine who looked like a biker from a bar in Bloomington.

Who on earth is this guy?

"Hop in kids! The taxi is ready to go," the biker laughingly chirped as he took his position and locked and loaded his M-60 machine gun. The pilots fired up the old gas engine on their vintage chopper and it belched to life, smoke billowing in all directions.

Will this thing fly?

The biker known as "Bunns" from New Castle, Indiana, was the door gunner, and the young officers were the pilots who were taking Riggs on his first combat flight in the place they called Nam. His veins warmed with the rush of adrenaline pumping through his body. The pilots spun the bird and raced the engines before roaring down the runway for a quick takeoff.

Is this thing going to fly? My God there's no seats or seat belts in this thing. What am I going to do here for a year? What?

The chopper shook and shivered its way into the thick afternoon air with the roar of a lion on a bad night of hunting. It burst airborne and began flying like it was hung on a wire, swinging back and forth, reminding Riggs a little of the Ferris Wheel at the annual fair back home.

Riggs, Glubo and the crew settled in for the hour or so flight north to Phu Bai. Glubo was right at home. He was screaming back and forth with Bunns; they were laughing together like nothing was wrong and they were at the bar downing a few.

I can't believe I'm here in Vietnam. Part of me wants to be and part of me wants to be back home in Indiana. I really want to be with Maggie. Wonder when I'll get mail? I gave her my address at the Fleet Marine Force but she won't know I'm going up here. I wonder if the mail will get up here? I know I miss her, that's for sure.

The time flew by as Riggs tripped out about life back in the world. As they approached Phu Bai, Bunns bellowed, …"sit on your helmets! You never know … the LZ might be hot."

Glubo immediately grabbed his steel pot, reached it down between his legs, set it upside down and sat on it. Riggs watched and followed orders like a good Marine, a good one that was scared and confused about his role in this new world of combat operations.

The chopper's engines gunned as it started a not so gentle curve. The body of the helicopter swung sideways with Bunns standing, machine gun at the ready. The tattooed Bunns was prepared for anything but Riggs was scared out of his mind.

For the first time he realized he was flying over the jungle of Vietnam with an unlikely new friend down below. He was landing, exposed to the elements in a hot war zone and he realized neither he nor Glubo had a weapon.

Is this crazy? Why didn't they give us our weapons? What are we doing out here ... what am I doing out here like this? It's an insane asylum for sure. I just know it.

The door gunner was wired, leaning out the door, jerking his machine gun back and forth, eyes popping out. He was ready to let loose given half a chance. If Riggs was scared when he left Da Nang he was terrified now.

He slid along the floor of the aging chopper, inching his way to the small window to his side. Peaking over the edge of the ten-inch square hole masquerading as a window, he found himself hiding behind the skin of the chopper-- skin not thick enough to stop a large mosquito, let alone a bullet from an AK.

It doesn't look dangerous down there. Grass huts, people walking around ... how bad can it be? It's filthy and I like to be clean but ...

Crack! Crack!

Glubo ducked as his smile disappeared like a zipper pulled hard shut. Riggs froze, eyes wide, as his nerves climbed through his throat to the top of his head.

The chopper switched directions and spun a hard right. Bunns leaned into his M-60 and cut loose with a long blast Brrrrp! Brrrrrrrp! Brrrrrrrrp! Empty cartridges pinged into the air and disappeared as the gunner blazed away with a crazed grin that showed his tar-stained teeth glistening in the afternoon sun.

They're shooting at us! What now? No rifles? Oh man, get us down in one piece. This is crazy.

The pilot spun his chopper in a short figure 8 while the gunner did his thing, working on emptying his belt of ammo. He was thrilled and it showed. Glubo recovered, grinning ear to ear as he turned towards Riggs who was clinging to his window.

"Hey, pig farmer … welcome to Nam." Glubo was matter of fact.

The old 34 hung on its thread and spun around again, circling its way to the ground in front of an old hangar that appeared frozen from the set of an old World War II movie. The chopper jerked as it slammed into the ground. Riggs and his unlikely companion had landed at the Phu Bai airstrip. They made it in one piece.

Glubo and Riggs crawled out of the chopper with their sea bags in tow; their egos fractured as they grabbed their gear for the walk to the hangar. Inside a Marine sat at a makeshift desk, hastily constructed of ammo boxes stacked about three feet high.

He looked up, unimpressed.

"Corporal, we're here with orders for the grunts," Glubo announced with a wide grin.

"So," the corporal moaned, "where you headin'?"

Riggs was a doormat no more.

"Corporal, we're going to 2nd Battalion 4th Marines. The DMZ," he said with some authority. "How far is that?"

He was doing well until the "how far is that comment."

"Well PFC Riggs … it's about 60 clicks that way," the corporal snidely remarked, stretching his arm and pointing his finger to the north.

Why do I put my foot in my mouth? I want to be part of this and do my duty. I can do it and I'm not going to walk on eggs anymore. I am not going to be intimidated.

"Well, how do we get there corporal?" Riggs asked, showing more than a little irritation.

"It's simple, my main man … go right over there, sign out your weapons and climb aboard the convoy that's lining up as we speak."

In the time it takes to walk around the block, the odd couple was sitting aboard another "6 by" heading north on Highway 1, racing to beat the sun dropping in the west and the storm clouds rolling in from the east.

My gosh! This is worse than riding a hay wagon back in Hope. Sure would be nice to have a big thick chocolate shake from the Dairy Barn back there too. I'm starved and no one seems to care.

The convoy rambled forward in a vain attempt at beating the setting sun. The caravan stretched along Highway 1, a row of twelve olive drab, box-like trucks, chocked full of Marines, mail and supplies heading north for Christmas.

About half way to Dong Ha, just after passing through an eerie looking village named Quang Tri, the heavens opened up and poured buckets of water down on Clayton Wesley Riggs.

"What the hell is this?" Riggs surprised himself by muttering an obscenity from a deep sleep. He'd settled in, curled up on his sea bag, just like he used to do by the TV when he was a kid. But he looked around and this wasn't kid's stuff out here on Highway 1; it was downright serious.

"It's the beginning of the monsoon, pig farmer. Ain't you seen rain before?" Glubo laughingly chided his truck mate.

What a place. What a place to fight a war. I'm starved, I'm soaked and I'm sick of the wop riding in this Godforsaken excuse for a vehicle we're in. Get me out of here. Maggie where are you?

Riggs couldn't help but feel sorry for himself as they bounced their way north, heading for the Dong Ha Airstrip.

I wonder what Maggie's doing right now? I wonder when I'll hear from her? How long does it take for mail to get from the states to Vietnam? I wish …

"Riggs?" Glubo leaned over to get his attention.

"Yea?" Riggs replied.

Glubo pushed his face up and close to Riggs to insure he could be heard. "Riggsy … you gotta get your head here … in Nam. You gotta get out of your girl's panties man, or you're gonna go home in one of those bags there," Glubo said, pointing to a box of body bags in their truck going along for the ride to Dong Ha.

Riggs looked up as the convoy slowed and appeared to be turning. The awkward green boxes with wheels made their way into a small village. It was full of strange smelling smoke, strange looking people with, what he would soon find, stranger sounding names.

Riggs was soon surrounded by large, leafy palm trees dripping from a deluge of water caused by the driving afternoon rains. The convoy had long lost its Huey chopper air cover and was 'driving clean' with no eyes to see any bad guys waiting in ambush along Highway 1.

The convoy inched out of the village canopy and into a ring of concertina wire surrounding the Dong Ha Marine Base. Inside, they made a sharp turn and headed towards what looked like an oversize outhouse sitting about 200 yards ahead.

It was near 1930 hours and getting darker by the minute. Riggs was sitting up surveying his new surroundings. The three-hour ride was made shorter by his frequent "trips" back to "the world" and life with Maggie O'Reilly.

One thing I know for sure ...Glubo is right. I gotta' get my head in this game. I'm here so I better "be" here and get with it. I'll figure out how to cope as time goes by but for now I have to be here.

As the convoy ground to a halt, Marines jumped out from every side, like cockroaches fleeing the dreaded light of day. Riggs jumped down, grabbed what was his life, now laced inside his sea bag, and followed Glubo along the south side of the now parked convoy.

The ground was mud, solid mud squealing, trying to suck the boots right off your feet. The rain was constant and the wet tiring.

Are we ever going to eat? Where the hell is the DMZ anyway? Is this it? What is that outhouse up there? Why I'm here I have to wonder.

Riggs's mind raced as he slogged along behind an almost jubilant Glubo.

Maybe that guy is really happy to be here, like he says. Could somebody be happy to be in a place like this? Can't imagine it!

Reaching the makeshift outhouse building, a shack serving as the air controller's house, alongside the steel airstrip, the terrible two, Riggs and Glubo, received the usual greeting.

"Lance Corporal, what do you want me to do about it?" came the caustic reply to Glubo's quest to get chow for him and Riggs.

"I want you to tell us where to get something, anything to eat." Glubo glared back, showing the first signs of strain, after a long couple of days. He wasn't to be denied.

"Over there in the corner … right there," the sergeant said pointing. "There's some c-rats … help yourself."

After a brief search of the leftovers in the corner, Riggs came up with a can of peaches and another of apricots. The food was depressing enough but the news of yet another chopper flight to reach his new outfit, Echo Company, 2nd Battalion 4th Marines made Riggs wish he were home with Maggie O'Reilly.

The driving rains, now a deluge, made the ground mush and the choices of beds, none. Riggs and Glubo kicked the pile of unwanted c-rats to the side and collapsed in the corner of the outhouse. Their weary, hunger driven bodies needed a break.

"Marines! Marines! Get out here now! We need help with incoming wounded."

What on earth?

4

December 12, 1967

The chopper ride from Dong Ha to Con Thien, Republic of Vietnam

The pilot spun the CH-46 twin rotor Chinook helicopter right above the control shack at the Dong Ha airstrip. It was 0500 and black as night with a steady drizzle driving rain through the cracks in the shed's roof.

Is he landing on us?

Riggs shot up looking for his boots, fear racing through his veins. He grabbed his new jungle boots and tried lacing them in the dark of night. It wasn't an easy task with a chopper whirling overhead, and he gave up in a pitch-dark fit of frustration.

"Get the hell out here. We got a chopper full of dead and dying. Move it!"

Oh my God!

The chopper landed a few feet from the outhouse where Riggs and Glubo were being rousted from a deep sleep. Its back door stood, gaping open like an ugly wound with its red nightlights glowing inside, making an eerie, strange aura drip over the bodies stacked inside. Disarray filled the floor of the shaking chopper.

Glubo jumped right in. Riggs stood in the dark, a red glow washing over his face and a heavy dose of confusion clouding his head. Marines appeared from all sides out of the night, dragging, carrying and helping the wounded from the rescuing chopper. The bodies were stacked three feet deep along the entire length of the inside of the Chinook chopper. Houdini couldn't tell the difference from the dead and the dying.

"Hurry up, hurry up, get'em off … we got another hot load to get!" the Crew Chief screamed at whoever was in earshot over the womp, womp, womp of the idling chopper blades, resting for a return trip to the jaws of hell.

I gotta' get inside. I gotta' help with this mess. I can't imagine I'm doing this or even what this is!

Riggs ran to the back door and stepped up and inside. The load of dead and wounded humanity was recently rescued from a battle raging on Dong Ha Mountain. They'd been surrounded and trapped for three days. The bad guys suddenly pulled back allowing the much-needed evacuation Riggs found himself standing knee deep in right now.

The Marines of 2–5 were locked in a bitter battle. These guys were stuck inside a ring of fire laid down by the North Vietnamese. The pilots went in for the rescue in spite of all the rain and fire filling the night air to bring these guys out and there was more to come.

"Hurry up!"

I got'em! I got'em! I know I can help. I know I can help!

Riggs was on his second pass into the knee-deep carnage and grabbed his first dead body.

I can't believe how heavy this guy is. I can't believe he's dead.

"Glubo. Glubo. I need help."

Riggs called out for help in picking up a badly decomposing Marine. The stench was not something a farm boy from Indiana or anyone else was used to. He swallowed hard and lifted the dead Marine with the help of Glubo … who seemed unfazed by the overwhelming stench of death.

By the time the chopper left for round two, it was daylight and nearing 0600. Clayton Riggs had been in country for just over twenty-four hours and had been shot at, starved, nearly drowned and just touched his first taste of death. He was a Marine and a real member of the Riggs family back in Hope, Indiana.

Riggs and Glubo made their way around the little base of Dong Ha. They found some real chow at the Force Recon mess area in the old French barracks. It was about 50 yards north of last night's outhouse bedroom but they couldn't see it in the dark of night. They listened as the second Chinook came and went with another load of misery.

I can't believe a crap breakfast tastes this good ... but it's delicious. I feel half rested and my stomach's full ... I just want to get to my outfit and get settled in. I need some sanity.

The day wore on like a bad dream. It was noon before a sergeant came by with news that Glubo was heading to Fox Company. He wasn't going to be with Riggs at Echo Company on Con Thien.

"It's out at Cam Lo, guy. Go over there and catch that convoy," the sergeant said with no interest at all.

It was just a routine day sending out stragglers like Riggs and Glubo to fill the holes left by days of battles and nights of anguish and despair.

Alone, sitting in silence, leaning against the old outhouse the sergeant called home, Riggs had too much time to think.

The Marine Corps really is "hurry up and wait." All day I've been here, now I can't get out to Con Thien.

I want to write home and don't have any paper. Man I want to write and tell Maggie what's happened so far. I want to tell her about last night. Maybe I can't write her; maybe she won't like it ... of course she won't. What am I thinking?

Mom, I can write her ... I can ... no I can't. You can't tell your Mom about death and dying and how you feel. How do I feel? I can't believe it but helping out back there was a rush, a real high. It surprised me. I felt it ... or did I? Did I just unload dead bodies?

I know I could tell Dad. I've listened to his stories for years. But no, he didn't talk about the details. He just talked about the glory, not the guts. He wouldn't want to hear.

I have to talk with somebody. If I don't talk I think I'll explode. Why am I excited? What am I feeling? What is right and wrong? What is truth? Maggie always wanted to know ... maybe I'd find it here in the midst of this madness. Maybe?

Riggs whiled away another long Nam afternoon awaiting word on a chopper that would take him for the fifteen-minute hop to Con Thien, wherever that was. It must be the DMZ.

I can't help but think of Maggie and her forever question "what is truth?" I wish she were here now and we could talk about it. Well, no I wouldn't want her here, seeing this, but I do wish I could see her. I wish we could sit down and talk, talk about everything.

Man I miss her. I'm alone. Right now I actually miss Glubo. I need someone, something to hold on to. I'm not sure what truth is or ever was after last night. I don't know but hope to find out.

A big, loud, noisy chopper, one Riggs had never seen before lumbered onto the runway right in front of him. It jerked him back to reality, a reality that both excited and frightened him. His emotions were jumbled, his thoughts, like looking at a plate of spaghetti.

The chopper taxied in front of the pig farmer and stopped like a giant bug, staring right at him. It had two big gas engines, one on either side. It was painted green and each engine had a big mouth painted on it with snarling teeth glaring out at the world. It was an old CH 37, the biggest chopper of the old armada.

"Riggs," the sergeant barked.

"Yessir!"

"That's your ride. As soon as they fill it with supplies … get on."

"Yessir!"

Riggs stood, watching as the supply troops loaded boxes of ammo, c-rations and bags of mail.

Mail? Mail? Oh man, are those mail bags? It's too early and too soon for me to get mail. But what it would do for me about now to get mail. I need to know that Maggie cares. She wouldn't have come to the airport to see me off if she didn't care. I know she cares.

The Crew Chief was ranting about something Riggs didn't understand. He walked up to the side door with cases of ammo still being loaded onto the back of the bug.

The noise of the idling chopper's engines was deafening. The two Marines couldn't hear one another over the roar all around them.

"What did you say?" screamed the helmeted Crew Chief at the top of his aching lungs.

"I need to get to Con Thien."

"WHAT!"

"I need to get to Con Thien."

The Crew Chief, visibly frustrated and seriously pissed off, grabbed a pad and pencil from a homemade pocket in his flak jacket. He scribbled a note and handed the paper to Riggs …

"You poor bastard, no one needs to go to Con Thien ... hop aboard."

Climbing inside, Riggs sank to depths lower than he'd been before.

What does that mean? "No one needs to go to Con Thien?" I don't care. I'm a Riggs and I'll figure out how to do this and survive. I will. I'll go out there and I'll come back.

In the depths of despair your deepest conversations are with yourself … and Riggs was starting to talk. Unsure of what he faced but mustering up the courage and determination to face it … he stood lost amidst the cargo and looked for a place to hang on.

The big bird with the big eyes began revving its engines. The salty Crew Chief was yelling into his radio, obviously mad as hell about something. He slammed his radio down and looked at Riggs, motioning him over.

As Riggs climbed around boxes of ammo unfastened for the ride to the front, the Crew Chief was writing him another note.

"This thing is 7000 pounds overweight and he's going in anyway. Hang on! This will be a wild ride!"

Information like that wasn't very reassuring to a new guy all alone in Nam for the first time. Fear shot up Riggs' throat … one more time. The chopper wallowed forward, crawling along, heading for the end of the steel matted runway clipped together on a hastily plowed strip of dirt somewhere near the DMZ.

7000 pounds overweight? Man that sounds like a lot and that guy is pissed. They wouldn't fly this if it wouldn't carry that kind of weight. Would they? I'm about to find out whether I want to or not. What a crazy place this is!

There was no time to worry or fret. The big, ugly green chopper lumbered along the runway, roaring, grunting and struggling in the thick afternoon air of the northern I Corp of South Vietnam. The entire shell of the chopper began to shake and shiver as it groaned skyward.

Riggs was trying hard not to swallow the huge lump in his throat. He was terrified of being in a chopper loaded with ammunition so heavy it could barely get off the ground. Once airborne, the UH-37 rolled to the north towards Con Thien, barely staying afloat in the thick, late afternoon air. Riggs looked out the window opposite the Crew Chief and got yet another shock as he saw the tree tops of Dong Ha just below.

Holy shit! We're just missing the tops of the trees with this thing. It's shaking like crazy and we're airborne and on our way. God, please get us to Con Thien.

Night was fast approaching as the sun slipped behind the mountains to the west. The big bird fought its way towards its target just above the treetops on its way to Con Thien. Riggs's new home soon popped up on the horizon and looked like nothing more than a dirty hilltop.

He peered out the window and focused on the land below. It no longer looked like a place he'd want Maggie O'Reilly to visit. He thought he was beginning to understand why the Crew Chief said, "no one needs to go to Con Thien."

The chopper banked hard right and Riggs got his first good look at his new home. He wasn't impressed.

Oh man this place looks like shit. The hills have holes pock marking the entire area. It's mud. Everywhere. Bunkers spot the edge of the hill. Litter everywhere. This looks like I'm flying into the county dump back home. How could I be coming here?

Suddenly the chopper door gunner jumped up. The M-60 was locked and loaded and the pilot's eyes darted left and right searching for danger. Riggs's ears were about to burst from the deafening noise caused by the roar of the two engines as they growled towards the final approach. The pilot manhandled the giant old chopper as it touched down, slamming into the muddy ground … knocking Riggs flat on his back.

He lay sprawled across the floor of the chopper. Lifting his head off the metal deck inside the UH-37, he heard yelling and screaming.

What the hell is going on? Are we being attacked?

Riggs jumped to his feet and clamored to get to a window.

What he didn't know was that the routine was normal for Con Thien. Riggs just didn't know they gang unloaded the choppers the second they touched down. As soon as a chopper landed every available Marine came running to off load the precious lifeline of supplies. The chopper was in, out, and back in the air in minutes. That was the drill. Choppers were a mortar magnet and the Marines of Echo 2–4 were tired of being on the receiving end of that fun.

My God they're throwing it all off in a pile. I don't get it?

Riggs grabbed a handle on the side of the chopper wall and made his way to the side door. The cargo was about gone. He looked around, grabbed his rifle, tossed his pack on his back and grabbed a mail sack on his way out of the butt of the big bird.

He stood amidst the mud and clutter of the off-loaded ammo and c-rats holding a huge sack of mail. Looking around, standing boot high in gray mud, Riggs was shocked at where he found himself.

What is this place? Guys scrambling around gray from head to toe ... beards on Marines, trash everywhere and mud holes to live in ... this is crazy like I thought.

"Hey, who the hell are you?" an ashen-faced marine yelled.

The guy greeting Riggs didn't look like a Marine at all. He looked like a bum in what used to be a Marine fatigue uniform. He was filthy dirty and wore a distant stare.

"I'm PFC Riggs. Reporting to Echo 2–4."

"Well, if you wanna' live to report, then you better get the hell out of the LZ."

The voice came from another direction. Turning, he could see another Marine who looked like he was a member of the walking dead.

Riggs could barely hear as the blades on the huge chopper whirled away and he realized they were loading wounded Marines on board along with two green body bags, obviously full of dead bodies.

Man this is the real deal. That could be Uncle Ben in Korea. But back then they didn't bring them home. They just buried them there. At least if I died here they wouldn't just bury me in the mud of Con Thien! Thank God for that ... but I'm goin' home.

Riggs took a direct hit, right square between the eyes. It was a serious dose of the painful reality of war. It splattered across his mind as he stood in the rain trying to make sense of the senseless. He found himself surrounded by young men who actually seemed comfortable in the midst of filth, anger and chaos.

"Marine!" A voice of authority called from the mist. "Come over here."

Riggs struggled to free his boots from the sopping wet gravity of the foot deep mud that was Con Thien. He followed the man who appeared to be the only one who looked like he might be in charge.

"I'm Lieutenant Vance," he said. "I'm in charge here."

Finally someone with whom Riggs could feel safe, someone he could look up to. He appeared to be the one sane man amongst the insanity of Vietnam.

"I'm PFC Clayton Riggs Sir," he said. "I'm to report to Echo 2–4."

"Well you found us PFC Riggs." The Lieutenant gave Riggs a short briefing before he realized what he was carrying. He stared at the bag Riggs absentmindedly held over his right shoulder.

"Riggs, is that a mail sack you've got?"

"Yessir!" Riggs said in a manner that gave away his recent graduation from Parris Island. He was still nervous and stood erect, even in the midst of Con Thien.

"Relax, Marine. I just want your mail sack."

He called a sergeant who passed the word. News of the new guy's arrival spread like a wild fire on a dry Montana summer.

Squad leaders, looking like the cast of a bad movie, began arriving to grab the mail containing precious word from home.

"Cooter," the lieutenant called to one of the vultures hovering around the fast depleting mailbag.

"Yea Sir," he replied.

"Take Riggs and show him his new home in the mud."

Riggs grabbed his gear and stumbled after a fast moving man covered in days of mud, with more days of beard hanging from his face. They reached an area of makeshift tents the Marines called "hooch's".

"Riggs … I'm Cooter, I'm from Texas and I'm your squad leader," said the seasoned veteran who'd just turned 20 years of age.

Who would have guessed a Texan with that accent?

"There's home, man," Cooter crooned on in the early evening.

He pointed to a three by four foot hole filled with water near the edge of the perimeter. The first thing Riggs noticed was that it didn't even have a "hooch" over it.

"Stay here and settle in. You're replacing Kug. You just met him."

"I did?" asked Riggs shyly, surprised.

"Yea, you did. He was in that last body bag we just loaded on the chopper."

Riggs put his pack down in the mud. Still standing, he could see the night creeping in around the fog-shrouded hill that he would now call home. He walked over and stepped down into the murky water that filled "his" hole, his new home, and sat down on the edge.

"Riggs," it was Cooter calling from his hole, which was in the middle of several water filled holes running left to right along the perimeter of the forward base at the edge of the DMZ.

"I'm passing out mail and you don't have none 'cause you just got here. Keep a watch out on the perimeter while we get caught up on the good stuff."

With that, his new squad leader disappeared into the muck and mire and darkness of the advancing night that was Con Thien. With the lieutenant gone also went Riggs's hope of companionship, at least for the next few minutes.

The night came fast, surrounding Clayton Wesley Riggs, but not as fast as the depression that he was feeling for the first time in his 19 years on earth. He had a sinking feeling and it wasn't the mushy ground he was now sitting on. It was the reality of his new home.

How am I going to live like this for a year? How am I going to cope with all that I see around me? How am I going to relate to these guys? Men my age surround me with faces like my father's. Faces that smile without laughter and eyes that see but offer no life. They're young men comfortable in carnage and devoid of innocence. I don't want to be one of them.

Riggs "tripped" deep this time, and deep always took a one-way street to his place of hope. It was a cold place on Lake Michigan in early December.

This is a long way from last December with Maggie. I feel better just thinking about her. Maybe my memories will get me through. Maybe I'll figure out her answer to what is truth. Maybe I will ... right here in the mud and muck of the DMZ. Maybe I'll make it. I have to make it. I have to make it back to Maggie O'Reilly.

Nightfall won the battle for Riggs's mind. Pleasant thoughts of a lifetime ago with a girl a lifetime away from a simple Riggs kid from Hope, were replaced with the fear that sailed in on the wings of darkness. A black sky was eerily accented by the stark contrast of the early evening fog that hung in the air like bad mascara on the girl you wouldn't want to take home to Mom.

Riggs was wired for a long night of new sights, new sounds and live animation that would take fright to a new level in a young pig farmer's life.

5

December 13, 1967
Con Thien, Vietnam

Boom! Boom!

"Incoming!"

The cry in the early mist of a monsoon morning was loud and clear and shook Clayton Wesley Riggs to the core.

BoomBoomBoom!

"Corpsman Up!"

Running, people crouching, then the "ratatatat" of automatic weapon's fire broke out on all sides.

Mortars rained in on Con Thien serving an irreverent reveille to the Marines of Echo 2–4. One more time, a rude awakening that was getting "ruder" everyday.

"Maline, you die!" The battle cry echoed from the tree line just outside the Marine perimeter.

"Dink bastard!" a surly Marine shot a nasty reply almost shrieking with laughter in the process.

As fast as the attack came, it went. A normal morning at an abnormal place called Con Thien. A former French outpost, Con Thien was the northern most American outpost, just a short mile from the DMZ.

"Riggs!" It was Cooter, scurrying along, crouched, crawling to the hole next to him.

"Yea, whatdaya' need?" Riggs replied with a shaky voice filled with fear.

Cobwebs still clouding sleepy eyes, he had just been rattled to life with sounds never before heard by him. He could barely talk.

"You got mail, you turd." Cooter moaned.

"Me?" Riggs shouted back with a mixture of excitement and amazement.

How could I have mail?

But it was true. Somehow Maggie O'Reilly had gotten Riggs's address and sent him mail and a package. She'd sent it soon after he left.

Unbelievable. I can't have mail yet! I just got here. I brought it in with me. Come on! Who could write to me that fast? Maggie? Come on, I'll bet they're just having fun at the new guy's expense.

"You sure Cooter?" Riggs asked, making sure this wasn't some kind of "new guy" prank.

"Riggs, it's like we say in Texas, 'lettin' the cat outta the bag is a whole lot easier than puttin' it back in.' I suggest if you want this shit you get your ass over to the LT's tent now. The shit'll hit the fan here again real soon … so hit it!"

Riggs made a beeline through the mud to the LT's tent. Sure enough, there was a tattered letter and a manila envelope. The envelope was all neatly taped and stuffed full of something; he had no idea what it was. He hadn't been this excited since his ninth birthday when his Dad presented him with his first rifle … a .22 caliber passed down from Grandpa Riggs.

He grabbed the letter and the package, stuffing it under his jungle jacket to protect it as best he could from the light rain still falling. Back in his new home, the three by four hole in the ground, he hurriedly dug inside his pack and pulled out his poncho. He placed the poncho over his head, protecting his "unwrapping" from the rain.

This is too precious to get wet, whatever it is. What on earth did she send me already? I can't believe her. I can't believe she did this for me. I really can't.

Oblivious to the battle zone around him, Riggs took his Marine K-bar and slit the end of the envelope. Sliding his hand inside, he pulled out a letter only one person could have written. He'd recognize the handwriting anywhere … it was Maggie's.

He carefully laid the big envelope on his lap, making sure it was free of the rain pecking on his poncho and opened the letter in the faint light of early morning.

It read …

November 12, 1967
11 o'clock in the morning
Bloomington, IN

Dear Clayton,

I came to the Well House today with my art pad to make a sketch of its walls from an angle I've not chosen before. But instead of the pencil leaning toward any of the beautiful images before me, it started forming words that I might say to you after three months of separation and silence.

All the bitterness and shock and hurt that I felt during the first weeks after you went away is now transforming into a mood of quiet resignation and helplessness, mixed with a touch of hope. I'm a bit overwhelmed with thoughts of all the things I wanted to say to you since you declared, "I am going to the war—this is my final decision—goodbye for now."

I know my reaction made me akin to a fair-weather friend, but what could I say to that? I do not want sadness and regret to divide us. You know I do not say, "I am sorry" easily, but I will say: Yes, I regret you chose to go to Vietnam to express your love of your country, but I also regret my anger and stony silence since your declaration.

I will make up for this emptiness—that might appear as forgetfulness— by a gift of letters. I will be honest with you and not hide my range of emotions, even if they appear to embrace bitter moods. But these as well may have already passed or transformed into something new between the time when I write them and you read them.

You may see these leaves as those that fall in autumn, or clouds that pass, just so you don't mistake them for inconsistency and fickleness. I want you to know I am a steady friend, and I will say true words. But if bitter, I will offer you sweet ones as well, which suits your sweet tooth better—or are they all still sweet as you used to tell me?

Instead of making my planned drawing of the old watering hole where our friendship started, I envisioned this colorful fall landscape and shelter soon being covered with white snow, and how the black branches will be bare, and I will soon need to bring those fancy sunflower seeds from the Farm Bureau to give to our fine-feathered fellows and ladies.

They count on us, and now that you are gone they will look to me and I cannot disappoint them. I was especially concerned about "The General" looking down from his favorite maple tree—you know he will be asking about you, but don't worry, I will explain everything and he will understand.

And this makes me think of "The Partridge in the Pear Tree" and your favorite holiday and all at once I know I will explain everything to you so that you too will understand. I decided what your Christmas gift would be …

You know how I favor my little games with words and pictures with silly clues and favorite tunes, but these will not be the usual twelve days of Christmas—no geese-a- laying or five golden rings. However, there may be some calling birds, ladies dancing and swimming swans, for we have seen these over the last year, haven't we?

I am designing this holiday offering to be opened in parcels, one envelope for each of the twelve months I have known you, and this for the thirteenth. I pray that my writing will give you a part of me that no one else has ever had or will ever have. I shall share with you my thoughts, feelings and inner self that will be yours and yours alone.

Since you always admired my "Catholic girl's school" script and my rambling haiku and my miniature sketches, I will write down some poems with all

the proper curlicues and Emily Dickinson dashes, and I will throw in some drawings too. I am asking that you please open one of these dozen letters each day, starting on December 13. Clayton, please have a safe and happy holiday season. I think about you every day and pray for your safety. How I look forward to the day you may join me on this bench again.
Yours truly,

Maggie

Clayton Wesley Riggs sat in the rain but he wasn't taking in the water. He was drinking in a mixture of love and hope, a blend of the awe and respect he felt for Maggie and a determination to make it home at all costs.

Maggie O'Reilly can make me feel better from ten thousand miles away. Maggie is the girl of my dreams.

Whomp, Whomp, Whomp …

"INCOMING!"

Riggs grabbed his precious letter, hastily folded it and stuffed it in the big manila envelope. He hit the muddy deck face first, wrapping his "Christmas gifts" in his spare jungle jacket.

I'll guard this with my life. I love Christmas even in this hellhole of a place.

BOOM … BOOM … BOOM!

Mortars whistled in on all sides and broke up the memory dance of Clayton Riggs as if to say, "you're here now GI and you die."

Riggs lay in the mud listening, watching, and waiting to see what people were doing. All he saw was a well-trained response. No one panicked, no one got excited … everybody just did what needed done. All the while Riggs was face down in the mud, frightened to death he might die and more frightened he might live and not get to read his first letter later today. The shelling continued throughout the day and frayed his nerves to a raggedy edge.

I can't imagine she feels that way. I can't believe she found my address, wrote the letters and made this package for me. It's the hope I need to make it through the insanity of this place. She is my hope.

The day dragged on like a spaghetti western playing at the local movie house. The shelling stopped when night started. It was a long day as PFC Riggs slid down in the slime pit he called home. He took out the first letter and leaned his upper body over, protecting the paper Maggie O'Reilly wrote on. He didn't even want a mark on it.

He sat quietly, looking at the letter she'd prepared for the first day. In the dim of a monsoon evening he read …

November 13, 1967
7 o'clock in the evening
Bloomington, IN

-Cardinal in the Well House Tree-

Dear Clayton,

This morning the light sifted through the trees and came to my eyes with a brilliant splash as I shooed away the gold and red leaves that had found a seat at our bench.

After I sat down, I felt the warmth of the sun on my back. For the second time in two days, I put aside my pencil and paper and closed my eyes while memories of times we spent in this place and others rolled over me like cool sea breezes—only these smelled like earth and trees and rain.

I could feel you sitting next to me, where we last met—how many months ago? Only three, but it seems more like three years. Instead of the General, whom I had hoped to see, a bright red cardinal has shown up today to tell me he is well. He too moved his head in a jerky fashion, looking this way and that, but he doesn't bully the other birds when I throw them crumbs. The General has no such manners.

These birds seem to tolerate each other's weaknesses, or they are worn down and have come to accept the community they live in. Now as a collective they need to build their strength for the winter, though many are happy to live for the pleasure of today—who blames them? — If you were here you could tell me their types and give them at least the dignity of knowing what family they belong to.

I only know the Indiana State Bird and everyone knows the Blue Jay. So red and blue are represented here, but only the white dove of peace could give us our flag's full palette. Where is she? I look for her everyday, and that is my patriotism, in hoping to fulfill this one sweep of color and pattern. Even if these stripes and stars elude me, I can still see these lights at night in the sky, and the various roads we take to our fates in these stripes—all parallel in this case. We go forward together.

I told you I am not so angry at your decision anymore, but I will admit this anger was also mixed up with some deep hurt that you left me here alone in a way I have never felt aloneness before. So I am going to show you some of the places I traveled in my mind that have hopefully been colored with the better palette of poetry and art—not that it does not too protest!

You would not recognize me if I were divorced from all forms of protest. But now it is your absence that I feel to argue with even in accepting our current far-away corners of the planet we inhabit. I have never had a good friend be so far from me on the face of this earth, but in a strange way, at the same time, never have I had a friend so close.

Since I am starting my picture gallery of memories with our Well House, I must say something about the difference between the times we spent here a year ago and how it is here now. To capture any of the flavors of my mood, I have to look to Mother Nature and her landscape in front of me for some blanket to sit down for a rest and a look up into the sky while lying on my back.

I am reading haiku for my poetry class. Perhaps you know of this ancient Japanese poem of three lines with 5, 7, and then 5 syllables—ideally contemplative, about some creature or image of nature. Of course there is no tradition or even perhaps respect for the likes of my haiku—no excuse for my running-away-with-it, filling it with ironic twists in non-stop stanzas piled one over the other in a mass. It is only "My Way", not "The Way."

"Any Way," the point here Clayton, is when you first told me you were going to the war I wrote this poem to you. I thought, "Here I am abandoned on the shores of this small town, like Ophelia forsaken by Hamlet—off balance in her steps, or Sappho the poetess, or Ariadne when she was left by Theseus after she showed him the way to slay the dragon and saved him with the golden thread so that he might make his way out of the maze."

I never saved you from anything, have I, except temporary loneliness perhaps. And I have no magic thread to help you decide which way to turn or how to find your way out of the maze you are in—a place that must be as terrifying as any beast.

Of course, unlike these ladies I would never drown myself or throw myself off the cliffs for anyone. However, since I will always be honest and share my feelings, I will also continue to show you my writing and artwork—for as you see I have enclosed one of the first sketches I ever made for you of the Well House—on the first day we met.

In this poem Ophelia floats downstream in a cloudy vision as she joins the ocean of beings, which have gone before her to the sea—she too cannot see her way out of her narrow path. Underneath her are the wrecks of old battles, long-forgotten bones of men mix with the broken bones of ships. We Irish have a history of losing friends and family to the seas, and the ocean speaks to us not only as a friend who gives life and food but also takes it away—but this is not really me, Clayton.

Instead of taking refuge in these cold waters of death, I still look to my sister Beverly and my friend Judy for company when my emotions are in turmoil thinking of you gone to war.

Now I have regained a little of my humor, and maybe I will find some things to laugh about, so feel free to consider these lines a bit morose. Yet, I see them as full of hope, or at least a ray of hope, and what more can one expect but this one line of light coming from the sky to warm us and make our next steps more sure?

This stream of haiku is about the wave we move upon to pass into the larger waters of life—that unending space that seems to have opened up for me in the last year. It is about going with the flow, waiting for the longer days of light and the flowers of spring, the season of new beginnings.

"Downstream"

The stream flows onward
As red haired Ophelia
Is joined by sisters

Her view of the sky
Is pure cloud not telescopes
Reaching their limits

Her skirts billow out
Farther than deepest curtseys
Catching no branches

Her palms face upward
And fingers glisten playing
The strings of cold winds

Underneath green leagues
Fathom a weight cast iron
Ruin of shipwrecks

Bleaching limbs askew
Split plank decks washing onto
Her the living moss

She will learn to live
Unsure if he'll survive to
Celebrate Christ's Mass

She will learn to breathe
Over water under air
While still seeing spring

He will surely live
To unveil hidden clues to
This blue treasure map

My dear Clayton, wherever this finds you, I hope it will provide for you comfort as your friendship does to me.

Yours truly,

Maggie

Maggie touched Riggs with more than her words. Her pure spirit lifted him high above the fog shrouding the blanket of darkness on Con Thien. It lifted him high above the mud where he had curled up, lost in the words of someone he cared deeply about, who was far, far away. He wasn't sure what her poems meant but he was starting to feel her presence in her every word.

"Riggs. Riggs. Who the hell is Riggs?"

It was the voice of someone Riggs didn't really know. It was Moto … a fireplug of a Marine who was as different as he was tough.

"Riggs … get that damned flashlight out. You're coming with me. We got an early patrol."

6

December 14, 1967
Con Thien, Vietnam

The night was a short one for PFC Riggs, real short; but then all nights were for the Marines of Con Thien.

I'm ready. I know I can do this. I'll do it for Grandpa. I have to do this and do it well enough to go home. Go home to see Maggie. Maggie. I don't want to think about her right now. I can't. She takes me to such a good place ... and then here I am, and this place is bad.

His mind was overcome with a rainbow of emotions. It was a kaleidoscope of blacks and dark blues, purples and olive drab. If there were truth to be found here, it was in being focused so you could live another day. It was 0400 hours. It was dark, wet, and looking like another day of genuine misery with a group of young men ten thousand miles from the arms of their loved ones.

"Riggs, this is the real deal. No bullshit around here. Stay focused and stay awake. Got it?" He didn't know Moto but he understood what was important. When Moto said something, he meant it.

"I got it," Riggs replied with a confidence that betrayed the fear that welled up inside his stomach like a bad burger.

"You damned well better," came the dagger shooting back from Moto. He was a fighter and a survivor and no new guy would ruin his day and send him home in a bag.

The 16-man patrol loaded up, slinging their combat harness of ammo, water and medical kits across their already tired and sore shoulders. It was a routine that was old the very first time you did it.

Everyone saddled up, moving like a line of cats creeping off into the darkness. Moto's patrol disappeared into the dark of night. Clayton Riggs was heading to the bush. Their mission ... an early morning ambush.

I can't believe I'm way back here at the back of the column. I think there are only three guys behind me. Quiet? I must be quiet but I can hear my heart beat I am so scared.

Every sound, every step, every breath was magnified a thousand times. Riggs was wired for sound as he followed the column walking off into the unknown blackness that surrounded them.

They can't hear us. I know they can't. It's pitch black. Okay ... stay calm, stay calm. I can do this, I can.

Riggs desperately battled his emotions in a vain attempt to convince himself he could handle combat. He knew he'd measure up when the bullets started flying. He was playing a game of false bravado, a charade, a game everyone new to the game of combat played. It was an eternal battle of the mind. To survive you must win.

Why are we stopping? We've only been going a few minutes? What is it? What's going on? I can't see a thing!

Riggs could hear whispers coming from the front of the column. It was 0445. The squad was just a few hundred yards to the front of the north side of the Con Thien perimeter. It was time for an ambush to catch bad guys moving around just before daylight.

Moto moved quickly, setting up security on each end of the patrol. He methodically went about placing each Marine exactly where he wanted him in the underbrush along the jungle trail. Riggs was tucked away in a thicket, shivering with fear and wishing he were back at his new home on Con Thien.

Wow. I'm here. This is it; this is what it's all about. Quiet. Quiet. What was that? Don't breathe. Was that someone walking?

Riggs was edgy and sweating bullets that dripped from the tip of his nose. He didn't know what to expect. He didn't know what was real and what he imagined.

As near as he could tell he was maybe five or six feet off the trail. It was dark and morning couldn't come soon enough for the boy from Hope.

Maybe nothing will happen. Maybe this will be a dry run. That's okay with me. It's not raining much right now and we'll get back to the hill and have some time to rest. And time to read ... I've got another letter. Eleven more letters ... no I can't think about that right now. I ... what was that?

Noises ... walking ... talking ... there was movement all around and the Marines were waiting to kill the unknown prey.

That's not English they're speaking, that's for sure! This must be it. I know it is. This is it!

He tensed every muscle in his frightened body. His hands froze as he squeezed them tight around the stock of his automatic M-14. Riggs's knuckles ached as he gripped his rifle. He was sure his grip would leave fingerprints in the aging wood of the only protection that stood between him and a terrifying unseen enemy.

You couldn't get a hair between his trigger finger and the half moon metal that would unleash the 7.62-millimeter shells poised to take down the enemy silently approaching in the night.

The young man from Hope, crouched and frozen with fear, tried frantically to convince himself of his superiority when hell paid a visit ... to PFC Clayton Wesley Riggs.

Brrrrp! Brrrp! Brrrrrrrrp!

M-14's opened up the entire length of the trail. Every rifle reported from the exact spot where Moto placed them. Riggs heard Moto yelling, screaming directions to his Marines.

Boom! Boom! Boom!

Grenades blew the night apart, with Moto's end finding most of the action. Explosions echoed in every octave on a scale of destruction Riggs could have only imagined a few short days ago. Bullets whizzed by Riggs's ears for the first time in his life, prompting the space between his finger and his trigger to vanish into a staccato of individual explosions as his 14 sent hot lead flying through the eerie silver of the morning light.

My God. My God. Be with me. Let me live!

Moto tripped the ambush when he set off his Claymore, an eight by eight inch portable mine designed to blow out in one inch square pieces, each one blazing towards the target. They were white hot, delivering death in a heartbeat. Once Moto triggered the ambush, the Marines of Echo 2–4 hooked it out with M-14's and grenades, fighting on until the unluckiest man lost.

This is insane!

"Corpsman! Corpsman! The cries that broke the early dawn of another bad day in Nam echoed all around. The rains had picked up and the misery along with it. Driving rain and streaking bullets combined to frighten the strongest of men.

The terror of Riggs's first firefight vanished in the light of a new day. As suddenly as it started, it stopped … for an instant. As he looked around and surveyed what first light revealed, it reminded him of the scene of the car wreck he drove upon his junior year at Hope High. A family of six, an unrecognizable mess, the carnage and the horror of it all came back as if it were yesterday.

Moto ran by, screaming in a calm voice, organizing everyone into a new defensive position.

How can he be that way? He's ... almost calm?

"Riggs!" Moto yelled in his face with an air of authority he hadn't heard before. He was as scared of him as he was his situation.

"Right here, you cover this area … now! You got it?"

Riggs nodded and immediately jumped up and ran over the trail to the area Moto had mandated. As he ran and stepped one foot across the trail he was startled by a figure running in the jungle twilight that surrounded the fighting Marines.

"Halt!" Riggs yelled at the racing figure trying to reach the dense undergrowth. Just as the daunting figure jumped, Riggs fired a burst from his M-14 on full auto. The world stopped in its tracks.

In a blur Moto appeared out of nowhere and sprayed the area as he ran head long into the bush.

Holy ...

Riggs instinctively but reluctantly followed Moto, rifle at the ready.

"You're a lucky pig farmer asshole," Moto grunted. "You got his ass. But get this … there are no 'halts' in Nam. You shoot to kill. Got it?"

Riggs got it.

He also got more than he bargained for, the image of a dead person, one he'd just killed, chiseled hard into his psyche like the engraving on the monuments back home.

I just killed a person. He looked strange. He was small and dark and oriental and ... well, dead. Dead because I killed him. I haven't even been here a week yet and I've killed another human being. God forgive me please.

Riggs learned there's no time or place for reflection in the bush of Vietnam. Daylight showed its face as morning and early afternoon turned into a blur. The Marines waited as another squad came from Con Thien. They came to help secure the area and clean up the aftermath of what Riggs would learn … was a very small skirmish in a nasty war.

The aftermath … seven dead gooks and two dead Marines, with another two Marines wounded.

"Riggs, grab this poncho," a fellow grunt yelled from behind him.

It was now 1415 hours, mid afternoon and Riggs had not just killed someone, he was now carrying a poncho filled with impending grief for an unsuspecting family back home. He and three other Marines were doing their best to carry the body of a comrade back up a slippery, dirty hill in the Republic of South Vietnam.

Back home on Con Thien, Riggs and the others grabbed c-rats, some not so fresh water and sat back to savor the life they still had. Impromptu shelters, mere "lean-tos," were springing up over the holes, now filled with more water than before. They were the homes of the Marines of Con Thien.

I've had two hours sleep in the last twenty-four. I've killed a man and carried another dead man up our hill. I can't believe it! I'm starved and I'm bone tired. I don't know what I want other than to read a letter from Maggie and to eat something. And I hope I forget what just happened out there.

Riggs chowed down on a can of Beans and Weenies, a White Bread, and crackers and cheese. He actually felt full for the first time since he'd arrived in Nam. He didn't have a headache anymore and wanted desperately to get dry and get some much needed rest.

The unrelenting rains drove Riggs and Cooter to scavenge the hill. They salvaged a couple plastic camo tarps from the holes of the unfortunate and recently departed. The two "hole mates," Cooter and Riggs, came back and fashioned a small rain cover over their home in the rain soaked ground. In a few minutes they completed their project. The driving downpour missed Riggs, who was alone while Cooter went to be with Moto for a "debrief" of the day's happenings.

Alone at last, Riggs had thoughts of Maggie and thoughts of the one elusive thing he missed the most … sleep. It was 1620 hours and Riggs was sound asleep in a muddy hole, ten thousand miles from happiness, sanity and Maggie O'Reilly.

7

December 14, 1967 – Evening
Con Thien, Vietnam

It was dark, damp and Riggs awoke to the sound of mortars whump, whump, whumping into the other side of the Con Thien perimeter. He slid deeper into his muddy hole, realizing after just two days, he was becoming a little numb to the dangers of life in the DMZ.

The incoming mortar barrage was short with no apparent casualties. There was no cry of "Corpsman Up" and that had to be good. Rousing his faculties and waking his wits from the deep sleep he'd so rudely emerged from, he remembered his letters from Maggie.

After all, this was the 2nd day of Christmas and Clayton Riggs needed a dose of Maggie's goodness.

November 14, 1967
Bloomington, Indiana

"There never was a good war or a bad peace."
-Benjamin Franklin
September 11, 1773

My dear Clayton,

Where are you my friend? If I had wings, I would have a chance to trace your route to some tree house; I could fly to you like in those old folk songs, to land in some high tree to keep an eye on you in the forests of your journey.

Would I be a bold blue jay like The General, all blustery and full of confidence, with no blue coat of happiness perhaps, but the blue cut of a soldier's jacket, or the common cop on the street? Or would I be an Indiana cardinal whose males wear the bright coat of battle while the females hide their brown feathers to protect themselves and their babies? Or would I be a red-winged black bird or a redheaded green parrot?

This sounds a bit more like me, perhaps, but in truth I would not want to be the parrot who only repeats what she has heard from others instead of thinking and speaking for herself—you surely know me well enough to know I cannot but speak out.

Yet, of all the birds I might be, you may guess my final choice. I would be the dove of peace that brings an olive branch from the far forests of Vietnam and finds itself in the Indiana University Woods within a few feet of our Well House, a dove of peace for the world outside and in our own yard. Beside me would be my friend, not my adversary, not the dove of war (you might say this creature does not exist), but a dove of peace that chooses fight instead of flight.

Are you not a dove of peace caught in the form of a soldier at war? And why can't birds of different feathers also be together? Perhaps these are the things that wintertime hardships and wartime give us, forcing us to ponder our humanity and connectedness to others.

Even at our worst, with no wings of angels, we all turn to some kind of hope that man is by nature good. I believe this. And if we shed ourselves of the dark veils that keep us from knowing each other and caring more, underneath, we are all, most of all, kind at heart. It is that small percentage of monsters I worry about.

It's these very monsters that love the thrill and excitement of war, like children at their games. But now the games are real! The soldiers are not plastic pieces that can be blown up and put back together like some Humpty Dumpty, nor are they pretend superheroes with bullets bouncing off their chests.

But funny, in my mind, I see you as one of these make believe heroes who do not need to dodge bullets at all—they might buzz quite close to you and it is tragic that they might reach some of your friends. But in my vision you are protected by something, perhaps even just the power of prayer—not just mine but of your mother and father and sister and even the animals at your father's farm.

They must all look to you for your next appearance at their supper table. But of course many people pray for the safety of those at war, and what good has this done them?

One of my classmates named Jim is taking a journalism class and he told me about Ernie Pyle. Of course, you must know more about him than I do, such a famous Hoosier and hero journalist of our last big war. Did you know that he had a premonition that he would die on that little Pacific island?

He went home from reporting about the European front, but he could not stay away and felt he had to write about his soldiers in other parts of the world fighting this war. My friend said Mr. Pyle's last column found in his pocket was very dark—people might not want to hear their favorite reporter talk about the real visions of war—all the dead men. Jim read me a quote from the letter, for he had taken notes and he had them with him, and these are the lines that made me think of what you might be going through.

I expect you might have some of the same feelings, for you of all people cherish even the smallest lives—you are almost a Buddhist in not even killing a bug unnecessarily—and I thought of how you told your father when you were a boy you would kill no more chickens with your hands and how any animal taken in hunting would be used for food, all of it, never merely for sport. (oh how I prattle!)

Perhaps I was thinking not to send you the quote from Mr. Pyle after all, but you know me—I will do it and you will read it and know this is not me trying to be mean or sad or scared but simply trying to walk in your shoes and see what you see. Not because I want to see it all but because I want to keep company with you, be next to you, somehow, for all the unnatural things that happen to you—

This is what he said in this last column he never finished—

"But there are many of the living who have had burned into their brains forever the unnatural sight of cold dead men scattered over the hillsides and in the ditches along the high rows of hedge throughout the world.

Dead men by mass production - in one country after another - month after month and year after year. Dead men in winter and dead men in summer.

Dead men in such familiar promiscuity that they become monotonous.

Dead men in such monstrous infinity that you come almost to hate them.

These are the things that you at home need not even try to understand. To you at home they are columns of figures, or he is a near one who went away and just didn't come back. You didn't see him lying so grotesque and pasty beside the gravel road in France.

We saw him; saw him by the multiple thousands. That's the difference..."

I accept that there is a difference between what you and I see, but I do not want you to think I am one who does not understand, as Mr. Pyle suggests, because I do not have the men who have fallen into these ditches burned into my brain.

I have seen them too, in my mind, and I will try to know what you know. But I do not see you among them. Never have I seen you like this. But maybe this is Pyle's point—I do not imagine MY friend like the others. I am not ready for that vision and will never be.

When I imagined myself telling you stories of how men and boys find a way out of the draft, I know none of them would ever suit you—lying, fleeing, declaring yourself as a conscientious objector.

I do appreciate your dedication to your family traditions, for how can I say I am not dedicated to what I was taught by mine? Just because my parents taught me that life is too precious to waste on useless wars, perhaps one day someone will be able to tell us what the true use of this war is.

History looking back on this—what will they say? How will they commemorate all the lives lost? How will they account for the costs?

So today's letter is about conflict that I feel both close and very far away at the same time. The far view is like the visit I took from high up that came into focus when I came down from my perch.

Three weeks ago on Halloween I went to the Tower on the seventh floor of the Union Building—you might recall it as the Bryan Room perhaps, as we were in that room—do you remember?

The red furniture and red and navy oriental rugs and antiques and the beautiful long and narrow windows with the ornate patterns and shapes give you a view of three sides of campus. You asked me why the university would have such a lofty room named for him. Was he a visionary you asked? A hero or a leader with a long view of the institution?

On this hallowed eve, afternoon really, I got off on the top floor of the elevator and walked up the two flights of steps to the room, and by chance it was not locked, as it should be, so I was able to slip in.

I shut the door behind me and looked out the window facing north to Seventh Street. There you could see the students gathering to hear Dean Rusk speak at the Auditorium. There they were, small patches of color and movement—and I was thinking what a great painting this would make with these bits of moving life in their anti-war banners and their American flags all thrown together with those in masks and Halloween costumes. This was a very colorful parade indeed, for the leaves were still full of splendor and the air smelled so crispy and good.

I looked down on people below who would soon be forming into two dueling groups—the war is galvanizing and separating and the gathering looked like the flow of cells under the microscope grouping and regrouping to stage their new assault on each other's views.

I was thinking," if you were here with me, would you and I walk down Seventh Street together to see our Secretary of State talk of how great the war in Vietnam is going and the importance of sending our citizens to fight this war over someone else's land grab?"

I know for sure you would be the gentleman, always the one to go along with what the lady or the girl has asked of you. So then I questioned myself: would I ask you to join us even with no sign, no armband of peace, no slogans—would you stand with me on this side as people around you are shouting at that man who condones and controls major moves of this war policy?

Would your name be among the signatures on the petition going around after Rusk left that apologized for the rude manners of the anti-war protesters—there were quite a lot of signatures! Two students went to Washington D.C. to make their apology in person, but maybe just to make a spectacle of themselves and rub shoulders with famous politicians.

I felt sick reading of their touring the very capital that symbolizes the American gift and power of free speech—why should they apologize for those who are against the war and speak out? The doves speak with the same passion as the hawks, and maybe more so.

Where would we be if our own heroes of the 18th century did not speak out against the tyranny of the all-powerful colonial British? These brownnosers know nothing of history.

But another curious issue that I raised in my own conscience as a friend—would I keep you company if you were with your companions in a show of "support" for our troops? As in support them in their choice of war?

How they call it "support" is a question here, for bringing them home in boxes, if they can be brought home at all after falling in that battleground, is not support as I define it. I feel it is we who are showing the real support for these soldiers in bringing this war to a close before it takes more lives. Not just warrior lives, either—it is women and children and old people and poor people who suffer and die.

As I looked down at these students, small figures walking on the street and sidewalk and grass of Dunn Meadow, there were people throwing Frisbees to each other at the most amazing distances, riding by on bikes, in buses and cars—there was no sound coming from them.

When I left the Tower I rushed down each flight of stairs, not even bothering with the elevator, but instead dizzying myself by hurrying down the steps. Upon reaching the doors to the outside the silence lifted and the air was filled with all the sounds that had been muffled and cut out from above. There was the wind scooting the leaves along the walk with a soft scraping sound, the conversation and shouts of people passing with their banners and buttons. Some were in Halloween costumes and the children were ready for the tricks and treats, laughing and carrying bags, and jumping into leaf piles. Dogs barking, a distant siren, and the smell of burning leaves — all these kept me company like shadow puppets trying to lull me into some state of normalcy.

This was not just another day. It was one of your favorite holidays even! Here next to me were some of my friends and colleagues against arms. I ran into a group of them going to the lecture and joined them. One of these *friends of a friend even looked a bit like you so I had another excuse to think of you and imagine you there whether with me or near me or behind me. With us or them or by yourself I could feel you there weighing some of the opinions of my group with your quiet questions—would they also doubt their cause? No, I suppose not.*

But you know how I feel—Ernie Pyle had the "Good War" behind him, the war that had meaning to many people on the earth opposed to evil. What do President Johnson and Dean Rusk have compared to this?

Nothing so eloquent or daring or moving as Ernie Pyle, that's for sure. I love your Hoosier reporter for having the nerve to tell us what he saw, and to forgive us back home if we could not understand it in its entirety. That was kind of him, for he gave us a way out of our amnesia, but I will not forget, nor will I be one back home who does not see the bodies.

I will see everything you see, Clayton, even if you do not write any of this or tell me any of this ever again in our lives. Can you see me? I am sitting next to you, even if I take up no space or leave behind no shadow. Just as you stood next to me in the Bryan Room looking down, I could hear you laughing before we both went down to join the others. The way you laugh, soft and low and long, a bit wistful, not a laugh of joy but of understanding.

Yours,

Maggie

PS: This one maple leaf I enclose with my drawing of the Well House must serve as formal representative of all those that are blanketing the campus, and I chose it because its one tip is yellow, its belly is orange, and the other tip a bright violet red. Not all of its neighbors exhibit this level of flexibility, and it seems like the right one to send to you.

War? Ernie Pyle? Conflict? Protests? There's a lot of conflict here. Truth? I don't know about that one. She's always after me to answer that one. What is truth? I sure don't know what it is. Except I know how I feel about her. She's special, so very special. I can't imagine what's going on back there or what it all might mean. All the protests and people actually against our country and against the war, it makes me sick! I am so thankful for Maggie. I don't know if I understand her sometimes but I know she is special to me. She is so pretty and kind and sensitive and she's as flexible as the beautiful maple leaf she sent and as strong as the tree it fell from. That's Maggie. I am so thankful to know her. God ... please watch over her.

Riggs needed sleep. Night duty was bad. Why did he have to follow a great letter from Maggie with another bad night in Nam? Truth was … none of it really mattered, he was in Con Thien and Con Thien was getting inside of him.

He drifted off with Cooter standing guard nearby. His thoughts were of Dean Rusk, war, the IU Campus, maple leaves and Maggie O'Reilly.

8

December15, 1967
Con Thien, Vietnam

Night duty on the line is a Number 10 – dinky dao. Riggs learned the local lingo like high school slang back home. Number 1 meant something was good to the Vietnamese, a way of communicating okay to the American troops. On the other end, Number 10 was their way of saying something was bad. The locals picked up a little English and were quick to let the Marines know where they stood. You heard it everywhere.

It was 0300. Every Marine on the hill was on edge. Riggs basked in the glow left by the letter from Maggie O'Reilly. He sat in disbelief that she felt the way she did. He knew how he felt but always felt she was just being a good friend. They were too different to be more than friends. But reading her words made him think. They also made him feel good about himself and so much better about them.

"Pssst! Pssst! Riggs," came a quiet whisper coming from the position to his right. Riggs's adrenaline was pumping overtime at the mere thought of more action.

"I got movement!" came another, more urgent, frightened whisper in the night. Riggs reached out to shake Cooter just as the night sky lit up like the Fourth of July. Bullets sang in the night, whizzing overhead, cracking as they broke the night air, so close to his ears he could feel them pass by. Tracers painted the night as rounds of deadly AK fire filled the black of night as Con Thien got hit from the ground.

"What the hell?" Cooter came to life with a shock. He and Riggs lay side by side in their foxholes, blazing away with their automatic M-14's.

BOOM! BOOM! Grenades broke the night on both sides of the concertina wire that served as the line of demarcation between good and evil. Madness flew in both directions as the enemy hurled themselves in a major probe of the Marine lines.

KAAABOOOOM!

A huge explosion rang out to the right of Riggs and Cooter.

"Holy shit!" screamed Cooter. "It's sappers!"

Class was in session and Riggs was about to learn a serious lesson. Sappers were bad guys with huge satchel charges who threw themselves on the wire protecting the Marine compound and gave their life in the process.

Earth shattering, ear-splitting combat erupted on all sides. The din of a calm night gave way to chaos and turmoil that lasted just over an hour. Several NVA regulars breached the perimeter with a blitz in a maniacal race to kill anything in their path and serve notice just who was in charge of the DMZ.

Moto stood tall, blasting away with an M-60 machine gun. To Riggs, a rookie combatant, it was something out of a movie. When he saw Moto in the light of the flares he froze in disbelief, empty of imagination.

Marine artillery roared in so close it buried everyone's face down in the mud. Round after round landed, exploding in a deafening blast that sent enemy soldiers flying in the air.

My God there's one ... they're in here ... Cooter!

Riggs barely had time to react when an NVA regular, a shadow in the silvery background of mortar illumination, came running like a wild bull right at Cooter who was kneeling, back to the bad guy, helping a fallen Marine from his squad.

BRRRRRRRRRRP!

Riggs cut loose with a full magazine, sending the intruder twisting to his death right before his eyes. He turned the other way only to pull the trigger and hear the deafening CLICK of an empty rifle. He was out of ammo. He fumbled with his cartridge belt in a desperate attempt to find another magazine before another NVA came roaring in his face.

Where is it? Where is it? I need ammo!

Riggs's blinding fear disappeared as the roar of Moto's M-60 split the night behind him. He was beside the fumbling Riggs and mowed down a row of five or six gooks running headlong at the trio. The fight continued for nearly two hours moving from dark to light.

Daylight brought quiet and the heat of day to the Marines of Echo 2-4. They had held strong once again on a little mound of dirt known as Con Thien. But holding strong had come with a price ... to both sides.

The retreat of forward elements of the 324th B Division had left behind 37 of their dead, now laying in various stages of disarray, inside and outside the perimeter of Clayton Wesley Riggs's new hometown.

He escaped without a scratch, losing only another layer of innocence. Cooter was lucky. He had only a minor shrapnel wound. Then there was Moto, who ran around the hill in full view of God and all those NVA. He didn't get a scratch. He was too mean to die or so it seemed to Riggs.

The Marines spent much of the day cleaning up the battlefield and caring for the wounded. Riggs helped a grunt zip four dead Marines in their green body bags for the long and lonely ride home. That was one job he already knew he hated.

It was around 1700 hours before the sound of the whirling blades on the Medevac choppers made it through the fog of an early evening monsoon day. A day when the rains might have been the tears of a crying world about to receive even more bad news from a war they cared little about.

When the choppers left, Riggs lay in his hole like one of the hundreds of spent cartridges strewn across the muddy ground of Con Thien.

What am I doing here? What is this all about? I'm killing people like I used to when I played war with my cousin. Running in the woods on our farm or his ... man, we'd play all day. Only this isn't play, this is war and it's terrible. Truth? Maggie O'Reilly, the truth is, people are dying and I'm not sure why. That's the only truth I see right now. And I know the truth is I miss you.

"Get some sleep, we're going out again at 0100." It was Moto. He never looked tired or worn out... he never looked angry or even frightened ... he always looked the same ... determined and mean. Only Cooter seemed to like him. Riggs had never seen anyone quite like Moto and wasn't sure he wanted to either.

I don't like that guy. I know I need him around at times like last night but I don't like him. I really don't.

Riggs was instantly lost in thought.

What a roller coaster I'm riding over here. One minute I'm in heaven with Maggie and the next, we're in hell. Up and down. This is worse than the big roller coaster at Cedar Point. Wow. Cedar Point. I'd rather be there right now with Maggie than here in this slime pit. This place works on your mind.

I can't believe I can go from being on top of the world one minute and frightened out of my mind the next. What if Maggie is right? What if war is wrong? What is true? I've only been here a few days and there's not much truth around this place.

"Riggs! You asshole! Quit day dreamin' and get some sleep."

Moto caught Riggs by surprise and scared his heart out of his chest and up his throat.

"Yessir! Riggs barely mumbled a faint answer from his stupor.

"I'm not a 'yessir' … get your head out yur' ass … now. We're goin'out at 0100 and you be ready!"

Those were Moto's parting words. They were words Riggs would take to heart. He didn't like Moto but he knew he'd better listen to him if he wanted to go back home to Hope. He crawled in his foxhole, put his poncho on and fumbled in his backpack for his letter. It was his third letter and the 3rd day of Christmas. The farm kid from Hope needed a mental lift after the carnage of the last few hours.

9

December 15, 1967
Con Thien, Vietnam

Riggs carefully unfolded the precious letter from his special friend. He tried desperately to pretend all was normal in an abnormal world.

November 15, 1967
Bloomington, Indiana

Three Cornish Hens—
—As seen from our picnic basket

Dear Clayton,

A few weeks back I went with my friend Judy to Riddle Point to look at the lake—she had never seen it and I even remembered the way from our visit last spring—seven miles out Tenth and then left at Tunnel Road. The name reminded me of the "tunnel vision" I thought I had after spending the day with you—such a small world we created between us with a bridge to the real world that might look narrow from the outside.

I was thinking as we approached the lake in her car how appropriate it is we are going to Lake Lemon, for it was a bit sour seeing the place without the redbuds and flowering trees and ducks—without sitting down to lunch with you on a warm patch of grass.

Instead of a new beginning to the season of abundant growth Judy and I found the signs of its fall, beautiful as they are. And unlike our visit in May we saw no eagles nor did any animals approach to talk to us or beg a bite of something to eat. I imagine if you were there with us it might have been quite different.

Judy is quiet and reserved like you but she might not think to coax the birds and squirrels to come closer the way you do, or she might never try to explain the treat in your hands, or what makes it right for them to trust you.

Judy went walking up the shoreline on the other side of the sandy dirt area. I stayed behind on the bench with a book but I spent most of my time looking out at the water.

There was one family there, a couple with two small children and a dog—the typical American scene, only they were walking by, not sitting down to rest as I was. Actually the parents were walking and the kids were running wild—then they moved out of my sight and it was only me going back in my mind to the time we spent there just half a year ago. It seems like ten years, or sometimes ten days—I am not sure which.

Do you remember what was in the basket I prepared for us? I think you do, since you had some very particular things to say about "my kind of food"—as if you and I were from different planets or species. It was only the cheeses and artichoke hearts I think that were actually mysterious to you, other than the size of the "puny chickens" as you called them.

I had fixed four Cornish hens with sage marinade—not three, but in keeping with our third day of Christmas letters, it will be three for the record—and you had joked about how chickens that puny would never even get to the neck-wringing stage on your farm and were they corny for the corn feed they liked or their own goofy natures they started out with.

Then you asked what they might think of their basket neighbors—the boiled eggs in particular, that must have looked huge in comparison, like the product of Super Hens and all the confusion this might create in this already confused community. So you had them talking to each other, squabbling and near fisticuffs (remember how you loved that word?) about who got *"dressed first" by me, and who got "dressed best" and how a few bits of sage dressing does not an outfit make, and how at least a leaf of fresh basil wrapped round the middle would offer some covering or badly needed coloring in such a sad sack line-up of baked birds. Or even a tomato vest might do!*

You also thought they might feel more comfortable keeping company not with themselves or the big eggs but with the Italian candies in the basket, which resembled, after all, eggs of a reasonable size. But that again was another illusion you announced, since these were only filled with hazelnuts, not new life of another silly chicken. What appeared to be perhaps white feathers of a newly sprung chick were actually coconut flakes! You never had hazelnuts I remember, and you were surprised to find them in the center of the candies. And then you told me of the only place you had eaten coconut, in your mother's coconut crème pie.

I have forgotten none of these things—does that surprise you? These thoughts go way past the details I wrote in my journal about places we went, way into parts of our conversations that still resonate due to their unique flavor. So many things you said were something quite new to me, and your approach to all living things was so like the way my parents had raised me. This we shall always have in common, no matter what comes of either of us.

You know I will never make that coconut crème pie properly even with your mother's blessings and the secret recipe she was so kind to share with me—I will tell NO ONE of the lemon zest and coconut in the crust, I PROMISE.

I will be going home for Thanksgiving of course, and will try to make that pie for my family. I am so sorry you cannot be there to judge. Even if out of your sweet nature you would not criticize my effort, I would be able to tell if you were hiding something from me.

You know that you can hide very little from me? Did you know that even a wrinkle of doubt passing over your face will cast some shadow in my mind and that I will read you like a book not read by candlelight but in the full light of a summer afternoon?

Did you know that your shyness and the quiet you present in company is not the "you" inside that I know has many things to say about this and that—and your confidence in yourself is not shyness at all, but just your unwillingness to always prove yourself in the face of another or at the expense of another! I remember this look of quiet goes right away as soon as anything threatens your friends and family, even your furry and feathery friends, and then your quiet look turns to fierceness.

When that man at the lake asked us for matches or a lighter just to get closer and talk to us, and you looked at him like he could be the enemy or the friend, and you were ready to tip either way if he looked at me for one more moment without turning away. I know you hated the way he gazed at me, and you were torn about how to react. I will not forget that, feeling totally protected but sure that your judgment would be sound on how to talk to him. And it was.

But now I've gone wandering, for I was talking about how I might be successful at making this cocoa nutty family heirloom of yours for my family. If I get eggs straight from the chickens and fresh butter like your mother does, I might have a chance, but the stuff I buy in the store does not do it right.

It's the little things that make a difference in cooking, don't you think? But maybe that is the same for most anything successful—we like to notice details and we are sometimes happy with the most humble or simple offering. I was thinking of how on top of your kindness toward your baby sister and all beings smaller and weaker than you, there are many small things you do to make it clear to them you care.

Beth is only seven but you never talk down to her, treating her like the baby in the family who understands nothing of the grown-up world. And the way you scratch Bob behind the ears when he rests at your feet—he knows this is something you do because he likes it.

No dog is man's best friend just because he is a man. But when you are kind to me I know it is not because I am weaker or younger—of course, I am ahead of you by nearly one year—or because I need some special kindness from you but because you are by nature this way. It is spontaneous and almost non-thinking, and I cannot reconcile this with you in a war zone, except I am sure you risk your own life every day to save your friends. This would be your way.

But enough of this! I was telling you about the peaceful countryside of your fair state, and how the seasons have turned to ready themselves for the hard winter coming. The lake looks like a sheet of granite as the sky covers up in clouds. There are squirrels gathering and digging not far from where I sit leaning on the picnic table. The sun is stingy now and the year 1967 draws quickly to a close.

It has been an amazing year altogether and I hope the next will be better and wiser and not so violent. But something tells me it is not to be, and the best I can do is pray for an end to the fighting and most especially for your safety.

Is this fair? If I pray for you in particular would this make it more likely that you will be okay? That your friends might fall instead? But I have told you that today I will talk of the good times we had, not of the war—why do I keep returning to it?

When Judy came back from her walk up the shore we didn't stay very long. A cool wind gave us a chill, and the sun was going down, so we headed back in time for *something she had to do. But when I stayed with you in this same spot it seemed the sun was taking a slow turn in the sky and time passed with no obvious hurry to meet any deadline.*

I remember the strawberries I brought were so large, from California probably, and you told me of those you grow at home, how small and sweet they were, and how soft too, for they seem to breed them with a touch of cardboard for help in shipping—your suggestion.

The strawberry stain on my blouse never really came out. You told me the strawberries from your garden would never dare stain my silks, and that is when I caught you in a real lie that you had to confess to. We debated who had the best food growing up—my family with its city markets and imported goods from around the world, or your garden basket from the farm where everything was fresh and quick to the table from the land.

But our picnic was not only about food, was it? It was also the first time I saw you outside in the trees and hills that you said reminded you of your home. I learned much about you and your family and your home, as you did about mine.

And the beautiful quilt that we sat on—that too was a family heirloom. When you told me the intertwining loops were called the Wedding Ring pattern, often favored for a bride's wedding gift, I could see the string of vows that marriage involves, like the string of rings on the quilt.

And when I told you it was too fancy to sit on outside, you said that there was no better time than now to enjoy it, that it had lasted for two or three generations of living, not being hung on a wall. I like that—living art, not stuck out of reach, behind frames.

And you were right—the quilt did make the picnic special and that pattern of circles holding each other securely but not tightly seems like the way you hold onto life. You have the ability to make even a simple thing like sharing a meal outside appear as a very grand and casual event at the same time. Perhaps because you, my friend, are so grand and casual and that's why everything you do has these qualities.

Do you blush when I talk to you like this Clayton? I prefer this red on your cheek to any other red that might come from you—please keep it all inside your skin and be safe.

Yours,

Maggie

10

December 16, 1967
Con Thien, Vietnam

A warm glow rolled through Riggs covering him from head to toe. There was a special kind of magic in Maggie's message. He was cold, filthy and dripping wet on the outside but inside, he was a new man. Riggs knew he'd walk through hell to hear Maggie O'Reilly's voice one more time. To go on one more picnic. To share one more sunset or sunrise. He couldn't imagine a quilt so fine as the one Maggie talked of in her letter. How could he imagine something so special in the midst of the mud and filth where he now sat?

The picnic and the lake ... what a day that was ... and to know how she feels ... and I have to be here. I will be home. I will.

It was 0 dark 30 … 12:30 am in civilian time, not a time many Marines at Con Thien could remember. Even Riggs was having trouble recalling life back home and he'd only been here a few long days. If it weren't for Maggie's letters he would be lost in time.

Oh man. I gotta' get my mind focused and on this place not on Maggie. I still can't believe she took the time to send me those letters. I've got one a day for twelve days, nine more to go. Her letters keep me going and keep me ...

"Riggsy … you ready?" It was Cooter. He was walking point tonight and Riggs was about to find out he was walking second. Vance and Moto weren't about to let a new guy walk point. But they wanted Riggs up to speed so up front was the order of the day.

Cooter, Riggs and the other two Marines in their Fire Team picked up their gear and headed to the center of their humble hilltop base for last minute instructions.

"Did you get your head outta' yur ass?" Moto's first words to Riggs picked up where he left off. Riggs bristled in the dew of the very early morning.

What the hell has he got against me? I've done what I'm supposed to ...

It wasn't long before Maggie O'Reilly, a fall picnic and the fragrance of a pig farm were the furthest things from his mind.

"Remember Riggs, even a kick in the ass is a step forward." It was Cooter, a smile on his blackened face, teeth glowing, leaning near his ear and whispering to his new friend and new back-up point man.

At least somebody here is nice. But how on earth do you whisper in a Texas drawl? I'm beginning to really like this guy.

Lt. Vance gave the patrol a short briefing on the operation. Moto would lead a group of 18 out to the north and west. If all went well they would circle behind any bad guys near the base and hit them near dawn when they tried to make their way back into the thick, humid jungle of the DMZ.

Another group of twenty Marines were heading out the opposite direction to loop around to the south and west. Their objective was similar ... encircle the NVA who were now brazen enough to challenge the Marines of Con Thien almost every night.

It was 0100 and time to venture into the dark and mist, into NVA country. Cooter stood next to Riggs, Moto readied the others.

"Cooter, one of these days I'm telling Moto what I think of him," Riggs whispered a little louder than he should have.

"Riggsy, as we say in Texas ... speak your mind, but make damned sure you ride a fast horse, " Cooter responded.

"Saddle up," Moto growled like a bulldog going for a bone.

Cooter led the way to the perimeter. Stopping, he turned and said, "Riggs, you cover my back man ... this is the badlands out there. No mistakes."

"You don't worry Coot, I'm here."

Riggs walked a little taller, as he stepped gingerly through the concertina wire, knowing at least he was trusted by Cooter. He knew Cooter was counting on him. He also knew Moto wouldn't let him walk second in the column if he didn't trust him. He knew that for sure.

It feels good to be trusted, to be counted on. I feel like Dad and Grandpa looked when I saw them talk about their wars. Well, now I got my own. I can do this. I know I can.

Walking off into the night felt like a bad Halloween trick back home that had gone sour. The night was chilly and the fog was thick and dripping. The fog was weird; it was waist high, giving everyone a ghoulish feeling as they moved deeper into their fears. Cooter looked like half a man walking in front of Riggs as they descended the hill into the ravine that would lead them away from the base.

I hate the way this feels out here. This area scares me to death. The jungle is closing in around us. They could be anywhere … just like last time. Where are they? How do you know?

Cooter moved like a cat ready to pounce on an unsuspecting mouse near the barn back home. He measured every step as if it was going to be his last. Riggs had to stay closer than he liked. It was so dark he could barely make out Cooter's half silhouette moving through the dark jungle, closing, swallowing them from all sides. Riggs stepped up his pace to stay close enough not to lose him, but staying far enough away that if Cooter hit a booby trap, he'd survive.

What the heck was that? Cooters still moving? I heard something ... I know I did. Why doesn't he stop? Why doesn't he slow down? What's he doing? Man I am scared!

Cooter had been through here before and he didn't like it either. It was an area with steep sides, tall grass and sagging jungle trees with huge leaves that dripped from the heavy dew. It was a great place for an ambush and every Marine knew it.

Riggs was spooked but Cooter wasn't going to waste time with every noise that broke the nighttime silence. He was hell bent on getting through what the old salts called 'the draw' before something bad came down. It was not an area to half step, hesitate or stop.

Glancing at his watch, Riggs knew they'd been moving now for an hour. It was a little after 0200.

I need a break man, slow down. I don't like the pace any better than I like the place. How do we know we're not racing into an ambush ourselves? I don't like it. I'm beat, exhausted but no one cares. What am I doing here?

They were now deep in the eerie jungles north of Con Thien; the land rolled gently, providing great cover to whoever got there first. Cooter hoped it was he and his patrol of eighteen not so merry young men.

They reached a Y in the trail and Cooter stopped to make sure this was the spot where he was to change direction and lead his group to the west. Riggs, tired and sore, shuffled up behind him, leaning over his pack where he was sure he could hear him …

"Hey man let's take a short break and get our bearings." Riggs was unsure and nervous.

"Riggsy," Cooter said, pausing. "Nobody ever drowned in their own sweat … suck it up … we've got a ways to go."

Man how could I do that? He'll never trust me now. What am I thinking? Am I thinking? Why did I do that? I always do something to mess things up.

The confidence and camaraderie Riggs felt just over an hour ago had vanished into the stifling night air. He felt like a little boy back home when the pigs got away when he was doing the feeding. His confidence waned and his mind shook from his self-inflicted pain of disbelieving his own abilities.

Before Riggs got his bearings, Cooter took off on a trail heading to the left. The pace was faster than before and they went on for another hour. It was near 0330 when they stopped to set up their position. Moto directed them into position for a modified ambush, hoping to spring death on an unsuspecting NVA team doping along in the early morning.

Thank God we stopped. I need a break. I need sleep and I want to get this over and go back to Con Thien. I need another letter from my best friend. I need to get home when this is over. I don't need to be out here doing this.

The small group of lonely Marines sat, enduring an unnerving silence. Then the background music of Vietnam shattered the night with the distant sounds of mortars dropping on Con Thien. They were receiving a heavy barrage of incoming. The enemy mortars were firing from near their position. The radio began to crackle with information, noise and Moto, who'd joined the fray and was receiving direction from Lieutenant Vance.

I never thought I'd feel good about being out here in the black of night but it sounds better than the alternative right now. Con Thien is getting it again. There'll be more wounded and more death when we get back tomorrow.

Cooter was summoned to the center with Moto.

This can't be good. When these two get together something is about to come down. Man, I'm out here on the end and I'm alone. This is not good. What's going on? What are they talking about?

Riggs was wired, tense, and fighting with himself to keep his courage. His nerves were on his fingertips as his trigger finger tightened its grip around the half moon metal piece that connected him with burning death. One squeeze and death would spew its ugly answer into an unsuspecting enemy.

Man that incoming sounds bad. Con Thien is getting hit like nothing I've seen. Oh no, I can hear the whomp of the outgoing mortars right in front of us ... I know that sound now. I know it. It's out here in front of us. They don't know we're here.

Vance radioed Moto with the painful news. Our patrol was too close to the NVA mortar man in front of us to allow Marine mortars or artillery to respond. Con Thien was getting pounded and the only one who could stop it was Moto's patrol.

Cooter clamored back, motioning Riggs and the rest to fall in behind him. His Fire Team crept their way towards the whomp, whomp, whomp of the outgoing enemy mortars.

This is insane. It is just insane. I can't see a thing.

With silent steps in the pitch black of night, eighteen Marines, led by Cooter and his four man Fire Team, inched closer to an unseen enemy who was destroying their comrades a few hundred yards away.

Riggs's mind fought for focus. He needed to be front and center for the inevitable firefight about to erupt. He thought his heart would explode with each beat. His mind began to drift, floating to somewhere stateside, hoping upon hope to survive, to nurture a friendship that made him whole. Hoping he would survive to fight another day and return to the girl of his dreams.

Voices! They're not our voices. They're the high pitch ying yang I heard outside our lines last night. My God. My God we have snuck up on'em. My God. It's time.

Riggs was amazed he and the team could move around in total darkness. The fire teams each split up, three with four men each and two with three. Spreading out in a line, poised like a lion protecting her cubs. Ready to attack an invisible foe making a deadly noise that rained death on a distant hill.

BOOM! BOOM! BOOM!

The Marines attacked with Moto leading the way with grenades flying in the night. Screams pierced the air like a shrill foghorn in a cold bay. Screams have their own language; they speak of pain, fright and misery. It was a language understood by all.

BRRRP! BOOM! Brrrrp. Brrrrp.

The fighting was heavy with tracers flying like streaks of fireworks in the night sky. The smell of black powder fought the stench of death for control of the night.

"Move! Move!" It was Cooter up and running into the darkness. Riggs and the remaining Marines of their fire team were off chasing their Texan leader.

This is nuts. It's chaos. It doesn't make sense!

Riggs ran forward shooting his M-14 from the hip on full auto. He was chasing friends headlong into an invisible enemy. Side by side with people he'd met a few days before but would love for a lifetime. Racing in the night, firing wildly at people firing at him, Riggs jumped over a mass he could barely see and …

"Riggs, Riggs wake the hell up!"

"Riggs you're okay buddy, get up … we gotta' get up and outta' here man." Cooter was trying desperately to wake Riggs from wherever he found himself, unconscious on the jungle floor. He was out cold.

"What the hell's wrong with him?" Moto asked, mystified that anyone was flat on his back and not bleeding.

"Look at his head" Cooter said, "He must have run into that tree branch up there," he said, pointing just above Moto's head. "We can't find a scratch on him but he must have knocked himself out."

Moto grinned an evil grin, one he'd trademarked some time ago following a human wave assault in Helicopter Valley. He stepped over to where Riggs was laying on his back.

"Pig farmer … get the hell up!" Moto screamed reaching down and slapping him across the face a couple times like a scene from a bad John Wayne movie.

Riggs rolled his head back and forth and finally his eyes popped open. He looked up, shocked to see Moto, Cooter and the morning sky right before his eyes.

Where on earth am I? What's going on? What happened to me? Where are the NVA?

Up and on his feet, the cobwebs began to leave his aching head as Riggs began to realize what had happened. A grizzled looking Moto reached down to hand Riggs his helmet. He realized it wasn't a tree limb that took the pig farmer to the deck.

"Damn!" Moto growled. "You're one lucky pig farmer."

He reached out and showed Riggs a torn hole that went straight through the right side of his helmet. He had taken a direct hit from an AK-47 round and lived to tell about it.

How can that be? That thing missed my head by an inch. Oh my God how can that be?

Moto gathered his tattered group and led them back to Con Thien. They'd stood tall and done good. They had knocked out an NVA mortar position … even if by accident. But then the whole war seemed to be one big accident didn't it?

At Con Thien the news wasn't as good. Moto's legions had all come back standing, with only two wounded and one real, real lucky guy by the name of PFC Riggs. The NVA had at least a dozen killed and who knows how many wounded. They wouldn't be happy about this surprise in their backyard.

The Marines at Con Thien, the ones on the receiving end of the mortars, weren't so lucky. They suffered 4 dead and 6 wounded. The choppers were on their way and the unlucky among them were being zipped up for the ride home.

"Hey Riggs, I heard what happened. I need to check you out." It was the Doc, that's what all Corpsman were called in the Marine Corps. No one ever seemed to know if they had a real name or not.

"I'm fine," Riggs replied meekly.

He was hiding a splitting headache, as well as all the other aches and pains that made him feel like he'd been beaten about the head and shoulders all night long.

While the Doc checked him over Riggs was off, drifting along in his own reality, one of his own making, thanks to a special friend back home.

I never knew a black man until the Marines. The first I really was close to was in Boot camp and I really couldn't know them there. But this guy, this Corpsman, Doc, he is so kind, so nice ... he doesn't seem like he belongs in a place like this. But do any of us belong here? We're just a bunch of young people looking for more body bags and more misery about to start the long ride home. Truth? Maggie wants to know what truth is ... I don't see it here.

The Corpsman left, pronouncing Riggs ready and well … and real lucky.

"You'll be fine but get some rest today, as best you can." Doc walked off to watch over the wounded that were lined up awaiting evacuation.

I can't believe what just happened to me. But I don't remember a thing. Just getting up to run, running for my life and the lives of my fellow Marines. I wasn't sure where I was running or what I was doing really. Then I wake up and see Moto and Cooter and the morning sky. I got shot and it missed. I can't believe it.

I just want this over. I just want to go home and sleep in my bed. I want to go walk with Maggie in the park. I want her to tell me the things she writes. I want to go on that picnic again and even eat those little puny birds. I want so bad to be out of here and back home with Maggie.

The rains ratcheted back from a downpour to a slight drizzle. After living days on end with water pouring from the sky, a slight drizzle was like no rain at all. The monsoon made life miserable for anyone that dared live in its path. It was 0950 and Riggs was dead to the world and only wanted peace however he had to get it.

He fell back in his hole, head laying back on a water-logged pack, he drifted off thinking about what might have been and most of all … what he hoped would be.

11

December 16, 1967
Con Thien, Vietnam

Riggs didn't return to the living for several hours. He woke up feeling very different than when he slipped off the cliff into a deep sleep. His head still ached and so did the rest of his weary body.

Why didn't that bullet hit me? Why am I still standing and others are on their way home in a bag? I didn't see a flash of light or a long tunnel but this is more than luck. If you want the truth I know that's it. That bullet missed me by a half an inch and there's a reason.

Riggs hadn't written home to anyone, not his Mom, Dad or Maggie. He was too busy fighting, sleeping and the little time he had he was reading letters from Maggie. Now he wanted to write. He wanted to write and tell everyone what had happened. He wanted to tell Maggie this new truth he had just experienced.

Can I tell her stuff like this? Can I share this stuff with her the way she feels about war? Do I want to share it with her? She is so pure, so natural, so kind and caring. I don't know if I can share it. I don't know if I want to. Maybe it's mine to live with and understand.

He had perimeter watch in two hours. He reached into his pack and pulled out the plastic bag that was home to the greatest gift Clayton Wesley Riggs had ever received. It was a gift he couldn't have imagined just a short time ago. Now he wanted to savor each and every one of the letters from Maggie O'Reilly. This was her special gift with her message of the Twelve Days of Christmas.

This was the fourth day of the twelve gifts that went straight to Riggs's heart. He carefully opened the bag with all the anticipation of a four year old on Christmas morning. He took out his green, upside down L-shaped flashlight, braving the wrath of Moto. He slid down into his foxhole, covering up with his poncho as a final move to push the world of Vietnam far out of sight.

November 16, 1967
Bloomington, Indiana
"A song for every heart"

Dear Clayton,

I went to an event at the School of Music last night, a violin concerto at the Auditorium. I entered the hall and glided to the same place we sat when we heard the female quartet singing those beautiful melodies last spring.

For some reason sitting in the same spot made me feel that you were still right next to me—because the place was empty and reserved for you. Remember how the girls looked so sweet as they sang, and one nearly closed her eyes during her solo, seeming to be calling out from another world than the auditorium. I felt the same way.

Last night during the violin solo I closed my eyes too and thought of you during your favorite season and what songs you might sing to yourself or your friends to bring a touch of home to mind. Or what tunes your grandfather played on his hand-made fiddle—the songs with such clever names. I also thought of the visit we made to the violin shop where you asked Ole Dahl about the recipe for what did you call it? Not the violin glaze (I'm thinking of cooking here) but the stain made with resins and herbs. You told him how your grandfather's secret was passed down just like your mother's recipe for coconut crème pie.

Last night I wore the same black dress that I had on when we went to the opera—do you remember it? (But without the pearl necklace and bracelet.) Of course, no one told me that I "clean up good" as you did, and my date was my girlfriend Judy, not the handsome guy in the dark gray suit and silver cuff links and creamy shirt and silk tie.

I remember having to drag you into Whitesides to look at suits, after your confessing you hadn't worn one since your granduncle's funeral and you didn't look good in them. And how you were proved wrong not by me (for you did not believe me) but by all the women who turned their heads to look at you at the concert making me think you looked too good and perhaps I might even be jealous if you returned their gaze. But you never did—such a gentleman you are.

And when that Brook Brothers fit you perfectly you wouldn't let me buy it for you, even though you knew it was my dad's money for me to use, as I like. I told you the things he wastes it on including me and all my indulgences, and you said it was his hard work that made him rich so I shouldn't waste it.

I had to remind you he was spoiled as a child, never really having to work but wanting to and he in turn spoiled his wife and children so that they would never have to work for some "crooked money grubbers." You were so nice to wonder out loud why he was not a moneygrubber and why I was not spoiled yet. When I bought the suit behind your back you did not spoil my pleasure, did you? Secretly you must have known that suit had your name on it, as the man who fitted you had said.

And since Honey Jones can be a big man off-campus, I too feel free to call you honey without offending you, right? Hoosiers do things like that, call strangers by sweet names and make it sound most natural and respectful too.

This is something I have learned in my new home, though coming from me it does not have the same tone as from Mr. Jones or from you my friend. But the way he says it also sounds different from the way you do. No one has ever called me anything so sweet as you telling me "honey, you clean up good." And no one has looked at me the way you did before or since, no matter what I wear.

You always surprise me Clayton, even if your last surprise was very sad and totally scary. My mind returns to all the good surprises you gave me—not that I condone the one real prank you played on me—this I will not forgive! When after the curtain went down at intermission you took my hand to lead me out into the crowd and we went outside to look at the stars.

You twirled me around to make my skirt float like a boat and you said that someday you might set sail, with me as the masthead steering the way. If I had known where the stars would take you I might have gone in the opposite direction away from all this—my way.

At the time this surprised me, how comfortable you were in your new suit and silver links. When you accepted my help to get your tie knotted and the links in their proper place, you said you'd never been fussed over so. Let this not be the last time I get to link you into those shirtsleeves!

When you come home they can hose you down so to be spanking clean and crispy for another event that warrants your fancy duds. Tell your mother not to let those hungry country moths find their dinner in your Brooks Brothers, okay? I am now attached to the jacket in a doubly personal way, since I got to wear it too when you walked me home.

Last night when the girl singing of spring started her solo, all these images of blooming trees and flowers came back to me, how you collected a bundle of petals from the branches of the flowering crabapple and made them rain down upon me so that I was dotted and sprinkled like a cake of powdered sugar patterns.

Then you sang that song to me about wishing to be a crabapple hanging from the tree (you added the crab to apple, didn't you?) and every time my Cindy comes she takes a bite of me. You sang, "Get along home, Maggie, Maggie" instead of Cindy, Cindy and this surprised me too.

When I asked you how you learned to sing so well you told me of your grandmother talking to you during your visits to that special church where you learned shape-note singing in four parts and you compared the four part harmonies of the Southern Harmony songbooks to the four girls singing.

How the harmonies and rhythms at that church were almost as complex as your untrained singers who maybe didn't know how to read real music, and that's why the shape notes were created. They could read from shape instead of placement on the page. I still haven't heard your four-part harmonies with notes made of diamonds and squares too, so that also will be left for another day.

The wind is blowing outside and the branches scratch at my window, trying to tell me some secret. Like the quartet we heard singing, I bring you winds from the four corners of the earth to soothe your weary soul as it journeys in a strange land. I fear that you know no sound sleep, and that your rest escapes you. You worried even when your animals suffered the smallest discomfort, though you cared little for your own comfort.

I do not think too much on the present or the future now, for they are so uncertain, so I am more comfortable looking to the past—our past when I think of you. But the cloud of the past always contains the lining of the future. I will not be greedy and ask for a silver lining, any lining at all will do, just so there is a future.

Thanksgiving is upon us but I won't give true thanks until you are home. I miss you Clay. I miss all of our times together, the laughs, the debates, our walks, the picnics and the drives in the country. There will always be a song in my heart for the memories we have shared.

Already the campus is quieter as people leave to meet with their family and friends. So this calling girl calls out to you her own solo--please take care, be safe, and come home soon.

Maggie

That is so sweet. She is so special. How I wish I could go home and be with her. I wish we could sit at the Well House and talk like we did last year. I want to talk for hours on end so I can tell her what this is like. She could make sense of my feelings. I have to write and tell her how I feel. It is just so ... so ... I don't know anymore; it's hard to put in words what I feel right now except that I know I am a better person for knowing Maggie O'Reilly. I just want to be with her.

Riggs was changing in a way he didn't understand. Life was different. He was no longer the kid back on the farm in Hope, Indiana. He lost his innocence his first day in Vietnam and through these letters realized he had gained a special friend. He didn't understand his feelings or the things he was seeing … nothing made sense anymore.

12

December 17, 1967
Con Thien, Vietnam

"Riggs!" It was Cooter.

Oh man. I'm tired, I feel like crap. All I can think of is Maggie and here we go again. Out in the wilds where I don't wanna' be.

"Yea … whatdya' need?" replied a bedraggled, reluctant Riggs.

"Hey man, the Doc says you stay in today. We're goin' out on a daylight patrol so you keep the home fires burnin'."

I have to go. Now I feel bad. I don't want to stay here if they're going out. You have to go out with your team. No way.

"Cooter, come on. I want to go out with you guys."

Cooter had been in Nam for nearly a year. He wasn't long for the place, as he'd be rotating home soon. He stayed alive by knowing people. He knew Riggs didn't really mean it. He knew he wouldn't go himself if he didn't have to. He knew he was just suffering from the guilt of not doing what he knew he was trained to do.

"Riggsy … you earned the break, take it," Cooter slyly replied, as he started walking away.

"I give you my word Cooter, I'm okay."

Cooter stopped, turned in the early morning light, looking back at Riggs with a hint of a grin creeping across his bearded face.

"Riggsy, the best way to keep your word is to not give it foolishly."

Well that's not foolish to want to go with your troops. I hate it out there but I feel worse back here with them out there. I just don't feel right. I know I should go but he's leaving me.

Cooter walked away with Riggs lost in his own thoughts about keeping his word and about being a sitting duck all day on Con Thien.

I hate sitting here waiting for more incoming. After the bombs, come the cries for Corpsman up! Oh man I don't want to get blown up. I don't want to go home like those guys yesterday. I want my arms and legs. I want to walk and talk and be with Maggie and back on my farm. I want to go to college.

Riggs was banished to the hill for the whole day. It was 0640 and his team was leaving. He was guarding a perimeter that no one would challenge in the light of day. It was going to be a long, boring day unless the mortars came. He heard someone walking and turned around to find Lt. Vance behind him.

"PFC … how are you feeling?"

"Fine Sir, I wanted to go with my squad," Riggs replied, feeling like he'd skipped school and been caught by Grandpa. He always felt like he couldn't let his family down.

"Well, Riggs, you take the day and get ready for tomorrow. Doc thinks it's best. Appreciate what happened to you, most people don't get another chance like you have."

The Lieutenant surprised Riggs when he sat down and talked about the situation he faced on Con Thien. The NVA were closing in and trying to surround the base. He was hoping for a cease-fire with the approaching holidays. He was worried about their ability to hold out without more reinforcements.

Riggs hadn't been in the Corps long and had never sat and talked with a Lieutenant. They were God and you didn't approach them without a reason. It seemed Vance had a reason. He needed someone to share his concerns with, even if it was a new PFC.

Man, what does all that mean? I don't know what we're doing here. I don't know what to do about the NVA except go follow the others, especially Moto, and shoot them when I see them. None of this makes sense to me except they're Communists and we're Americans and we fight for freedom. What do I do now?

Riggs drifted in and out of reality most of the day. He still wasn't feeling well and was privately glad when the Doc held him back. He spent the day waffling between being the Marine his family wanted him to be and being the person Maggie O'Reilly was sure he was. He slept the day away.

I can't believe I've slept this much. I can't believe we haven't been shelled ... no mortars for a whole day? Don't believe it. They must be saving up for a big night. I don't feel right being here with the guys out there. At least I haven't heard any fighting. I hope they get back soon. I hope they're all okay.

The monsoon rains were even having a lazy day. The torrential downpour of a few days ago gave way to a soft, pattering drizzle. The heat that came with each afternoon made the humidity hang like a sagging tent that covered all of Con Thien.

I can't believe it's almost 1600. They should be back by now. I need to read my letter for today. I need a lift. I still can't accept that somebody like Maggie really likes me. I haven't really dated anybody. I don't know what it's supposed to feel like.

Well I guess I did date for a while when I was back in school. Can't believe I remembered her. Erin Vandivoort. Man, that seems like so long ago. She was nice, ran track like I did. We had a lot of fun that year.

I can't believe how far she could run. She outran me and I always thought I was in shape. I wonder what she's doing. I heard she went to school at Texas A & M of all places. I'll have to fix her up with Cooter. No, Erin wouldn't like a real bubba. She was too nice.

Riggs walked over to the center supply tent and got his daily handout of c-rations. When you were starving, it was time for some bean and franks and a little white bread, as horrible as it was. It wasn't much but it was filling. After chowing down it was nearly 1700. Night lurked nearby and with it the unknown of what another night in the DMZ might bring. Moto and Cooter were due back any minute.

I need to read my letter before something happens or it gets dark. What a novelty ... reading in the light of day. And I don't have Moto here to harass me. I love reading these letters. I can't believe it's me and she remembered all those things we did. She is amazing. I have a hard time believing we're friends.

Nervous with anticipation, Riggs began to read.

November 17, 1967
Chicago, Illinois
"A ring on each finger"

Dear Clayton,

Yesterday, I wrote my letter to you in the early morning before getting on the train to come home for what may be one of the more somber Thanksgiving vacations I've seen around here so far—my mother got into an argument this morning at church, with one of her very old friends, whose son is in the army but not overseas. This woman was complaining about all the war protesters, how they were undermining the morale of the troops and so on, and Mother said to her they cared more about the soldiers than anyone, that they were trying to save their lives for Christ's sake!

That did it—the woman attacked her for taking the Lord's name in vain while defending the draft dodgers and "peace nuts!" The woman gave Mother such a face full of venom. I'm telling you, if looks could wither she would be a puddle like the Wicked Witch of the West.

Mother answered that we should literally support peace for the sake of Christ, for he was all about loving your neighbors, not killing them. He would never approve of war for global power or money or land grabs, and that if He were here He'd be leading the troops protesting such idiocy and waste of young lives.

He would not be leading the troops into battle on foreign soil, where boys become murderers of innocent women and children.

It was t-e-n-s-e. I doubt the two will ever speak to each other again—not because of Mother—she is used to this sort of thing, for she is very outspoken and gets into trouble for it. (The apple falls not far from the tree, I can hear you thinking!) I started to say something about how Christ actually proclaimed He had come to bring the sword that would pit brother against brother, but Mother's look withered me and I shut up and sister and I pulled her on home. (Father never seems to be around for these scenes, though he finds them most amusing when he is told about them.)

It will just not go away, will it? The topic, that is. I planned to write you a nice letter about the gift of the five golden rings and the five golden fingers of the piano-playing hands of Hoagy Carmichael, but the incident at church has colored the day as it tints my pages as well. But since life is filled with bad and good, so too must my letters be.

Now that the bad is out of the way, I shall escape to my memories about you and what five rings might mean to me. It is the turning point in the Christmas song, the high separate note that makes the chorus twist into a different stream—a time to pause and change directions. Can you recall any time when you have seen five rings together—even if they are not all gold? (That's a hint) No, not the Olympic symbol, or the circles of the wedding ring pattern on the quilt, though these might both qualify.

Do you recall when we were walking from campus down Kirkwood to the square? It must have been March; we had just finished midterms, and we went into Williams Jewelry shop to look for a gift for your sister Beth. You thought I might be able to choose a necklace or bracelet a seven-year-old would wear.

After we found that lovely charm bracelet for your sis, I was distracted by the glass case with the velvet-lined shelves adorned with rings. Those rings had the most beautiful stones, the stones you could identify more easily than I could. When I decided to buy one, I asked your opinion of the amethyst in gold I had on the ring finger of my right hand.

You started looking at the others, discussing their qualities and teasing me about how I was hasty to reject them. "What about this one?" you asked as you picked up another and put it on my first finger and "that one" you said as you put it on my middle finger and "this little one" you said was for my little finger.

You teased me about how I was not so much a goldilocks with a "this one is too small and this one is just right" but a Crimsylocks, and what a good Indiana University student I was with creamy skin, a real campus patriot and every bit the Hoosier girl. All the while, you're trying to find the right size ring for each finger choosing from among the colors to make a rainbow of my hand—a blue sapphire, a purple amethyst, an aquamarine, a yellow citrine, a red ruby, a green emerald, a burgundy garnet—perhaps to confuse me. Finally you put one on my thumb and said, "Why not? You could start a new fashion."

So what does this mean to me? And why would this be a turning point for me or you—or for us?

It was something to do with a vision I had as I looked down at my hand that you were touching—for the first time. It was such a gentle touch, so casual, but really my hand was fire and ice, all tingly, not with all the semi-precious stones but with this sense that we had stepped over a line.

No, not anything so bright or simple as a man putting a ring on a lady's finger and all that it implies—though it was some of that too, giving you my hand to adorn, if not adore. There was something else too—what is it? I don't know! I don't know what it was then, but now I see how my hand is occupied with gifts for you in these letters.

The first being the gift of my drawing, the first one of you that I made, and the second I must say is my hand in a fist of protest over the injustices of war, a fist that may never unfurl in apathy, and the third is the gift of a picnic basket of dishes I made by hand for you, and the fourth, the ways of my hand that binds not only *the tie to your shirt but our friendship as well—But what is the fifth gift from my hand?*

Do you remember when, on our walk on a Halloween afternoon, you took me into the Book Nook and told me how Hoagy Carmichael used to visit this place and the Gables around the corner---and how 39 years ago to the day, he first recorded "Stardust?" I found his new biography, Sometimes I Wonder on the shelves. When I asked why you had refused your piano lessons, and that if you had continued you might be able to play like Hoagy, you answered, "Sometimes I wonder..."

I had to laugh at your silly ways of teasing me with words. By chance I turned right to the page of his book where he talks about his cousin's rhubarb pie. You guaranteed your mother's would beat out his cousin Amanda's any day of the week and I decided to make rhubarb pie instead of the coconut cream pie for Thanksgiving last year. (If you would get that recipe for me.)

You said you would have to tap your ancestors' accumulated skills in stealth and military strategy to get it from your mother—bribery or torture, whatever worked, but not to hold my breath. After all, coconut crème pie is one thing, but rhubarb pie is something else—and it was. You were an untested soldier up against a formidable, experienced opponent.

Anyway, to drive my point home—since you never answered me properly about your neglect of music lessons, I found the score for "Stardust" in the Book Nook and bought it, dragged you over to the Union to the lounge with the white piano and played it for you. You commented that it was a curiosity how my small hands could cover such a wide range of notes.

In case you have not already cheated to see what surprises I have for you in this letter, you will recognize that score and my note to you about what might have been if you had been a good boy and listened to your mother, or was it your musical grandmother? When you look at this sheet of musical notes I feel sure you will hear some of these sounds from your Hoosier homeland, as I hear so many of those from you—the words you said to me, and the way you touched every finger of my hand with a golden glow of warmth and friendship.

My hand is raised to wave a goodbye for now...before I do, I shall answer the question I myself raised but never finished. The turning point in this letter symbolizes my strategy in gift giving, and the inadequacy of all those ladies dancing and maids-a-milking and lord's-a-leaping, for they will not do any longer to express my gifts to you.

I move away from tradition and holiday predictability to something made just for your eyes...this is the place of change just as in the song. From now on, my Christmas offerings will be parts of myself that no one else can give to you. Do not doubt, my friend, that I have seven more gifts for you that I shall reveal like "The Dance of the Seven Veils."

So you must stay safe for me and wait patiently for at least another week so that you might know the secrets of my heart. You have always shared so many with me. I will tell you how your mother's holiday pie turns out. When I next see you, I shall expect you to use your newly acquired skills to steal into your family's tradition for next year's dessert. I understand there are some very good cakes, too. But for now, I must make you very homesick for your mother's cooking. The first cut of pie this year, I shall dedicate to you.

Love,

Maggie

Riggs sat quietly, tears welling up in his eyes, his heart touched by the words of a young woman far away. They were words he often struggled to understand but his heart was touched in a way he couldn't express.

That is so beautiful. She is a friend like I can't imagine. Maggie you make things beautiful even in a horrible place. Those words touch my soul. What a tremendous gift to give someone ... I just can't imagine it's me. I really can't.

I have to get home. When my time is up I will. I must go home to this wonderful person who makes everything better for me. She lives in a world I could never imagine. Yet, she brings me in to be part of her wonderful life.

"Riggs! Riggs!" Lieutenant Vance was calling from across the garbage pit they called home. "Get over here," he breathlessly muttered with an urgency Riggs hadn't heard before.

"Riggs!"

Without grabbing a thing but his M-14, Riggs was up and running across the small, muddy compound to the LT's tent.

What's this about? Where are Moto and Cooter? We can't hear any fighting. We haven't been shelled either. Vance was weird; there was something odd in his voice. There's something about to come down. I just don't know what.

Riggs's mind rattled about as he reached the old French bunker that was now the Command Post for Echo Company. He was greeted by a full house. There were over a dozen Marines packed inside the tiny plaster and block building masquerading as a legitimate headquarters.

Glancing at his watch, Riggs realized it was nearly 1900 hours. The ritual of an evil and dark night was just beginning. As light disappeared the dark took up positions to protect an unseen enemy.

"Gentlemen, listen up," Vance said as firmly as an unsure twenty-five-year old officer a year out of college could muster.

"Moto's patrol is staying out all night."

What the hell is this? They aren't prepared for that. They didn't plan on being out this long. I don't like what I'm hearing.

Riggs didn't like Moto but he didn't want to spend a night on perimeter duty without him. He hadn't forgotten what happened the other night. He hadn't been in country long but he'd been here long enough to know this wasn't a planned action.

"They are currently positioned to the west-northwest about 1800 meters from here. They're right about here," he said pointing to a dog-eared map with his dirty finger, a finger this guy would never wear back in the world.

That is nearly where we were the other night when we got in all that shit. What are they still doing out there? What are we going to do? Who is in charge around here tonight?

The Lieutenant explained that they were watching a large concentration of NVA moving in the area. It wasn't safe for them to move out of their position. They were staying put until the area became clear and then a new decision would be made.

"I've asked Corporal Hertz here to organize a rescue force ... just in case." The LT babbled on about the purpose and objective, or as Marine Officers were fond of calling it ... Commander's Intent. It seemed to Riggs the "Commander's Intent" was to save their own ass.

Here we go again. This gets crazier by the day. The dozen of us are going to go out and bring back another dozen or so facing a large enemy force? Shit. Oh, I don't want to swear. I want to do my part but I'm not sure how any of this makes any sense. Sitting here on a hill where they can see you and then fighting, dying and the living coming back to do it another day.

Maggie may be right ... what are we doing here?

"Are there any questions?" Corporal Hertz asked with an attitude born of his second tour in country.

Everyone left the LT's tent knowing the plan was to be packed up, locked, loaded and ready to go on a moment's notice. Moto would lay low unless he was literally stumbled upon. That'd be tough for him to "lay low." That wasn't something Moto liked to hear or was even capable of doing. He seemed to love a good fight.

The briefing ended and everyone disappeared into the darkness, stumbling, struggling to find their way like a dozen young zombies departing for a night of no good. It was 2010 hours when Riggs got back to his dirt home. The monsoon was coming to life and the rains returned and came down in buckets. The driving pellets peppered the canvas tarp covering Riggs's bunker. His hole was overflowing with water that had the consistency of chocolate milk.

First order of business was meeting his new hole mate, a Lance Corporal by the name of John Recalde, a Mormon kid from California. They were fast perimeter friends but neither wanted to be where they were at this moment. But they knew above all else they had to be there for one another. It was the law of the Corps. You never let a fellow Marine down. Semper Fi … always faithful.

I sure hope this will be a long, boring, uneventful night. I really do. I don't want be in an all night firefight ever again. Ever.

13

December 18, 1967
Con Thien, Vietnam

It was nearly 0200 and Riggs was on his third watch of the night. To ensure each Marine could stay awake, they took turns, an hour on and an hour off. Regardless of what they did, staying awake was tough, staring into the fog and black of night for 60 straight minutes was maddening.

Man this is hard. I want to freak out here all night, alone. I know Recalde is lying next to me but it's like standing a long night shift at the local graveyard. I'm alone.

Maggie. What a beautiful person. She has a way of making me feel something special with her words. She writes and I can hear her saying those words to me. She is so thoughtful and kind. Even here she makes everything okay. I need some rhubarb pie.

Recalde was in a deep sleep with Riggs in a thick fog when their world took an ugly turn.

KABOOOOM!

My God what was th...

Boom! Boom! Boom!

"Grenades!" someone screamed.

The NVA force Moto had been watching had moved around his patrol under the cover of darkness and attacked Con Thien on Riggs's and Recalde's side of the world. Moto might have to come to rescue them! The world caved in with a crushing smash in the night.

"Sappers!" rang the desperate cry from the trapped animals of Echo 2–4. Those left on the hill now numbered less than 100 strong.

Sappers!

BAROOOOM!

A huge explosion shattered the night and blew dirt, muck and hot shrapnel through the blindness of a dreadful night. A staccato of gunfire roared across Con Thien shaking the living to their senses.

This has gotta' be hell without the heat. Combat's insanity.

Riggs and Recalde blazed away at the screaming cut outs, silhouetted in the wavering light of flares fired into the sky by the mortar men feverishly firing from behind them from the center of the base camp.

The night on Con Thien sounded like a child's birthday party gone wild with the happiness removed and nothing left but noise and chaos. Riggs and the others were fighting for their lives.

Where are they? How many? Do we have the ammo? My God will they over run us? Where the hell are Moto and the others? We need them now. Now!

Riggs's mind raced as he fought off the unseen bad guys firing streaks of steel into the night. Bullets whizzed by, cracking with a deafening whiz of fear multiplied a thousand times.

"Corpsman! Corpsman!" came the now familiar cry, like a chorus starting on cue when the orchestra of sadness and insanity played its ragged, sad symphony.

"AHHHHYYYYYY!"

OH GOD NO!

Recalde jumped up in front of Riggs, M-14 extended, arms stretched with his barrel unleashing a full magazine of twenty rounds of 7.62 mm armor piercing ammo, firing full automatic into the chest and stomach of a dark figure running, screaming towards their position.

The screaming figure fell forward, barely missing Recalde and landing next to Riggs. Recalde sidestepped the falling NVA and kept firing in the same direction. Riggs pushed the now dead body out of his hole, rolled it, slid down behind it and started using it as cover. It gave him a makeshift wall to hide behind.

Screw it. I gotta do it. I gotta survive.

Riggs blasted away from his foxhole, rifle resting across the NVA soldier's dead body. He emptied another magazine into the night.

No atheists in a foxhole? That's because everyone's praying to stay alive. We have to fight and survive this chaos. Keep firing. Keep firing. Keep going we can make it. We can win!

On a night like this only the quick and the lucky survive. No one cared which one they were, they just wanted to be standing when the terror vanished into tomorrow morning and the bandits returned to wherever they went to spend the day.

In combat you never know when the tide will turn, or even if it will. You never know if you'll win or if the guy you're taught to hate will prevail in the game led by people that aren't even on the ground to play the game. Riggs was learning the leaders of this war were rarely within fighting distance of the death and destruction.

The maniacal assault of the NVA stopped as suddenly as it started. It was nearly 0430. Riggs, Recalde and what was left of Lieutenant Vance's crew were left to clean up a mess that was getting worse by the day. Now there were bodies on both sides to contend with and it was quite a sight for the approaching dawn of a new day.

It was dawn's early light before the cleanup was complete. The wounded were cleaned and comforted and the dead packed up. When the final score was tallied one Marine was dead and four wounded bad enough for evacuation. There were 8 dead gooks littering the landscape in front of Recalde and Riggs's house. It was two hours of hell on a hilltop far from Indiana's peaceful, rolling farmlands and the little pig farm Riggs could only hope to see again.

What a sick place to be and a sicker game to play.

14

December 18, 1967
Con Thien, Vietnam

"What were you assholes doing up here?"

Moto always had a way with words. As it turned out, his patrol had been cut off by the NVA when they launched their predawn attack. There were so few Marines on the patrol, the best they could do was set up a small ambush and harass the bad guys as they made their hasty retreat.

"Man … I want to be in another one of those human wave assaults. I wanna sit here and have their stupid asses come at me."

I can't believe that guy. He's been in too much of this stuff. He is the only one who doesn't talk about going home. He likes this stuff. He really does like being here, I swear. I can't imagine it but he does.

Riggs was lost in disbelief. How could anyone like war?

How could anyone possibly like combat? How could you like killing anything, let alone anyone? How could you? I hate being around him except he seems to always come out on top.

Night rushed in, as a sudden blackness suffocated the miserable lot of young men living in the bad lands of the DMZ. The day flew away like a chopper taking fire. Each twenty-four hours came to frighten the life out of the fortunate few still living.

It was 2300 hours when word came down that the entire base was on full alert. That meant no one would be sleeping tonight. The unstoppable monsoon rains were once again the order of the day. Being wet was as common as taking a piss in the mud. Life was getting worse for the Marines of Echo 2-4.

I remember the picnic Maggie wrote about. It was something like I'd never experienced before. I sure wish I were home with Maggie right now and not in this stinking hole doing this lousy job ... for what? I guess Dad would feel different. Was Korea like this? I guess it was freezing all the time ... that would be worse.

Riggs realized he still had time for one more letter from Maggie. Her letters were the bread of life in an otherwise "famished" existence in a faraway land called Vietnam. He grabbed his dripping, mud-soaked poncho from his hole, his M1A1 Marine Corp green flashlight and slid down into his watery hole like a gator waiting for its prey.

I sure hope Moto doesn't see me. I think he would be worse than the NVA. I hope I never have to find out. He would come over here with a good reason to have a piece of me. I don't need that confrontation but I sure do need Maggie. Here goes!

The kid from Hope needed a reason to continue his own hope for one more day.

November 20, 1967
Chicago
"Reflections from a distant star"

Dear Clayton,

Today is Monday, the day of the Moon, and surely I feel moonlike in my endless reflection of light from a distant star, sitting here at night in my old study, leafing through a stack of creamy white letterhead and stationery to find the right paper for my letter to you.

Even though I am at home now with my family, a place and people I have known far longer than you and the state of Indiana, my mind still escapes every day—often at night when you are awake perhaps—to campus trails we walked.

If I were to follow the paths traced over again and again, from the center of this pattern, of course, would emerge the Well House, the hub of our wheel of time together. If you are talking space, then I might follow one trajectory line as if some heavenly draftsman made one curvy line from the IU Woods through the center of the Well House to Owen Hall to Beck chapel to Venus-on-the-half-shell as some call it-- the new fountain near the *auditorium, featuring the lady, whom you liked better than I did.*

Were you scolding me when you declared visual artists are tough critics of art forms, and that the lady's proportions, though "off" as I had charged (though her fins were okay) were appreciated by amateurs such as yourself.

When I asked you if you were a connoisseur of female forms, you said of course, all men with eyes to see were specialists in this area and you looked at me slowly from my red Maryjanes up to the ribbons in my hair so-to-speak with a look so cool, so treacherous and guileless at the same time, you almost made me lose my balance and leave the ground in a cloud of embarrassment.

How do you do this? Am I to doubt your innocence? No one has ever looked at me like that, and I did not expect this of you. But now I find myself waiting for your next gaze, which I imagine, might or might not stay on my eyes.

I was thinking about our talks about campus legends and myths like Ernie Pyle and Hoagy Carmichael and Chancellor Wells, and how when we were sitting at the Well House one early morning to watch the woods wake up soon after sunrise, who should appear on that quiet empty hour, but Herman B himself, disappearing into the little door to the side of the Owen Hall steps! You said he looked like the busy White Rabbit disappearing around the corner quickly, watching his clock to make some very important date. He must be magic.

On the last day of classes before break, I sauntered into Beck Chapel and sat in the front pew just in the spot where I sat during one of our visits.

I remember you standing near the organ in front of the Bible placed on a table, facing the pews, when you opened the pages—-was it by chance--to that beautiful passage from Corinthians?

I thought as you readied yourself to read, straightening a tie you didn't have on, combing back your hair with your fingers, clearing your throat, rolling up your sleeves, that I would hear a sermon at least the length of a few sentences. With all the ceremony and drama of a good Baptist preacher you then raised your arms to speak. "Help one another," you said, those three words only.

Such a wonderful synthesis of the whole Christian message, even less selfish than "do unto others" which only implies helping others but does not clarify how—for what if we do not know how to accept help ourselves? What if we are self-haters?

No matter what you face each day Clayton, do not loathe yourself even if you hate your job, promise me this. I fear a bit for your self- esteem my friend, even though yours was never fragile. But I know you, how your manner is always to care for others before yourself, and how difficult it must be for you to see anyone as your enemy. So even if the "enemy within" is now "without" and all around you, I still see you as one without foes. Maybe looking at my sketches of those gravestones has made me morbid, but how can I not think of this? I can only wish the death surrounding you would be as peaceful as those inhabiting the grounds of Beck Chapel.

As I walk on this campus path, the one we walked more than once, I follow the Jordan River upstream, bending and bypassing Ballantine, bubbling and lengthening out behind the Lilly Library, leaning east to pass the peeling barracks where we used to stop and listen to pianists practicing their arpeggios. We have walked this wavy line east as I follow my thoughts east where they lead of course to you.

If only I could make my way like a dove around the coast of Africa to the heart of Asia to visit you from a tree—not one ruined by napalm and all the deadly chemicals used to defoliate the fair countryside of

Vietnam. I shall always be there with you, Clayton, right by your side.

In my next letter I will send you a poem, something new, for I have to read and write new poems everyday for my creative writing seminar, and I am feeling inspired with so many images and emotions running through my textbooks and mind stream. For seven is my lucky number, and I am hoping the seventh letter will be lucky for both of us.

All the best from yours truly,

Maggie

(Enclosed is my sketch of Beck Chapel and the cemetery)

As he placed the letter back in the plastic bag, he noticed another page, one he hadn't seen. He carefully unfolded the tired, faded page only to see it wasn't a letter but a beautiful drawing Maggie had sketched.

Wow! It's a beautiful picture of the Beck Chapel, complete with gravestones. Incredible. That is exactly what she described. What I wouldn't give to be there now. I have to get home when my time is up. I will.

DUNN

15

December 19, 1967
Con Thien, Vietnam

"Riggs! Cooter! Where the hell are you?" Moto growled in the dark of the night.

"Riggs."

What does he want? It's 0300 and we're off tonight.

Riggs rolled over as if he didn't hear the aggravating voice invading his precious time off. He was interrupting his dream time, time to trip out and go back and see Maggie.

"Cooter, get the hell up … Riggs you too."

Cooter rolled over and squinted, looking up into the misty night. He reached out and gave Riggs a shove, rustling his poncho in the process. He could hear the drizzle, continuing its steady mantra on the makeshift lean-to that was their home.

Moto squatted down in the muddy hole and peered into the black of night at Cooter and Riggs. Moto was always after Cooter to toe the straight and narrow of being ready for anything.

"Cooter … do you have your boots off again?" Moto said as he wiped his eyes and filthy face at the same time. The standard procedure was to sleep with your boots on in case of attack. Cooter wasn't into standard procedures.

Cooter sat up a little straighter and squeaked out a weak reply to Moto, who was always ready for anything.

"Moto … just 'cause a man takes off his boots doesn't mean he plans to swim the Gulf."

Moto wasn't having any shit from anyone, especially in the middle of the night. He was upset with Cooter, and Riggs wasn't up yet either.

"What on God's green earth does he want?" Riggs groaned, waking up from inside his poncho while trying to make sense of Cooter's Texas charades at the expense of Moto.

"I don't know what either of you means, I just want your asses out here right now!" Moto grunted, a first for him when Riggs was talking. Moto didn't understand either one of them-- he just wanted them up and ready. Moto didn't dislike Riggs either, but he was uncomfortable around him. Riggs was just too damned nice for his liking.

"I have no idea … what the hell do you want Moto? It's O dark early and this was our night off from guard," Cooter whined in one of his few moments of obvious frustration.

"I need to pass along the fact that things aren't lookin' too good out here at our home away from home. The LT and I were talkin'. The gooks are closin' in around us."

Riggs pulled himself up and out of his soaking poncho. The cobwebs of a short night were hard to shake but Moto's line that *things aren't lookin' too good* cleared his head like a strong wind on a still day.

Could things look worse than they have been? Moto thinks we're all in trouble. He likes this stuff and we don't so we're all in trouble. What does this mean?

"At first light we have to start digging in. We've gotta' go deeper than we are. The choppers are coming as soon as the fog lifts to bring us more sandbags." Moto's voice had a hint of concern that Riggs hadn't heard before.

"So what does all that mean? I mean ya'all can just "imagine" yourselves into a panic if ya' want but we've been kickin' some gook ass around here lately so why the poor mouthing now. What's up?" Cooter wasn't buying the bad news.

Why do we have to get up at 0300 to find out we have to dig in deeper at daylight? Moto doesn't make sense and neither does this war. Why did I drop out of IU? Why am I here? I just want to sleep.

"Moto … what does this have to do with gettin' me up at night? I need some Z's!" Cooter wanted to sleep as much as Riggs but Moto wasn't having anyone sacked out when he was wound up like a top.

"Coot … I'm tellin' you and the Pig Farmer this … those little beady-eyed assholes aren't playin' games. That probe last night, them cutting us off and coming through the wire … somethin's up.

Something big." Moto was holding court, not because he wanted to have a fireside chat, but because he was going to be ready for whatever came. He was a survivor. He was worried.

"Why do we have to dig in deeper?" Riggs meekly asked, more afraid of Moto about now than he was the NVA.

"Riggs, always remember your horse hears and smells more than you do." Cooter struck again with his Texas wisdom, a wisdom that drove Riggs crazy, but it was better than listening to Moto.

"Riggs, our horse is our main man Moto. And if he says we dig ... we dig." Cooter was putting an end to the O dark early encounter.

Riggs was mentally trying to get his foot out of his mouth as Moto climbed out and sloshed off into the dark. He felt like a little kid back on the farm.

Why don't I feel a part of this team? Well I guess I do but not when Moto is around. Why? It's something strange ... I just feel inferior to him. I'm never going to like it here. I'll tolerate everything but I won't like it. I have to be here but I don't have to like it.

I don't like to kill people. I don't like to live in the mud and eat out of a can with a plastic spoon. I don't like to drink warm water with critters floating in it. I don't ...

Riggs drifted off for more much needed rest but morning came early, earlier than he liked.

"Get your Marine Corps asses up and start diggin'. It's time for assholes and elbows, gentlemen." Moto was back and so was the driving rain. Moto was the worse of the two.

The hill came alive to the ping, slosh and splash, as the Marines dug deeper. It was mushy digging as the E tools had to be pried from the water logged ground with tired hands. Hands of Marines, mostly young hands, weary of the grind of fighting death on both sides of a conflict no one understood.

The day wore on like a bad pair of socks... the kind with a hole in the heel that rides up your foot as you walk and wears a hole in your skin and makes every square inch of your life miserable.

Womp! Womp! Womp!

"Mortars!" The cry reverberated across the slimy little ridge the Marines called home. Marines everywhere jumped into their holes, now much deeper and more secure after a day of slow digging.

The splash of men landing in their new holes could be heard across the muddy base. It made the hill sound like a pond when you surprise a bunch of frogs and they fly headlong with reckless abandon into the water in a vain attempt to masquerade their presence.

The mortars were soon a minor distraction. Even Riggs was now immune to the dangers of incoming. The Marines of Con Thien were making the most of a real bad situation and for some … 'most' wasn't good enough. The crew defending this remote real estate knew what was next.

"Corpsman Up!" The now familiar cry for help rang out across the land like an echo reflecting from the incoming barrage. Like drowned rats, Marines scurried about preparing for the inevitable approach of the Medevac choppers. Mortar magnets. Hit the deck for another round.

Riggs hustled back to his hole. This medical stuff was none of his business. Cooter was already prepared for the worst, sitting deep inside his watery house in the ground, adorned in helmet and flack jacket, vainly defending what he could.

"Riggsy, I can't believe it." Cooter moaned in a way Riggs hadn't heard before.

"What does that mean Cooter?" Riggs asked.

"It means they're loading up Rizzo, that's what it means. I went through boot camp with him. It means he was from back east, Massachusetts I think. It means I'm tired of this place."

Cooter sat dejectedly staring off into the concertina perimeter as if to say, "It's payback time."

Before Riggs could say anything Cooter continued as if he had a need to explain the unexplainable.

"You know Riggsy, Rizzo was a good guy. But I hated to take him on patrol. He was always doing something stupid, stumbling around. He was tough as nails but he scared me. I still loved that big ole' guy. I wanted to go home and take him hunting."

Riggs sat listening as the choppers whirred in providing background music in the distance of life.

"The last time I went out with him I told him what my Daddy said…'Cooter, if you're careless by nature, you'll have to learn to be careful by necessity.' I don't know if he got it or not, but it won't matter now."

Riggs didn't know if it would matter or not but there wasn't time to worry about it. The choppers were coming low and fast. The Huey gun ships streaked across either side of the base with a whoosh and they were gone, spinning in the distance for another protective pass.

The Medevac spun around to the north and made a beeline straight over Cooter's and Riggs's makeshift digs.

"Womp, Womp, Womp."

The blades whirled overhead spraying bullets of rain that peppered the skin of the tired Marines below.

"Grab the damn tent!" Cooter yelled as the wind swept across their foxhole.

The two hole mates, forced friends in a strange place, struggled to hang on to the only protection from the weather that they had. The "comm" wire they'd tied it down with was a blessing, even if a small one.

The Medevac came and went like a bad cold. Cooter watched in the distance, rain pouring over him like a shower back home, as his fleeting friend, Rizzo, was placed on board, adorned in his green body bag for the ten thousand mile ride home to Massachusetts. He was just another package of misery heading to unsuspecting loved ones back in the world.

"I'll take first watch tonight buddy." Cooter had resigned himself to a night of somber thinking as he had volunteered for first one up on another long and sleepless night.

The frightening black of a Nam night lurked nearby. Riggs settled in, laying his old wet poncho out on the ground in the corner of his newly expanded bedroom in the dirt. He sat down backwards pulling his knees forward, covering himself with his newly acquired dry poncho that carried a Swiss cheese look from all the incoming shrapnel.

I can't believe I've only been here a week. So much has happened. So much. I can't believe I'm here. I had no idea what Dad and Grandpa were talking about. I had no idea what it's like to see people die. I don't know what war is for. I don't know why we do it.

Maggie ... where are you tonight? I have no stars to look at and imagine you're looking at them too. The sky is always black. It's like we're living in a different world than you Maggie. There is no sense to be made of being here. No truth that I can see.

Are you right? Am I right? Is Dad right? Is there a right? I don't really know; I can only hope to find out. I miss my family. I miss my sister Beth. She's growing up without her big brother.

It was almost magic-like, how dark appeared out of nowhere. One minute you can see and the next you're in a black box. Riggs looked up and it was dark. Real dark. It was cold and damp now and it would soon be time to spell out Cooter and go on watch for another long Nam night.

But he knew he was never going to survive another night without another dose of his best friend. He reached for what was now the usual ... the M1A1 flashlight, the poncho over the head and another gift from the girl who was changing his life.

November 22, 1967
Chicago, IL

"A pig named Wilbur"

Dear Clayton,

It is late in the evening, after a day of preparation for the Grande Fete tomorrow, and I am writing to you from the desk in my room—nothing has been moved or changed since I left for college fifteen months ago—it seems such a long time now.

Mother has placed a bouquet of yellow roses on the mantle above the fireplace, where I spent so many hours sitting and reading, writing in my journal, making sketches, listening to music or just staring into the fire like a mystic or a mute.

My books are on the shelves in their multi-colored jackets, including some of my favorites from childhood, some that I never saw as belonging only to the very young, or belonging in put-away boxes of my past.

Before sitting to write you I pulled down my beloved Charlotte's Web and leafed through the pages, stopping here and there to read a passage or look at the drawings, in particular, those of the fair near the book's end.

When I was a child reading Charlotte's Web, I always wanted to go to a real country fair or real working farm and see the animals, not the small country estate of my grandmother's that really was no farm at all.

So the chance to visit your parents' farm last June brought the promise of my childhood dream, and I was not disappointed. Just like Charlotte introducing Wilbur to the farmyard inhabitants, you introduced me to many animals as if they were members of your family. Some you even gave first and last names.

Was it Serious George the cow, who always looked particularly mournful and was never particularly curious? (He must have been named for the monkey in the kid's book, right?) And Sweet Jessie the lamb who followed you everywhere and came when called, named for Jesus.

Felix the Dirty Dog would never come when called, but sometimes he would curl into a ball on your lap, just like a cat, after dragging himself through the muddy woods and digging his nose in the dirt.

He was demoralized when you hosed him down to make him presentable, and when he slunk away with sad eyes dripping water with tail between his legs, you waited until he was out of sight to laugh at him, for he was sensitive to criticism.

You surprised me with your story of how animals were aware of their appearances, and when you shaved your dogs into their summer coats sometimes they would hide for hours until their hunger brought them out.

The chickens were not given the same consideration. They were all Peckerhead number 1 through 30 or so, and I suspect you didn't really remember the order they came in, or didn't care. And weren't the pigs all Porky's *of sorts, though they were given the grace of a first name even if they all started with P—whether it was Pudgie Porky, Puddin' Head Porker, and Petunia Porklette, the little one who loved eating flowers over any other treat?*

When I asked you who named them, you admitted it was mostly your doing, and also your sister's, since farmers tend to see their cattle and fowl as food and not friends, and they hope perhaps to distance themselves from those doomed for slaughter.

This was Wilbur the pig's problem, wasn't it? Charlotte the spider loved Wilbur, and this hope of saving him became her inspiration. It was her love that caused her to be creative and clever and figure out a solution to prevent Wilbur's death—and she used the power of words to make this pig into someone special in the world.

But do not think I am getting personal here my friend, with some analogy between you and Wilbur, for I cannot save you with words, can I, even if you are special and even if someday I might write about how amazing you are?

I remember asking you if you really did wash a pig with buttermilk to make his coat shine. You said you never did and you laughed at me when I told you that until I was eight years old and saw my first real pig, I thought they were pink and shiny, like in the cartoons.

I had so many questions about how the children prepared their animals to show in the fair and you promised to take me to the Monroe County Fair the next month so that I could see for myself. You are always good for promises, aren't you Clay?

I didn't need to remind you when it opened, as you were eager to get a jump on the offerings before the mold on the prize-hopping cakes and vegetables platters set in. This reminded you of Great Expectations in which the wedding cake was left to ruin on the table. You said your sister would never look at the food entries past the first three days for this reason, nor would either of you look at the animals after they had been suffering in the hot sun for many days.

You insisted we see it all while it was fresh. And I had my first taste of "elephant ears"--that great Hoosier fair delicacy of fried dough and powdered sugar. When the man from the NRA next to the elephant ear booth tried to get you to shoot a rifle into the target you refused, and hurried me over to the Ferris wheel just before it got dark.

Remember when it stopped at the top and we could see all the fading hills of the farmland that stretched out beyond? It was so humid, like breathing underwater—and patches of forest spread out like a patchwork blanket. The stars were just starting to show in the sky, and you said this is as close as we may get to those stars without boarding a plane.

You said we were on top of the world and it might not get much better than this, at least for a small town boy from the sticks. I promised to take you to Paris to the Eiffel Tower someday. You said you heard that after a man goes to Paris he can never go home again, and since you must go home in the end, we had best be content with seeing the stars from here for now.

We had been closer to the stars in a way, as close as we could be, when we visited the Kirkwood Observatory in the IU woods also as the sun was setting—do you remember what constellations we looked at? It's all a blur to me now, like the blur of the Milky Way, except for the place itself. I recall it was named after the astronomer who also lent his name to Kirkwood Avenue, and the fact its foot-wide refractor could magnify the sky 600 times.

It is now Wednesday, and I wonder if the observatory is open tonight as it was that Wednesday when the sound of those woods at twilight was hushed as we walked down the red brick paths. You pretended to get lost on the way to the observatory, leading me down the path while waiting for the sun to set. You then took another turn until I was totally disoriented. All the while you teased me about the different choices in my life I was considering, not knowing whether I would be an artist or a novelist or a reporter or a full-time professional agitator or a businesswoman or a nun or the first woman President of the United States—Democrat of course! At each turn you came up with another option for me.

When I asked about your options, you stopped abruptly and made one long step, saying you were going to take over the family farm and that was it. Now I imagine the other family tradition that you would follow, that of a Marine would put your other foot in its place, but you said nothing of this.

Also, you never mentioned the possibility of my becoming a farmer or a farmer's wife, that is, in fact the same thing, isn't it? For all these duties are ultimately shared on small farms. You said that you and your sister did many of the same chores, and your father shared all his concerns with your mother, even if their duties were divided.

I still think of the kindness of your mother towards me, never making me feel like a stranger or foreign city girl, as all of your family was kind. I hope that my mother's weird sense of humor and my father's belligerence on politics and my sister's questions did not offend you too much when you visited us at Thanksgiving.

This year my heart is not in it as it was the last year, for I was sharing new things with you, new tastes, new places and people, new to you, but now it is just the same for me and the routine is not exciting. I will not go to the Lyric Opera as we did, nor the Field Museum, nor any "blues" clubs this year. I will go back to the Art Institute of course to see what they have to see.

The next time you visit we can go back to the neighborhoods, the Swedish and the Chinese and to eat Russian or Mexican or whatever pleases you. I do not want to think of what you are having for your

Thanksgiving meal this year, or what you have to be thankful for day by day. I think being alive is the key, staying alive. Please stay safe Clayton, not just for your family or your family farm but for yourself and whatever your future brings--for us.

Tomorrow I shall spend all day in the kitchen, as I spent most of today in the grocery and markets. The first piece of rhubarb pie I will dedicate to your health and happiness and your parent's prosperity and so as not to live in too narrow a place, I will pray for world peace.

The things I am thankful for you know all about, for these letters are full of my memories of times we spent together. Also, I will look to the sight of seven swans a swimming the next time we visit the lake in the woods, when it is no longer a bitter lemon but a lovely blue and green of another summer day.

Yours,

Maggie

16

December 20, 1967
Con Thien, Vietnam

What am I doing here with Maggie half a world away? I want to be home with her. I want to spend time with her and learn more and be something I never dreamed I could be. She makes me feel a million miles tall even in the midst of this mess. I am a better person because of her and I can't imagine what might be possible. I can't imagine she said, "Come home for us." Us? Could she mean it?

Riggs was lost and alone, yet living in a tight little circle of Marines ten thousand miles from Hope, Indiana and Maggie O'Reilly. She gave him the only hope he felt right now. She gave him hope he never imagined possible.

He was torn right down the middle like Mrs. Templeton used to rip his math paper back at Hope Junior High School. He was searching for truth in a place that was flat empty of even a semblance of truth or common sense or anything remotely resembling it. He struggled furiously to maintain the aura of Maggie and her letters. He drifted off into the night.

"Riggsy … it's time my man," Cooter called to Riggs almost gently, waking him from a deep sleep.

"Time for what?" Riggs grumbled, uncharacteristically irritated that anyone would take him from the dreams he longed to fulfill.

"Time to hit the road," Cooter said, indifferent to life anywhere outside the cool, wet, miserable morning on Con Thien. It was 0400 and Riggs wasn't due up for watch for another long hour.

Here we go again. It's dark, it's early and ... man why me? Out in the driving rain ... for what? I just want to think about Maggie.

"Wake it up my man; you'll be back in time for another one of those letters from your Sweet Pea. You just hang tough."

Before Riggs could get his head clear of the dreams that comforted his weary sleep, Cooter was offering family wisdom one more time. "A woman's heart is like a campfire. If you don't tend to it regular, you'll lose it. You best start writin' back."

"Now what's that supposed to mean?" Riggs asked, getting up in the dark, slipping in the hillside slime and unable to see Cooter in the mist that sagged around the living like a damp blanket on a misty morning.

Cooter smiled his wry, yet kindly smile. It seemed so out of place in the midst of hell.

"It means my Daddy would tell ya' what I just said. It's about time you wrote that girl … wouldn't ya say?" Cooter asked with an air of authority.

Oh my gosh! I haven't even tried to write her. I've been reading those beautiful letters and thoughts and questions and I haven't as much as tried to write her. How could I be so selfish? That's exactly what it is ... selfish. Cooter's right.

Cooter didn't give Riggs time to fret over his selfishness. It was time to hit the road and get back to the bush. The last couple days had been a strange combination of silence and calm. If Moto was right and the NVA were trying to close in, then patrols in the bush were a necessary evil. One of many "evils" that were part of daily life in Nam.

"Okay guys, our job today is to recon the area north and west of here. The LT just had me over and told me that Force Recon has been out there and observed significant activity. They had to pull back. The weather is gonna get worse, choppers are having trouble getting in and out so the recon for Con Thien is now up to us."

Cooter spent the next several minutes outlining their assignment. Riggs was impressed with the level of detail in Cooter's briefing. He wasn't nearly as impressed with their assignment.

Recon? Man that sounds crazy to go out there with four men. I guess the real Recon guys do it but then they're trained for it. But now we have to go out and the choppers aren't going to be there for support. I don't get it, why us?

Riggs desperately grasped for something sensible, in a world where sense had long since vanished.

Thank God it's almost Christmas and we get a break. I'm sure there is a cease-fire and man we'll need it. That's when I'll write

Maggie. I'll write her a nice long letter and tell her how I really feel.

How do I feel? I don't know. I get that warm feeling just thinking about her. It's like I know I am supposed to be with her. I want that feeling to last forever. I don't care what it takes. And in that last letter it seems she feels the same way. I hope so.

Riggs wanted desperately to believe he was in love. He was sure Maggie was in love with him, not just "bestest friends" as she called it. But then again she hadn't said the words. The nagging doubt he felt returned like the monsoon that wouldn't go away.

She wouldn't want to be with me. She's just a good friend. A great friend really but she is from the other side of town. She likes me as a friend but she couldn't marry somebody from the farm, especially a pig farm. The differences are just too big. Now there's a truth for you. The truth is Maggie O'Reilly is too good for me.

Riggs was a good guy, solid and everybody but Moto seemed to know it. But he wasn't long on self-confidence. The whole "pig farmer" thing often made him ashamed to say where he came from. He had struggled with it at times in school and as long as he could remember.

He was proud of his dad and his family. Proud that they worked hard and loved their country. He was happy, most of the time, for the legacy they left him, a legacy of patriotism, love of country and Corps and a willingness to serve. But he was always filled with self-doubt at the worst times.

As the team loaded up for the patrol ahead, Riggs continued his games of deep introspection.

I love Mom and Dad; I just don't want to be a farmer. I once thought I did but I don't. I could never tell Dad that ... I don't want him feeling bad. He works so hard to make a living for us. Mom is there for him and all of us. It's just not for me. Someday I hope they'll understand and I hope I can tell them.

I want an education. I want a nice job ... I don't know, I mean I just want to earn a living and have someone like Maggie to come home to. I want the feeling she gives me. I want what I can become because of how she makes me feel. I don't know what I can tell her to make her understand my feelings. I hope she's just not being nice like Moto thinks ... he thinks she feels sorry for me. He's like that.

Maybe she is just being nice. Someone like her, who was raised with everything, who hates the military and war and so does her family, how could she fall for me? They protest for goodness sake. Always have protested. How could she like me ... really?

When I get home I ...

"Riggsy … reel it in and saddle up, it's time to come back to earth lover boy, we're headin' out," Cooter said.

Cooter and the others were waiting for him to adjust the straps on his cartridge belt. If you didn't get the gear set right you'd be miserable for a long, long time. Making the adjustments final, he tossed his gear over his shoulder, fastened it down and asked …

"What is Moto doing? Is he going out with us?"

"Riggs, as my Daddy used to say … you probably shouldn't interfere with somethin' that ain't botherin' ya' none," Cooter said as he walked towards the fog-shrouded perimeter without glancing back or caring about Moto or anyone else.

Riggs didn't understand his question anymore than Cooter's answer. He also didn't understand why he had a strange attraction to Moto, a guy he was afraid of and then some. Yet he couldn't deny he wished Moto were going with them. Moto acted like he wished Riggs had never even joined the Corps.

Cooter's four man Fire Team consisted of Riggs and two "boots" newer than he was.

"Riggs, you're on point and don't ask me why, just get going," Cooter said in a surprisingly cocky way.

Point? Me? Man that's tough.

The four Marines made their way to the exit point of the concertina that surrounded the perimeter corralling them in like a pen of chickens. Riggs made sure he notified the on duty Marines of their exodus. He wanted to make sure some war-weary grunt didn't wake up and start shooting or worse… fire off a claymore mine in their direction.

Riggs led the way and once outside their own lines, they descended into the fog of an early morning, like so many mornings before them. The monsoon kept hanging on like a bad cold. Staying dry was out of the question; it was just a matter of how wet you were going to be when you left the cover of your "lean to" and entered the dreary world of jungle patrols.

Man this is scary. I can't see a thing. Quiet. Quiet. I have to be quiet. I have to make it through this for my family and for Maggie O'Reilly. I have to make it ... easy ... quiet.

Riggs moved the small, ad hoc Recon team deliberately and quickly, penetrating the jungle, deeper into the badlands than anyone cared to be. Cooter hurried up behind him, trying to catch up and slow him down.

"Riggsy. Riggsy," Cooter whispered as loud as he could, making noise in the night as safely as he could, trying to catch up with the hustling Riggs.

"Riggs!" Cooter called again, this time louder than he cared to be on enemy turf.

Riggs stopped and turned, heart in his throat and head wired for the sound of anything remotely threatening to his small team. He stood duty-bound after years of stories of the Corps and no duty was more important than being entrusted with the responsibility of walking point.

Cooter came up and put his arm around a winded Riggs.

"Hurryin' won't help when you're lost my man."

"Lost?"

Riggs was shocked at his friend and leader's mention of being lost. He wasn't lost!

He'd been leading the team at a blistering pace and inadvertently passed the trail junction that was to take them north and west to their observation post. Cooter patiently explained the dilemma and Riggs turned and backtracked to where the trail split.

How can I do that? How could I have missed it? I don't have time for this. These Marines' lives are mine. Think. Focus. You can do this Clayton Riggs. You can do it. You're a Marine and by God you'll be a good one. You're a Marine returning to Maggie O'Reilly.

With time on the trail, Riggs began to settle down. Adrenaline pumped through his veins like a gusher from a Texas oil well. He was beginning to focus. He knew he would need to if he wanted to survive. He also knew he needed to put Maggie away in a place as far away as she really was somewhere back in Chicago.

Daylight began to unfold as he led his three wary followers deeper into the DMZ. When they finally arrived at the coordinates of their observation post they were about 4000 meters from home.

The trip had been tough but uneventful.

It's strange out here. Where are all the NVA? It's hell and then it's nothing. At least I made it. I got us here. I didn't hit a booby trap or walk us into an ambush. I knew I could do this ... I can.

Cooter stood next to Riggs, staring first at his map then at a steep hillside nearby.

"We're going up there?" Riggs asked in disbelief as he looked up a small hill with nothing but grass about 4 feet high. "I thought this was jungle? I thought ..."

Cooter interrupted and abruptly cut off Riggs. "Quit thinking. It is what it is."

Each member in turn helped camouflage the other. Improvising with sticks, mud, grass and anything they could find from the surrounding area. They reapplied their face paint to cover what the sweat of the walk had rinsed from their dirty faces.

Riggs moved first, then the entire team began a slow and silent ascent up the 150-foot grassy knoll that would be their new vantage point for the next few hours ... or more.

The team was to move in position and use the pair of 7 x 50 binoculars Cooter packed in to observe the jungle below. With Force Recon grounded due to weather, the goal was to gather information on enemy troop movement in the area.

I sure hope there's no "bad guys" out here today. We're exposed to everything up here. Everything. I mean how can we sit here in the midst of nothing? I mean we're just hiding in grass. Are we playing hide-n-seek back home? This is ridiculous.

Riggs crawled headlong into the unknown. He set the team into position, doing the low crawl the last 50 yards. Lieutenant Vance had been right. The view from the edge of the north side of the hill was tremendous. It was the right place and the wrong place at the same time.

The trek to their unlikely vantage point had taken nearly 4 hours. It was much longer than planned and the arrival of daylight caused the final few yards to be nose to the ground and butts down.

Well one thing for sure ... you can see all around from up here. If people weren't dying on all sides this place would be pretty. It's green and lush and hot. It's a pretty place. What am I thinking?

The assignment was to watch the area and pinpoint any and all enemy activity. Daylight was the time to scope things out and make their way back to base by nightfall. The four-hour journey would make for a short stay. With just four Marines, getting home by dark was a must.

Riggs took the binoculars and was fascinated with the power of the picture on the horizon as he studied the terrain before him.

Man if I'd had these babies back shooting groundhogs ... none of them would have gotten away.

By late afternoon there was no activity anywhere. The enemy seemed to be gone, the area vacant, except for four Marines hiding on a wind swept, grassy and very soggy hill very close to the North Vietnamese border.

The recon team hid quietly in a 10-foot circle. One Marine was on the 7 x 50's, while Cooter checked in with the LT on the radio. Two other team members were taking a break behind them. The four Marines rotated positions every hour.

Clank. Clank. Clank.

"What was that?" Cooter whispered nervously, spinning in the direction of the odd noise, a noise that had no business in this place or any place jungle.

Riggs sat straight up with a jerk, reaching for his M14 at the same time.

"What is it?" Cooter whispered to the grunt who was powering the binoculars. He spun around with fear framing his baby face. He motioned with his hands in an upward and outward fashion in the international symbol for "I don't have a clue."

Cooter was up and crawling on all fours towards his teammates.

Clank. Clank.

"There it is again." Cooter was ready to fly.

It was a frightening noise, terribly out of place on this dull hill a few clicks from North Vietnam. The small band of Marines, alone, felt abandoned by the world. Common sense focused their fear towards the unknown invader identified only as a noise terribly out of synch with where they found themselves. Sanity and safety were long gone, nowhere to be found.

Unable to see anything, Cooter frantically motioned for Riggs to come and bring the radio. Riggs grabbed the radio and slithered quietly over the five feet of terrain just as he was told to do. He was a Marine. Marines did not let other Marines down under any circumstances.

A look of "this is no time for debate" was etched in the frown that gripped Cooter's usually kind and controlled face. Riggs grabbed the binocs for a look himself while Cooter crawled further out to the edge of the hill. The edge hung out over a fifty-foot drop down to the jungle and river below. Riggs wasn't sure which river it was, it could have been the Ben Hai that divided North and South Vietnam but he couldn't be sure.

"Holy shit!" Cooter let out a squeak louder than was safe.

Riggs jerked his head towards his Fire Team leader. Without a look Cooter motioned Riggs beside him, pointing directly to the spot where he wanted him. Riggs quickly handed the 7 x 50's to the other team members who were frozen with fear of the unknown that lay over the cliff.

Reaching the edge, Riggs pushed himself forward in an effort to see what had Cooter so spooked. He stretched his head out through the brown, dry blades of grass surrounding his scared, stiff silhouette. He stretched his neck through the four-foot tall slivers that strained to conceal them.

Oh my God we're in trouble. There must be fifty of them. Uniforms ... what the hell are they clanking along? It's some sort of weapon. I can't make it out.

"Riggs, that's the NVA and they're packin' in a 50 caliber," Cooter whispered straight into his ear. Twisting back around, carefully and quietly Riggs put his mouth to Cooter's ear.

"Man we got to get out of here."

Cooter moved his head back and forth … the answer was no. He explained to his newly anointed point man that moving at all would give them away and they'd soon be dead meat.

I can't imagine staying here, right smack above the enemy and doing nothing. I can't believe we're going to just sit here. We need to get back. It's getting late and we can't just sit here and wait on them. What if they want this high ground? What if fifty of them decide to move up here? What then?

Cooter sent Riggs back with the others to assure them things were cool. Just a week ago other Marines were calming Riggs down, now Cooter sent him to do the same. This was a strange place to find yourself and a stranger role to play for a guy in country less than a month.

Riggs quietly gave instructions and pulled the others in a tight circle forming their own miniature perimeter. Those were Cooter's orders. He had crawled off about belly high to a snake watching the movement of the intruders.

The time passed like a bad movie on a cold night. It was near 1600 hours and with a four-hour hike back to Con Thien it would be 2000 hours at best when they got back to the relative safety of their home away from home. Those would be four dark and dangerous hours.

There was rustling in the bushes to the east side of the hill. The two Marines froze, Riggs rolled to the prone position, rifle at the ready, with his finger tensely tugging at the trigger of his M-14.

If I go I'm going out blazing. I won't go down without a fight. A Riggs will fight, that's for sure. I'm ready ... come on!

"Parnelli," came the muffled voice from the bushes dead center in front of Riggs. He realized it must be Cooter returning from crawling around scoping out the NVA. Nervous, frightened into tomorrow, Riggs mustered all the courage he owned.

"Jones," Riggs called out.

"Indy," came a terse reply as Cooter crawled over to Riggs like a pig to slop. His face told a story, a story of just how glad he was to be back.

I sure am glad to see him. I just realized with him gone I was in charge. I was in charge of what? The three of us? My God that's scary. I'm not ready to be in charge with three of us and fifty of them out there. What are we supposed to do?

It was frightening being in the DMZ alone, in small groups with the NVA crawling everywhere. They knew they needed to get out of the area with night draping its curtain all around them.

Cooter was back on the radio talking with the LT. He turned and his face said it all. They weren't going back in tonight. It was too late. The LT wanted them to find a safe place and get secure until morning.

"Saddle up!" Cooter ordered his team as if he were lassoing a cow in Texas. "Riggsy, we're looking for a thicket, some dense jungle where we can crawl inside for the night."

I don't understand this ... I guess I don't have to.

It was nearly 1700 when the small band of Marines got moving again. The rain picked up and daylight was vanishing before their eyes. Riggs was wired for sound as he led the four of them in search of a hiding place for a very long night.

I can do this. I can do this. We made it out. I got us out and I can get us back ... tomorrow. No letters tonight. I can't think about Maggie now. I have to get back and get these guys who are counting on me back. I can ... I know I can.

An hour of extreme effort into the return route, Cooter grabbed Riggs by the shoulder. "We turn here," he said, pointing up a hillside, thick with foliage.

"Up there? And get off the way we came?" Riggs asked in disbelief.

Cooter stared down at Riggs. "We get off the way we came 'cause if you know it so do they. Let's get movin' now."

I can do this.

Riggs led the group up the steep embankment. The terrain was pure muck, mud and jungle. The four Marines were on all fours clawing their way up, through the thick jungle floor. It was exactly what Cooter was looking for.

By the time they reached the top it was dark… pitch black according to the other grunts that were as terrified as Riggs had seen in his short time in hell.

"Okay," Cooter rolled out across a quiet tongue. "One man up at all times. Lay side-by-side and shoulder-to-shoulder. No turning, sleep on your back. One hour shifts then the guy next to you sits up, rifle on your lap. Any questions?"

There wasn't much to question. Four Marines, all alone, nearly three long miles in the black of night with water pouring out of a sky no one could see. It was like being in a black box filled with weeds and no top, water pouring in.

This is a long night in the making. I'm glad I'm on watch first. I'm wired. I couldn't possibly sleep. The rain is miserable. What was that? Footsteps? Was it?

Riggs sat bolt upright, rigid, hands clenching the M-14 that lay across his lap.

What was that? Is it someone walking? My God I don't want to fire into the night and give away our position if it's nothing. But what if they sneak up on us? What if they come on top of us?

His heart was beating like it would jump right out of his chest. He hoped they couldn't hear it *thumping*. It made him sick thinking of the possibility of NVA creeping up on them in the night.

Riggs glanced at his luminous watch, it was 2020 hours and he'd been on watch an hour and five minutes. It was time to pass it on.

"Cisco, Cisco," Riggs shook his partner who was lying next to him. Startled, Cisco jerked to life. "It's your time. Sit up here and get your rifle at the ready," Riggs told the new guy with an air of authority he hadn't felt before.

Cisco sat upright; Riggs reached over and confirmed that he was upright. He couldn't see a thing, he had to feel him sitting upright next to him, and it was darker than dark. Riggs lay back, resting his head on his pack and covering his face with his helmet. The rain was still dropping through the jungle canopy like little steel balls.

Oh God just get us through the night. Please give us just one more night God, just one more night. One night at a time and I'll be home again.

Riggs couldn't imagine there wasn't a hint of light anywhere. Up, down, sideways or backwards it was just dark. He also realized if he couldn't see, neither could the bad guys.

I'm tired. I'm cold. I'm hungry. I have no moon to imagine I can see Maggie looking at ... I can't imagine I'm here and ...

Riggs drifted off into a much-needed sleep.

17

December 21, 1967
On patrol in the jungle north of Con Thien

"Riggs. Riggs. Your turn."

The wheel had turned around. It was Riggs's second turn on watch. Tired, sore and barely awake, he sat up. It was just after midnight, twenty-four hundred hours in military time and an ugly hour no matter how you measure it.

Boy, this is O dark early. It's a new day. This will be my first to miss reading a letter. I could sure use one about now. I really could. I need something to make me feel better. I just want to get back to base. That's the best we can do right now.

Riggs made his watch and passed it back to the fellow Marines he shared the misery with. That's when things started changing. It was somewhere around 0400 when everyone was startled into consciousness.

"What's that?" Cooter cried loud enough to be heard.

Before they got their bearings, explosions were erupting in the early morning on Con Thien. They listened and could hear the boom-boom-boom, a quick succession of firing coming from somewhere in the not-so-distant hills, close to Riggs and his fellow recon team.

More explosions erupted on Con Thien. From their hidden vantage point Cooter's team could do nothing but listen. It was still the black of night and they were swallowed by their jungle hideaway.

"Charlie One – Charlie One this is Charlie Five-O do you read me?" Cooter was on the radio calling back to base for a status report. "Charlie One this is Five-O do you copy?"

There was a long silence; four Marines sat in the dark wet jungle waiting for word from the Mother Ship. The silence was soon broken with chatter from the Lieutenant calling reports, updates and casualties back to the Combat Operations Center at Dong Ha.

The NVA had apparently moved some heavy artillery and rockets into firing position. It was no longer just mortars dropping in … the heavy stuff was a different ballgame and the Marines of Echo 2-4 were in the game. The casualties were mounting, evidenced by the tone and details of the LT's calls to COC.

Cooter readied his small band to move out. He had been unable to raise the LT on the radio. The airwaves were busy with the noise of Forward Observers, FO's they were called, frantically ordering counter fire against positions whose locations were uncertain. Finally, the radio crackled with a call to the recon crew for information.

"Charlie Five O this is Charlie One," came the call from the Forward Observer on Con Thien.

Cooter took the call and did his best to describe where the sound was coming from in relationship to his position.

"As near as I can tell it's about 270 degrees from our position," Cooter said, using the luminous dial on his compass to come up with a reading based on what he could hear of the boom-boom-boom echoing in the night.

It wasn't much information but he did what he could. The firing seemed to stop as quickly as it started which always seemed to be the case. It was 0445 and the calm of morning returned as if nothing had happened.

I wonder what happened up there. Who got it? I can't imagine being here was a blessing but it might have been. A miserable night on the dirt floor of hell and I'm complaining. I need to be happy being lucky. I just want to be home.

Riggs's mental trip was interrupted when Cooter decided it was time to move.

"Riggs, onward and backward my friend … take us back to base."

It was still pitch black as they crawled out of hiding and struggled to reach the trail. The dawn of morning slowly began to light up the eastern sky. He realized for the first time the rain had nearly stopped.

Riggs edged forward dodging vines that tried to grab him from every direction. He struggled to get loose and keep moving, hugging the ground like a snake slithering to safety.

My God I can't believe this place. How did we get into here in the first place? Nothing should live in this place but snakes and bugs.

He reached the edge of the steep ridge they had climbed. Turning around, he got into a sitting position with his feet almost straight out and began to slide down the embankment. He was covered in mud and sliding down like a kid playing in the rain. But the stakes were much higher and he knew it.

I can't believe I'm doing this. I can't believe I'm living like this. I can't ... but it doesn't matter. I'm here and the truth is, we have to deal with what is, not what we wish it to be.

Before he could catch himself he began to slide faster and faster. Whoooosh ... he slid the last twenty feet and crashed into the trail below. It was a quagmire of mud and slop. Crashing with a splash at the bottom he looked up in time to see another Marine heading right towards him ...

Shit! I'm right under him.

The Marine landed on him and the two scrambled to get untangled and upright to defend themselves against the enemy that they were sure was watching nearby. To their surprise nothing happened. They were apparently alone.

Cooter and Cisco made it down without incident and the four grungy Marines regrouped. It was time to head in. Radio transmissions revealed Medevac choppers were on the way as soon as the fog lifted.

Riggs led the way and walked with a renewed confidence, a feeling that was growing at the same time his uncertainty about his legacy was shrinking. He was a kid with feelings like two trains passing in the night. He wasn't sure what he felt or where he should really be.

I just want to get back to Con Thien and then home. Simple goals. Just one more step, one more day and one more month. I can do it. Now I have to get around that corner in the trail right there. Quiet. I gotta' be quiet.

His favorite group was the Four Seasons and with every step Riggs couldn't get that one song out of his mind. It just kept playing in his head over and over again.

S-i-l-e-n-c-e is G-o-l-d-e-n but my eyes can seeee. Man it just stays there. Silence is Golden. Quiet. Be quiet. Silence sure is golden here. One more step of silence. Eyes wide, nerves on your fingers ... one more step.

It was nearly 0930 when the four weary Marines on Cooter's patrol made their way to the edge of the Con Thien perimeter. Cooter radioed ahead to make sure the jumpy Marines welcomed them in without a friendly fire incident.

"Boy you assholes missed some fun last night." Who else but Moto would see the world in a way that incoming was "fun".

He went on with a blow-by-blow description and a body count report. It was an ugly night and Riggs realized it really was a blessing to be in a slime pit out in the middle of nowhere rather than back at base with Moto.

Three killed and twelve wounded, eight of those had to be evacuated. That was the cause of all those choppers they could see coming in as they made their way home.

Cooter and Riggs made their way to their lean-to with the basement, their foxhole, and couldn't believe their eyes. The hole they called home was bracketed with two large holes the size of Volkswagen Beetles.

"Well Riggsy … some things are funny and some ain't. This ain't," Cooter offered philosophically without a trace of a smile.

Man if we'd have been in this hole we'd be dead from the concussion if not the explosions. Man we're lucky. We are lucky.

They cleaned out their foxhole of the dirt and debris from the artillery shells that landed on either side. Riggs uncovered his rucksack that held the treasure of his heart, his letters from Maggie. It was undamaged but covered in dirt that looked like it had been pasted on the sides of his rucksack.

He sat down, deciding he needed the boost that only Maggie O'Reilly could give him. Pulling the straps of his pack loose, he flipped open the top flap, reached inside and pulled out his plastic bag. It was untouched, just, as he'd left it.

Time to hear something good …

November 24, 1967
Chicago, IL

Dear Clayton,

This morning I lay in bed for fifteen or twenty minutes trying to decide whether I had enough strength to rise from a full night's sleep while attempting to digest the obscene amount of food eaten at the Thanksgiving feast. I feel like a stuffed goose or a "pig-in-the-blanket" lying here wrapped in my goose down blanket.

Your mother's strawberry rhubarb pie was a big hit, even though I had to change the ingredients for the crust. I cannot stand lard or the idea of it—not since I read Charlotte's Web, in fact. Since then, when I think of lard I imagine someone slaughtering someone's Wilbur for his flesh and fat. My butter crust was not as light and fluffy as it would be otherwise, but it was good enough. Only my grandmother had eaten a proper rhubarb pie before, since she lives out in the country and has a good patch of it springing up every year without being pushed.

Grandmother asked about you first off, and why that charming boy (the one that looks like Jimmy Stewart) was not at our Thanksgiving dinner. Before I could tell her where you were she had already decided that your parents would want you to be home for the Holiday. So, I had to say that your parents wanted you to be in Vietnam this year and you being such a good son and all had decided to mind them.

She approved of your minding your parents' wishes but that started my mother off on the "sheer idiocy" and meanness of this war and all the dead boys and dead Vietnamese who never hurt a flea. Look where our young men are now and that damned so-called Democrat Johnson, the so-called defender of civil rights, is responsible for all this tragedy. She said she used to love that man, his Lady Bird and even his Texas barbeques but now he's a sham, and that led to the subject of what

I had been doing lately in terms of politicking and war protests—this from my dad.

So I told them about the Dean Rusk event and various activities on campus and I also mentioned the Dow Chemical recruitment protest where a few of my friends were beaten up by cops and taken to jail. This was not unlike the rioting in Watts that got way out of hand, only there was no property damage or deaths or serious publicity, just a lot of injustice.

Dad reminded me he would be proud to post bail on his little jail bird if I so chose to be one and I told him at the time I had a paper due and couldn't afford the time away even if for a few hours. At least I showed up to as many of these protests as I could fit in. They had my column written for the Indiana Daily Student (IDS) framed in the hallway. By the way, this is the 100th year celebration for the IDS. What an accomplishment!

I wrote another column about Che Guevara's murder in response to a "letter to the editor" regarding the plague of communism and that Che was asking for it. The column detailed the plague of government-sanctioned murders of citizens all over the world and did the end really justify the means.

My dad said there are rumors that the government murdered Marilyn Monroe and my mother said she wondered about the death of Malcolm X and other Black Panthers saying the world is going to "hell in a hand basket." My sister just rolled her eyes.

To change the subject, perhaps, my grandmother asked me if I still planned to be a writer with my superior education and all. Mother then reminded me that my English teachers had such high hopes for me and what did I have in mind. Then mother went on to this line of questioning:

What kind of family would send an only son to the slaughter? Why did you choose to go if you were such a nice boy as I had insisted? Have you become a killing machine yet, things such as that. She's worried you are the only boy I have ever brought home, at least since I was old enough to look at boys, and wondered what my plans are with you.

So there I was trying to explain how your family had a history of military men and you were raised with guns and could shoot a bird from the sky (only you never would) and that you were more kind to animals than most people are to each other.

There I was the fence- sitter not condemning but not condoning, trying to make them understand why you were different. I explained to them that you were not a war monger or hater of communists or hater of anything and I watched them looking at me getting more agitated.

Dad finally said, "That's fine, Margaret, we understand, Margaret," and Grandmother changed the subject again by turning to the bouquet of flowers on the table that my sister had brought and talked of their beauty.

In this way the topic of dead soldiers turned to dead flowers. I decided live flowers were a brighter thought so I asked Grandmother what flower seeds she was buying for her garden this year.

So we were in a fine mood as you can see—I admit my mother had a few glasses of wine and as a result was a little more animated than usual. I had had some too, (my parents allowed it since I am almost drinking age, and they'd rather have me drink at home with family rather than out with friends and so on). As they talked of my grandmother's gardens of vegetables and flowers I didn't say much for I was thinking about the summers I spent playing in her garden as a child, which I will tell you about in another letter tomorrow. There were only five of us at the table since my mother was not in the mood to see her Republican war-mongering sisters or their cheerleading daughters (my two cousins who do not seem to have a thought in their heads other than marriage to a *doctor or lawyer), and my dad was not in the mood to see his drunken brawling beer-drinking brothers (he keeps his drinking to scotch and martinis and good wine).*

Last night before I went to sleep I remembered what we had seen at the observatory—it was the Andromeda galaxy—named for the daughter of some god who was to be sacrificed to the sea monsters because her mother bragged of her beauty to the wrong male god who became jealous. What an awful fate at the hands of a mean man! The ancient Greek gods seem to be full of jealousy—but I remember you told me Perseus had saved Andromeda—and she is very beautiful isn't she?

Looking up at her, you laughed at me when I told you that although I was grateful for knowing this, and that I was glad your astronomy class did not ignore the ancient myths, I might become a little jealous myself of your admiring another woman's beauty. You told me your professor did ignore the myths and you knew these stories as a child when you used to look at the sky and imagine what the people before time saw in it.

Then, you told me I should be careful that some classical Goddess might become jealous of my looks even if I didn't have a classical profile. You said my nose was rather short, as are my legs, and I looked more like a red-headed Doris Day. You warned me that goddesses keep up with modern standards of beauty and I should watch my step. I made you promise to rescue me if someone chained me up somewhere and you said if it is the Well House I would not have to wait long, for you would go there any time day or night.

Now after remembering this I am able to finish my poem that has something to do with the sky and stars and you. It is called "Starlight" (does this sound a bit like "Stardust"?) and it mixes up our visit to the observatory and sitting with you at the lake and at the Well House, for that's allowed in poetry as it is in my memories. The stars all blur together and spread out in a galaxy but are distinct and individual and full of stories if you look closely.

Your Maggie

Starlight
For Clayton

That body is heavenly
It shapes the stilled voice of sound
Above the milky cover that reveals
Its waves, curves and stories
His arms fold
His legs cross
Drifting upon the quilt of rings
Weightless in an unbroken place
The light of these eyes guides me
Looking to the face of Heaven
We are not supposed to see this easily
This artist is bold
To seek the name of the divine
In the mere fold of his hands
The lake in the woods
The fountain in the well
The lady chained by the sea
Watching the night for a sign
The mail for a note from her rescuer

Riggs laid back on his pack just like he'd done a few hours ago in the middle of the night on a distant "arm pit" of the world. Now home in Con Thien he actually felt safe for the first time in a long while.

I feel on top of the world just reading a letter. I can hear her voice. How can one person make you feel so good? How can I go from hating life to loving it? How can I feel good in this place?

I feel good but I don't think I could ever fit in her family. I don't know what to think of the talk of protests and what her mother said

... what kind of a family would send their son off to war? Well if they didn't, you wouldn't be sitting there questioning in your mansion would you?

Riggs was struggling with the special feeling he had growing for a girl a world away and the tension he felt from her family who was so different than his.

He wouldn't have much time to think about it because the activity of the day was digging deeper. Marines across Con Thien were digging deeper and filling sandbags, the new ration of bags dropped from the most recent choppers that came for the miserable cargo heading back to the world.

It was 1400 when the work was done and the LT passed the word that all hands could stand down. Riggs was beat. He was still flying high from his letter from Maggie, still troubled by the news of protests back home and he was at ground level when it came to staying awake. He needed sleep and he needed it now.

As he crawled inside his newly renovated hooch he realized for the first time the poncho laying across his roof was looking real bad. The shrapnel from the exploding rockets had made Swiss cheese of it and there was little left.

He was beyond caring at this point; he just needed sleep like he'd never needed it before. Riggs laid down to visions of Maggie O'Reilly a million miles and a lifetime away.

She is what I need. If I could spend my life with someone like her I would walk through hell and back. I will even find a way to live with her family. If only ...

Riggs drifted off in the muggy afternoon. The monsoon was back at full bore with no signs of letting up and life was wearing thin on even the toughest of the tough.

"Sleeping beauty, get your ass up," Moto growled with a smirk and a smile as he kicked Riggs awake. "Don't sleep your life away, it's a great day."

Riggs sat up and looked around in time to see Moto walking away with his patented strut. You could tell that walk a mile away.

What does he want? Where did he go?

Moto didn't want anything other than to keep Riggs and others on edge. He was a strange character. What made it even stranger was that he liked Riggs; he just had a strange way of showing it.

I've got to eat. I'm starved. But ... the letters, I've got one more to read today. I have to read it now.

It was nearly 1800 hours and he'd been dead to the world for nearly four hours, four hours of beautiful, uninterrupted sleep, Riggs wanted to read his last letter for today in the few minutes of daylight remaining. He leaned back and carefully unfolded the letter and began to read.

November 25, 1967
Chicago, IL

Well Honey, it's like I said (can you hear that particularly Hoosier drawl of Honey Jones as I write this? Maybe if you read out loud), I brought up the new autobiography of your fellow-Hoosier Hoagy Carmichael to read in my holiday leisure, after deciding that the writing of that other famous Hoosier, Ernie Pyle was too depressing and anyway I'm not in the mood for homework, since I am doing a paper on him—didn't I tell you? About the difference between his private and public writing on war—I got access to some copies of his private letters the journalism librarian had in her files, not even catalogued. So I am positively swimming in Hoosierdom.

Do you see what a good researcher I am when I find an interesting subject? Or maybe it is my family's telescope that sees only one angle on you while I access real memories, all those going into these pages. But do not let this scare you, for we are a gentle folk who are only hard on mean people and conglomerates who step on the little guys, and neither you nor your family is in this category.

My grandmother did ask me today if I was writing any love letters to you and I said "Sure! A good dozen of them! For a Christmas present!" She approved and told *me that she used to write "scandalous" love letters to her first boyfriend when she was just a teenager younger than I and he was off in the First World War.*

She said she knew they would make him happy and she also knew he wasn't coming back. (I told you she was psychic, right?) I teased her that I was surprised to hear that from her, a good Irish Catholic girl supposedly raised with good Victorian values and Christian modesty.

She laughed and said rebels were all over her family tree, some hanging from its branches by their necks (for horse thieving and fighting the Brits no doubt). Anyway, she came of age in the roaring twenties when it was the fashion to be a flapper. She did a few steps with her arms flapping like a chicken and feet shuffling and eyes popped out. I laughed and laughed and so did she.

I started thinking of twenty years later when her daughter (my mother) was raised. That's when it was fashionable to be like the tough-talking Hollywood broads, the Joan Crawford types, not the fifties "catch your man with Wonder Bread" Doris Day types (you don't really think I look that much like her do you?) when women were put back in the kitchen where they belonged. Then, twenty years later the sixties erupt and here comes the women's liberation and now I'm wondering what the eighties has in store—the first woman president! Yeah that's me, like you said...

Funny enough I actually had a sense of what my grandmother flapper was talking about cause I had just finished the chapters in <u>Sometimes I Wonder</u> where Hoagy talks about the era and how women rid themselves of their heavy clothing and were covering very little, along with their drinking and smoking—not just tobacco either—and their taking chances with love in the back seat of "tin lizzies" and so on.

Sorority girls when he was a student at IU were rather wild too, and the Indiana state legislature tried to pass a law making it illegal for any females on the streets to wear skirts higher than three inches above the ankle! (Though he didn't say that it passed—I'll have to look that up) The local boys were peddling bootleg booze in cahoots with gangland criminals with submachine guns and so forth. Wow! You must read this book when you return, at least the first half that talks about his nostalgia for his Indiana childhood and the IU campus and so on. It's a great history lesson.

The second part I skimmed through seems to be mostly about his music and the crazy musicians he met. Not unlike the ten-lords-a-leaping, they were all over the place dancing up a storm making wild sounds and drinking and driving dangerous cars—the real pioneers of jazz went through Indiana it seems or were made famous in Indiana like Bix Beiderbecke and so on. And of course the Chicago music scene was mentioned—Hoagy lived here too! Bix was a good friend of his, someone he called "a sweet soul" saying it was a worn-out-phrase.

I kind of sighed, thinking I hadn't heard it much but I could think of <u>someone else</u> it might describe beautifully. Bix was his special friend whom he admired because he made people feel it was still possible to "know and need—and be known and needed by—another human being." I like that he said that, cause Hoagy kept a bit to himself, didn't let too many people in, even though he had lots of friends by that time and wasn't lonely anymore.

There were some funny and fascinating details about the things he did and the early campus that might amuse you, and also some things he said that reminded me of places on campus we enjoyed too.

Remember you telling me when I got my first case of chiggers that sprinkling your ankles with sulfur was the only thing you knew to prevent them, and nail polish on top of the bumps they made would smother them and I was sick thinking of those little red bugs that didn't itch *cause of their bite but because they were crawling under my skin? Well it seems Hoagy got chiggers! He walked around for two days in long underwear coated with lard! Give me nail polish any day of the week.*

He also talked about his gang shooting craps behind the Observatory, and sitting on the low stone wall south of campus (the one on Third Street?), kind of a lover's perch where kids late at night stopped on their way back from the Book Nook!

That wall is where he first sat and started to put the notes together for "Stardust" while thinking about his high-school sweetheart named Dorothy Kelly (Hoosier boys do seem to appreciate Irish girls). She was the girl who first called him Hoagy instead of Hoag like his friends did or Hoagland like his mother did.

After he worked out the first notes, he went right over to the Book Nook to work them out on the piano, not the Book Nook around the corner but the Gables on Indiana just south of Kirkwood Avenue—I don't even remember what's there now. The photo in the book of Book Nook is not the little bookstore where I bought the music to Stardust—it was much bigger and full of small tables and just some books it seems, and the place for late night music sessions and all kinds of shenanigans.

He also talked about how the Bloomington campus was surrounded by "hundreds of thousands" of Ku Klux Klanners, who were more active in Indiana than in any other state. This must have been scary, since he was hanging out with the black folks in Buckland—the west side of town it must be.

Some of the moving passages were his talk of his "Hoosier heritage" and the maples and how they were made large by the composition of the soil and how "a world without trees was unthinkable." I loved his descriptions of Bloomington in the fall with its gold and red leaves and the smell when they were burned.

He was uncertain about what he would sacrifice for love, and what love would have to offer to him. He said weighing the pros and cons of love "leads to nothing but trouble." I think he was saying you have to just go with it, but I'm not sure.

He also talked about the quietness of campus in the summer when students were gone, and about playing in Dunn Meadow and running through the Jordan River as a young child. He described the campus buildings when he was a student as old and dusty and buggy. However, he felt his professors were good and he somehow managed with all his wild lifestyle as a musician and "sometimes student" to get his high school diploma, then college law degree.

He hated when his family moved away from Bloomington now and then when he was a child, and he always loved coming back. Hoagy talked about his closeness to his mother and how he got his unique musical ability to play a tune by memory from her. She was a very good ragtime piano player, and he watched her play music for the Indiana Theater movies when he was young. Music and their piano was the center of their lives!

This made me think of my childhood and smells and of the outdoors and certain places and what and who I was nostalgic for. There were so many things I loved in the city—I showed you some of them—but the city changes constantly and grows bigger and busier every day. My grandma talks about her home in Michigan (where I spent many summers as a child) that had also changed and grown too much since those days.

It was an odd town in the upper part of Michigan's mitten. The place was called Petoskey, and was used by Victorians as a summer home. Hemmingway spent time there for some reason. My grandmother lived there all year round and I stayed there part of every summer growing up. Petoskey is five times bigger now and I only have my memories of the streets with houses boarded up in the summer, some abandoned for good. I remember my sister and me breaking into one empty Victorian mansion through an unlatched window. We thought it might be haunted, for there were torn curtains in the window and the rose bushes were very wild peeking out of the weeds. Year after year it just got dustier until finally someone bought it and fixed it up. Though it was newly painted a fresh pretty apricot color, the charm went out of it, Beverly and I decided.

My grandma's garden was our favorite playground, for it had lots of places in which to hide. She was named Erin Casey O'Neill, and she had "two green thumbs" she used to say. She grew sprawling English-style gardens (for what is an Irish style? No style at all she said). It wasn't the kind of garden where flowers are herded into rows but where they all run into each other. Every color and species kept company with shells, unusual rocks, birdbaths and bird feeders, including sugar water for the hummingbirds. Her garden was really more than one, for it went all around the house. There were stone walkways and trellises of wisteria that formed an arch with the blossoms tumbling down in bunches.

There was always a fishpond that would freeze over in winter. We would help her scoop up the fish in the fall to keep in this old footed bathtub she kept in the basement where they would grow fat and fatter before going back into the pond for the short Michigan summer. Her brother was equally famous for breeding a certain kind of azalea (or was it rhododendron) that could stand the cold winters, and she would always grow a wall of Heavenly Blue morning glories up her fence—what a perfect name for these flowers that were so beautiful they had to close up and hide in the afternoon like Persephone who could only show her face half the time.

But like Persephone, my friend, I must go to my underground home to sleep, into the arms of Morpheus they say, not for six months but for at least six hours for it is now past midnight and this letter is far too long. May Mars the god of war protect you and Diana the goddess of the moon light your way in the night and "Stardust" keep our memories of good times in Bloomington alive.

Stay safe,

Maggie

18

December 22, 1967
Con Thien, Vietnam

"Incoming! Incoming!"

The rude awakening for Riggs and his newly found friends stretched a checkered pattern of destruction all across Con Thien. He was startled awake finding himself sleeping flat on his back at the edge of the bunker he shared with Cooter.

WOOOOSH … KABOOM! BOOM, BOOM.

"Get in here!" Cooter screamed from the bottom of their muddy bunker. It was jet black outside but for the multiple flashes of explosions from the incoming artillery landing in their midst.

Riggs instinctively rolled to his left, falling into the bunker and crashing down on top of Cooter.

"Ughh!" Cooter groaned when Riggs hit hard on his back.

He rolled off and into one corner. They were soon in opposite corners of their muddy bowl dug with their own hands to protect them. The renewed onslaught of the NVA gunners was frightening.

BOOM, BABOOM!

Corpsman up!

The cry for the Docs to do their thing accompanied any round of incoming. Marines were losing life and limb, while back home kids their same age were partying, calling it a protest and remaining ignorant to the reality of combat a half a globe away.

The artillery shells kept coming in wave after relentless wave. The only break for the beleaguered Marines came when the NVA reloaded for the next barrage. Huddled in the hole waiting for the next round of destruction, Cooter and Riggs grew close without saying a word.

The initial barrage lasted for nearly an hour. Daylight was coming and hopefully some semblance of peace and order. Riggs welcomed the respite from the violence of a bad night after some beautiful thoughts from someone far from the devastation of war.

"Riggsy, if you're gonna take the measure of a man take it now. This is bad shit." Cooter waxed philosophical. Riggs could do nothing but nod in agreement. They had both had enough of life in a miserable hole.

It's hard to make sense of life here in Nam. I don't know how I would respond to Maggie about truth. I don't see any here. I don't see it anywhere. I only feel it when I read her letters. They are long and that makes the time I am away from here even longer. I love to read about Hoosiers and Hoagy and life in the world.

When I think of truth I think of our enemy. I don't know the Vietnamese. I don't hate them. I don't hate anyone. An enemy to me is someone trying to hurt me or my friends or family. My enemy here is some unseen person firing at me from an unseen place.

I don't know about truth I only know about feelings.

Cooter climbed out of the hole with Riggs and brushed himself off. He barely took a step when you could hear the slightest firing off in the distant. He jumped back in the hole just as destruction rained in one more time.

BOOM. KABOOM!

The artillery rained in all day long, barrage after barrage with brief breaks at the will of someone unseen very far away. It was near 1630 hours before the incoming slacked off enough that the moles came out of their underground homes and life on Con Thien returned to normal.

"Riggsy, it's been real. I'm goin' over and get us some chow. Want some?"

It actually sounded good to Riggs. He was hungry, tired and needed a break from a life gone bad, very bad. He was now as numb as the rest, sitting, planning to eat, while the choppers came in to save the dying and retrieve the dead.

"Yea, I do actually. Cooter, anything but Ham and Momma's, please," Riggs begged, talking to his back as he walked away.

Anything but Ham and Momma's, oh I hate those things. All the C's taste awful, they're just gross. I hate all our chow but I'm starved.

"Hey asshole. Don't you dare read under that poncho tonight! You'll be an arty magnet for sure. One flash of light and we're cannon fodder. Got it?"

Moto didn't mince words. But why was he telling me that? He just wants to save his own butt that's for sure. I can't believe that guy.But I know he's right, they get a bead on us, heck they already got a bead on us, dead center.

I've got an hour of daylight and I have to read Maggie's letter. I need the lift after a day like this one. I need what she does for me. I need a diversion from those choppers over there. Cisco took a hit and I hear it's bad. He's out on that Medevac above me right now. I need Maggie.

Riggs picked up his rucksack and walked to the middle of the hill, not far from the LT's tent. He found some bushes and sat with his back to the bush, as well as the others nearby. He needed to be alone, especially hidden from Moto.

Reaching inside, he once again found his precious plastic bag. It was torn, muddy and no longer clear but inside was the most profound gift he had ever received. He knew there could be no other.

He pulled out the next letter and read …

November 26, 1967
Chicago, IL

Dear Clayton,

This morning I woke up feeling lousy so my family left me at home while they went to church. By the afternoon I was better so big sis and I decided to go to the movies. I was thinking I wanted to see "In the Heat of the Night" starring Sidney Poitier and Rod Steiger, but Beverly wanted to see "Bonnie and Clyde" so we went back and forth and finally decided to compromise with something more lighthearted and saw "The Graduate" instead. It was funny.

I wasn't really in the mood for the violence of gangsters or bigots anyway and was ready for some laughs. I saw a few soldiers at the theatre all in their *khaki and camouflage uniforms and imagined they were thinking the same thing.*

Christmas decorations have popped up overnight now that Thanksgiving is over and the streets look so beautiful with the horses and buggies with their bells jingling and snow flakes tumbling down on the streets and the kids laughing and happy. I ran into a couple of high school friends out shopping and they asked me how I was doing. I actually had to stop and think about what to say, for I am not really here nor there it seems.

Later at dinner Mother asked what movie we had gone to see and we told her about wavering on our movie choices, and how the Sidney Poitier film about racism in the south was too dismal. Mother said sometimes the north seems as bad as the south, and she told me about some of the things that had been going on in Chicago this year.

Though Chicago seems to be the only big city that did not have those huge race riots this year, last year's events on the west side were still vivid—along with all the other tragedies—those poor nurses killed by that sick man I won't even say his name, and Reverend King being hit with a rock during a peaceful demonstration where 2,000 white people were heckling him and his people. It was still a bad summer for Chicago.

But Dad said it wasn't over: just this month there were race fights at a high school on the north side, which spread to a couple other schools and in the end there were another couple thousand students throwing bricks and setting off fire alarms.

The discussion got even more dismal as Dad talked about the snowstorms and tornadoes. They mentioned how kind it was of you to write them a letter of concern after the April tornadoes that killed and injured so many people—dad said it caused more than $50 million in damage.

Chicago's "snowstorm of the century" had drifts over five feet and abandoned vehicles were left on the streets with only trains running. People were stranded away from home and then, the looters—what a mess. It even knocked down the new convention center on the lakefront. In the end there were another 50 plus deaths—mostly from heart attacks caused by men shoveling snow! And then they sent trains of snow to kids in Florida who had never seen it—the one silver lining in that cloud perhaps.

Actually one other good thing about the storm is some of the white folks who opposed black folks moving into their neighborhoods were stranded and had to get assistance from those poor residents, so it likely opened some eyes and brought people together, as they do in common catastrophes.

Open housing is still a big issue here—you might remember my parents talking about last summer's Puerto Rican Day parade violence around housing and job issues and this year Mother's involved in some campaign to help the coloreds find better housing.

She's my mentor—when people tell her she's a good person for helping the less fortunate she tells them death and destruction comes in all forms, to rich and poor alike, so we need to help each other. And besides, she says, it's more fun than having tea with her church group and society lady friends. She's gotten some of them involved too. I am so proud of them both and feel so lucky to be their daughter. We are both lucky in this department, aren't we?

So along with all the sad news about politics there are, thank goodness, some great arts offerings in my fair town. Some exciting developments—what I call good news at least—since you visited. Here's a tour of the highlights:

There is a new Picasso sculpture set up in August at the new Daley Civic Center—there is so much building going on! It's 50 feet high and over 162 tons! It's beautiful, though some are criticizing it. Why? I don't know—Pablo P. refused to take a dime for it. My parents went to the unveiling and said it was a magnificent event, including some of the private celebrations. (They were donors it seems.}

The Civic Center is also very modern in style, very glass boxy and all the new rage of high steel boxes with windows that reflect the passing clouds. My parents were also involved in the new Museum of Contemporary Art that just opened last month. I'm hoping to go tomorrow—I'm back to campus on Tuesday and will only miss one class (I'm sure I won't be the only one missing).

Lyric Opera's fall season has been canceled due to labor issues with the musicians, so there's nothing to see there. But the Auditorium Theatre reopened after being closed for years—with "A Midsummer Night's Dream"—sounds dreamy, right? Sorry to miss those ten-lords-leaping but maybe next year...

There have been no concerts that come close to The Beatles last summer—I will never forget that as long as I live—not that you could hear much for the screaming, especially when John did that little dance on stage. Those songs they sang still go over and over in my head—mostly "If I needed someone" and "Yesterday" have those mournful ballad style moods we Irish seem to be prone to. Some of my parents' acquaintances wouldn't let their kids go cause of John Lennon's statement about being more popular than Jesus—luckily my parents aren't so strict as that.

Dad's all excited about the new basketball team starting up—The Chicago Bulls it's called. He's also very proud of one of his friends, a surgeon here at the U of Chicago; his name escapes me, won the Nobel Prize in medicine for his work in treating prostate cancer. So that's good news for the guys—right? (Medicine and basketball are arts, too, after all)

I am still basking in the beauty of the Art Institute's Monet exhibit we went to last year, so I haven't even bothered to explore what they have at the moment. You shared with me after we stood staring so long at the huge blue and green and pink and purple canvases you felt just like one of those floating lilies on their broad pads. I began to feel like the water was moving all around us and we could just float away like one of those gorgeous flowers.

Perhaps I do not wish to replace my memories of being there with you with new ones of my visiting with my family or even worse, all alone. I just haven't been in the mood to look up old friends. The funny thing about you, even though you had never been to such a large city as Chicago, I now see you as part of my town since your visit. You were so natural and relaxed as if you could be at home anywhere, even though you joked about being the typical dumb farmer from down ways staring at the skyscrapers and all, or not knowing half the dishes served in half the restaurants we visited.

Seeing my town through your eyes has given me a new feeling for it, and I wish you were here with me now so we could explore some new and old places. I am sending your mother another two jars of the lingonberries she loved from the Swedish neighborhood where we stopped—didn't she call them a gooseberry of sorts? I promised my family next year to make a proper gooseberry pie to match the rhubarb. Boy! Are we getting country up here or what? At least when it comes to pies...

Sometimes, Clay, I feel so lonely for you, whether I am here or in Bloomington it doesn't seem to make a difference, and now I am missing the peace and quiet of that place too—though it is not the same campus. I have my friends, of course, but it's not like it used to be—it's more gray and cold and lonely and maybe it's just the winter season coming and all the soldiers killed and missing in action reported every day—I read there were over fifty MIA's just this month.

Of course I think of you and wonder what your life is like and what you are thinking. Sometimes I can almost feel you thinking of me too—your image comes to me all of a sudden and I can sense this line that connects us reaching across the ends of the globe and you feel so close and so far at the same time. Just as now I feel like I'm a city girl and a country girl at once in some odd way.

I expect to get a letter from you sometime soon, mister, so I will not scold you yet for any negligence on your part. And now I am almost ready to send you your Christmas gift, and I am ashamed to say I expect something from you too—now how's that for Christian charity and good will! I will learn to be more generous and not expect anything from others in return for a gift. Mine is not really that great—just a few sheets of paper (okay I admit it, lots and lots of sheets) and some pictures and poems here and there. But like Grandmother says, there is nothing more precious to a soldier in the field than a letter from a lady friend back home.

Cheers!

Your Magpie

How could I have met someone so special? How could I even know someone like this who is so different than I am? She is everything I am not. She is cultured, kind, and considerate, she's thoughtful and she makes me feel like the most special person on earth.

I just wish this could be more than a dear friendship. She said "your Maggie". She misses me and she thinks about me as I do her. Yet we are so different. We're from two different worlds in almost every way yet we are the same. Is that truth? Maybe.

But I can't let myself think this. I can't. She could never go against her family and be with someone like me. She must just feel sorry for me. Maybe that's it. And then there is the problem at hand, Vietnam.

I can't think too much about "the world" or the people in it if I am to make it back alive. I have to be focused for sure.

Riggs sat staring into the darkening sky as if it weren't there at all. Facing yet another night of uncertainty, he was tripping back in time searching for peace and hope. The only thing he was certain of was his feelings for Maggie and the hope and motivation she gave him. Her letters, even though at times troubling with the news from back home, were his lifelines.

"Riggsy, Riggsy … where the hell are you?" Cooter was back with the c-rats. Riggs sat frozen in time and thought. It was nearly 1700 hours and he'd been gone for an hour or more looking for chow and chewing the fat with his friends along the way.

"I'm over here. I'm comin," Riggs replied, desperately wanting to stay where he was and go unnoticed.

Man I long for some private time, time to think and make sense of my last two weeks. Two weeks has it been that long? Can't imagine it. I live to think about home, sis, Mom and Dad and Maggie.

"Get over here my man, we got lots to eat and lots to talk about." Cooter drawled like the good Texan he was. "And don't look at me that way … I got you ham and eggs not Ham and Momma's … but we don't have time to heatem' so get your P-38 and open em' up and dig in."

Riggs sat down, tossing his rucksack to the side, almost oblivious to the precious letters he guarded inside. He didn't like the look on Cooter's face. He could feel the fear seeping out of the squinting eyes of a seasoned vet due to rotate home in 30 days. That is, of course, if he made it that long.

As the two fast friends sat, chowing down on cold c-rats, the day slipped to night and darkness grabbed them like a bad dream. With the darkness came the incoming and with incoming came the inevitable cries of "Corpsman up."

I can't believe this stuff but I guess I'd better. Cooter always shoots straight with me so why not now? I guess the NVA we saw with the fifty calibers the other day on the Recon Patrol are what they're talking about.

What I don't know is what it all means. Encircling us? I guess that means they're everywhere all around us. They haven't been attacking but then they think they will. Something big coming ... isn't there supposed to be a cease-fire or is that a joke too? I just want to make it to Christmas ... that has always been special to me. There has to be a cease-fire ... there just does.

19

December 23, 1967
Con Thien, Vietnam

"Cooter, time for watch." It was time for Riggs to pass on his watch.

Cooter sat up, shaking the cobwebs from his weary mind. It was 0200 and the night was quiet so far. No incoming, no probing, no nothing. It was strange.

"No action huh?" Cooter asked quizzically.

"None yet," Riggs dryly replied. He was tired and just wanted to lie down for a well-deserved break.

I need sleep. I just need sleep. I wish just one night I would get to lie down and see the moon again. Just like I used to with Maggie at the Well House. Just once Lord just once. Let me lie down with my mirror and pretend she is looking back.

Cooter sat up straight. Something was happening; he wasn't sure what. He could feel it. He stuck his head up and out of his hole, cupping his hand around the back of his ear forming a small seashell to pick up noise in the distant. He did a time check ... 0240 hours. The silence was too good to be true.

He silently reached out and placed the tripods of his M-14 down and laid it out in front of him, at the same time stacking extra magazines to his right for easy access when everything hit the fan. He leaned back inside the hole and kicked Riggs.

"Riggs ... time for the show."

It can't be time for my watch. I don't want to get up right now. It's not my time. I can't climb out; I am bone dead tired.

"Riggs, get out here. It's time for some fun." Cooter spoke as low as he could while he gave him another push with his grey, muddy jungle boot.

"Time for what man? I hardly got to sleep," Riggs fired back angrily.

"Time for the shit to hit the fan, that's what time it is," Cooter said with more than a note of fear that raised Riggs from his slumber like a splinter in his rear. Riggs shot up grabbing his 14 and following Cooter's example, hastily dropped the tripods on his 14. Cooter was on the radio back to the LT who was housed in the middle of the base.

"Echo One this is Echo Tex over"

"Yea Echo Tex what is it?" came the quick reply from the man in charge.

"Echo One get ready ... I've got movement," responded Cooter.

Riggs still wasn't sure what the movement was but Cooter had been in Nam too long not to 'feel' it when the gooks were around. He could feel it like all the old salts that survived as long as he did. He pointed to the front and cupped his ear, motioning for Riggs to do the same.

Man this magnifies everything. Why didn't I figure that out? I don't hear anything though. I don't think ... there is like rustling or something. I can't make it out. Or is it ...

"Did you hear that?" Cooter asked with the forced whisper required to stay alive.

Shaking his head Riggs indicated he didn't hear a thing. Cooter knew what he heard and he wasn't standing down. It was now 0310 and life was falling in the shitter like a rock off a cliff.

There was a huge flash of light followed by an explosion. BOOOM!

Brrrrp! Brrrrp!

Small arms fire broke out everywhere around the perimeter. The NVA were attacking with a vengeance. Sappers hit the wire with a huge satchel charge designed to break a hole in the Marine lines just north of Riggs's position.

Marine mortars began lighting up the night with flares floating down, creating an eerie look in the dark of night. Riggs scanned the landscape in front of his position as silhouettes of enemy soldiers running and firing dotted his view as they tried to advance against Marine lines.

My God this is the worst I've seen. It's worse looking at them out there. It's the real thing. They are surrounding us!

The sound of battle was deafening. The roar of gunfire sounded like all of Echo Company was firing in unison, like a perverted orchestra with a pitch that kept getting higher and higher but there was no audience to enjoy this mess.

"Riggs get ready to fire the Claymore!" Cooter yelled above the chatter of M-14s aimed at people trying to kill them and the roar of AK-47's firing back with the same aim.

"Claymore? Where is it?" Riggs screamed.

"Right there man, grab the trigger and push the button when I tell you."

Riggs grabbed the little trigger assembly in his left hand. It was hooked to a wire leading to the Claymore unit standing twenty feet in front of their position. All the Marine positions had them and he'd heard a couple go off already.

The constant womp of mortars dropping in their tubes was now a methodical rhythm playing out behind Cooter and Riggs. The light show kept up, revealing the bad guys coming like cock roaches scurrying around when they see first light.

Suddenly the bizarre horizon in front of Riggs's hole was filled with human figures running, screaming and firing. It was a human wave assault complete with the blaring sound of bugles in the distance down over the front hill of Con Thien.

"NOW!" Cooter screamed with the shriek of a coyote.

Claymores exploded along the Marine lines left and right. Riggs was frozen staring straight at the running line of NVA when he pushed as hard as he could on the mine's trigger.

WAYOOOSH! BOOM!

There was a flash and a blur of things flying in the air with a muffled blast that shot outward straight in front of a shocked Riggs.

Oh my God bodies are flying through the air! I did that. I pulled that trigger. My God help me. Help me God!

The Marine Claymores slowed the attack. Just then, Riggs turned to a noise on his left, in time to see an NVA running towards the hole next door with a fixed bayonet, screaming like a rabid dog dying in the road. Then he realized the scream was from the Marine in the hole.

Riggs opened up with all he had in his 14.

Brrrrrp!

"Nooooooooo!"

He screamed as the Marine went down along with the venomous NVA. A fellow Marine bayoneted right before his eyes.

"Riggsy keep it up man they're still rollin' in," Cooter growled firing his 14 like John Wayne.

The fight went on right up to morning light. As dawn began breaking so did the NVA. They pulled back, slipping into the surrounding bush like a nasty nest of snakes slithering away to escape the footsteps encroaching danger.

Standing tall for the first time in days, Riggs and Cooter surveyed the carnage revealed by the sun rising slowly and hotly in the east.

It reminds me of the county garbage dump back home. It's just garbage every where that was only minutes and hours ago human beings. I don't know what to do or think or ... I don't know what has happened. I just know I am still standing. What does that mean?

"Cooter … we need a report, how many casualties?"

… It was the LT's radioman running around asking for a personal report.

Cooter was up and about, looking, asking questions of the survivors and making sure the dead were dead … on both sides.

The news never seemed to be good and today it was awful. Ten more dead, fourteen wounded, eight of them seriously. The PFC in the next hole, Bugger Phillips, was reportedly from Massillon, Ohio and had a brother; some said two, in the Marines and Vietnam. Whatever was the truth … this Bugger died of a bayonet right before Clayton Wesley Riggs? He saw him die and then had to help put him in his body bag for the trip home to Ohio.

Home? Home, my God where is home? What I wouldn't give to be home sleeping in my bed. What would it be like to sleep with clean sheets and take a warm shower? Home to get up and go and see Maggie O'Reilly and walk where we used to walk and talk like we used to talk. What would it be like? I don't know what I'll be like in a year; it's only been a month.

Riggs thought he'd had bad days in his young life but none like this one. The strength of the Marines of Echo 2-4 was now down to under a hundred men, probably half strength for a grunt company.

Cooter, Moto and Riggs had survived, while several others nearby weren't so lucky. The LT came through untouched, except for a growing sense of depression over the reality of leadership in the midst of such madness and the mounting loss of his young troops.

Riggs retired to ponder what to do next. The options were few, the light was slipping away, it was nearly 1800 hours and another night on the edge of sanity awaited the Marines of Echo 2 – 4 living on the edge of mankind in Con Thien, Vietnam.

He sat in what was left of his home, a battered hole in the ground surrounded by the site and smell of death, the countless deaths of many North Vietnamese and a few more young Marines.

I gotta' talk with Maggie. I just have to talk with Maggie.

Riggs sat down dejected, exhausted and looking for the lift he couldn't imagine even Maggie could give him.

November 28, 1967
Bloomington, IN

Dear Clayton,

Well here I am back at the apartment with the girls, hearing about what they did over break—they all went home of course, mostly to small towns nearby. The train ride to Bloomington put me to sleep—I tried to read and then to write but eventually I just looked out the window and the movement of the train on the tracks finally wore me down into some dreamless slumber land.

My roommates asked me what I did in the Windy City. I told them about this and that and how the Christmas season is so beautiful there with fancy window displays in the department stores and bagpipe players on the street (not eleven pipers piping but only one or two) and going here to see this and there to see that. Somehow in the retelling, even the glorious skyscrapers and museums and everything seemed to become smaller and less grand in light of what is going on in this world. Just like in the narrowness of my little world—or is it the narrowness of my own bedroom at the apartment in comparison to my bedroom at home?

Riggs sat alone, quiet, tears running down his filthy cheeks, savoring every word of Maggie's letter, appreciating it as never before.

What I wouldn't give to be there with her right now. I would love to smell her perfume, to look into her eyes and touch her hand, to brush back her hair. I can't imagine life like that now, I don't know if I ever will.

He took a deep breath and picked her letter back up and began to read one more time.

I know I seem to find escape in the beauty of art and literature and struggle to find a way to make them a permanent part of my life. But I hope never to turn my back on the real world of people as well. Of course I have been forced a bit into thinking more about what is to be a permanent part of my life. At dinner yesterday my dad asked me what were my plans? Would I ...

** Get married and have a house of curtain climbers, like most good Irishwomen do? (My sister said why not? cause I think this is what her plans are)*

** Join the hippies and become a professional agitator? —Not that any of them seem to have a real job or a profession he said with a laugh—(my mother said Isn't that the point? and I confessed I wanted a real job someday)*

** Or make free love with the hippies and not worry about it? (I told him I didn't know what free love means but it sounded good to me—I certainly never thought to charge for it)*

**Or become a farmer? (Though he says "whatever makes me happy" he also said he's hoping I use my head more than my hands, which almost started me talking* on how much thought and brains goes into farming, and Grandmother added luck)

* Or turn into a charity queen? (If my inheritance or marriage to a stockbroker allows it)

*Or be a baker? (He teases me for my experiments with pies, all the while asking for seconds or even thirds)

*Or train to be a firewoman or any of the other men's jobs that are now opening up to women?

Mother said, "Now Dexter, she's only a junior this year, she's exploring her options."

But dad said I needed to be thinking about what my major will be, whether it was journalism or English literature or music or whatever.

I told him that I'm still taking classes in all these areas, and am still getting basic requirements out of the way, and wasn't it some ancient Greek philosopher who said society's great worry was how to keep our children from committing suicide at age twenty?

That seemed to make him quiet for a moment. Grandmother didn't say a word but looked at me in that knowing way, not really worrying but with a bit of concern perhaps mixed with this funny little smile now and then. She knows me so well.

When I was young staying with her during the summer she never acknowledged my "moods" at all, and if I became crabby or bored when my sister went to camp instead of going to Petoskey she would give me something to do, helping her in the garden or kitchen or shopping for a new book or even just taking a walk. This would always work.

To this day if I find myself getting irritated or blaming others for my sorrows I always turn to a good book or make a drawing or write a poem or write a letter or listen to music or play the piano or whatever. But I also realized something else about myself: I still do not turn to my friends so much, but keep whatever it is troubling me mostly to myself.

There are a couple exceptions of course. As different as Beverly and I are, we have remained quite close. Maybe it's because it was just the two of us growing up and my parents were not always having my aunts and uncles and cousins over since mother would tend to get in arguments with them on politics and current affairs and how they were raising us girls. Beverly, of course, being the oldest was spoiled and did just what she pleased, which usually had a lot to do with watching out for Number One.

We have beaten each other up often enough as kids that it is hard to hold back anything from her. Once you've exchanged blows dozens of times it seems to open things up a bit—not that I'm saying that the new fangled psychoanalysis is for me. You know, where you take your frustrations out on some symbol like beating a pillow or hitting a punching bag that is supposed to represent your enemies and so on. I still prefer beating up my sister! I even leave my dolls and stuffed animals at peace, the ones that still line the bed of my old bedroom.

But Beverly was more brassy and sassy and full of her oh-so-pretty self and she's also a bit of a flirt. I was always the quiet one with my head stuck in books, with the better grades at school and way too shy to chase boys (though you were quite sweet to say she didn't hold a candle to my looks—no one has ever said that to me before and I do wonder if you really meant it or were just being kind...)

But now Beverly said she <u>thinks</u> she's falling in love and she wanted to talk about that mostly. I asked her what does she mean she <u>thinks</u> she is. I've always imagined this was something really big you know. After all, poets and writers and singers have been going on and on about it for centuries. There are a few clues to the process in history.

She said maybe she didn't read as much as I do but, of course, the magazines all go on and on about it and *she feels it might be true love and isn't that what girls dream about all their lives? Isn't the most important day of their life their marriage?*

And to this I had to say I wasn't so sure—the most important role of your life being defined only in relation to another person and anyway, being just a housewife sounded boring . . .

But then, even as I was saying these things, I had to admit I was in no position to judge or even comment much on the subject based on my meager experience. Of course, we Christians might agree that Jesus is the role model for serving others, but in my mind, at least, these others are supposed to begin not end with family.

The kid from Hope was mesmerized by what Maggie had to say. Moto and the others would have never understood these words nor cared enough to listen to her meanderings about art, poetry and a sister possibly in love. But Riggs was transported out of misery into the arms of peace and love by her words.

Love? I don't know anymore about any of these things. I know I feel better being as close to her as the words in her letter. Jesus? God? I don't know anymore. How could there be love and peace and Jesus Christ in a place like this? I know what Mom taught me and what they said at Church but that was before all of this! I don't know much anymore, least of all about these things, Maggie.

A life that includes service to others is more rewarding than taking care of just your own, for that is a small number and the world is so much larger than that. Making a contribution to society in the larger picture, while making your family proud and serving them, is what we're raised to believe. But she laughed and said, just stay out of trouble and Mom and Dad will be fine! Take care of yourself first and then you can care for others. She has a point I suppose, for if you are a mess yourself what good are you to others?

But then I tried to explain to Beverly what was happening to me, that the difference between others and myself seems to dissolve at times, and I can't always locate the line that separates us. And I can't decide now what I want to do or be for the rest of my life when I have just started to really live it—you know, away from home, for the first time having to figure it out myself. And of course I had to admit to her and myself that I wanted it all—true love and a good family and good friends and good works and good art and good books and good jobs and good friends and respect from others and respect for myself... even if the outer world closes in on my little world and keeps me from getting it.

So what is the other exception to my little place of quiet and self-sufficiency? It is you Clayton. You are more than a friend or a confidant. You are now part of that space I live in that is not separate or alone or lonely even. Though I miss you I do not feel lonely. You are there all the time even if I can't see you or hear your voice at the moment. Be sure I am thinking of you every day and pray every night for your health and happiness and long life.

It is getting late now and my roommate is telling me to turn out the light already and leave something to say for tomorrow... so I am taking her advice...

Love always,

Maggie

Darkness reached around Clayton Wesley Riggs the way he wished Maggie O'Reilly could. The more he read her letters he knew she would reach around him and it made all the difference in his now miserable life.

It's hard to imagine just a few minutes ago I was so depressed, so angry, so lost ... and her one letter has brought me back to the Well House where life is the way it should be to me. Oh how I wish I were at the Well House now. I wish I could help her with her decisions and her future. I wish I could walk with her and I know she could heal the wounds in my soul. I know she could.

Riggs and nearly a hundred other men, young and old, longed for “the world” as they called it, ten thousand miles away. They longed for peace in the coming Christmas season … but peace would elude the crew from Echo 2-4 like the enemy they fought almost daily.

20

December 24, 1967
Christmas Eve in the DMZ

It's the eleventh day of fighting in a row. Will they ever relieve us? Will we ever get out of here? Or are we all destined to leave like the guy yesterday who went down right before my eyes and I can still see him now! Is this truth? Our destiny is a plastic body bag? Not for me. I will go home, I know I will.

Clayton Riggs, newly arrived in Vietnam, only two short weeks ago, was already a seasoned vet. He struggled to get his head around all that happened to him and his new best friends … the Marines of Con Thien. The last few days were a blur.

Riggs arrived in country on December 13, weeks out of Parris Island and a lifetime from Hope, Indiana. Today was Christmas Eve but there wasn't anyone celebrating on either side of the DMZ.

He was a grunt, and life for the grunts was a world away from his farm in Hope. Since the day of his arrival Riggs witnessed the NVA's offensive in the hills north and west of this pile of dirt he now called home.

"Riggsy, you're a piece of work," Cooter said, oozing his usual Texas affection. "We're in a serious game of tag and guess damned what … we're it!"

Clayton Wesley Riggs, country boy, pig farmer and corn grower extraordinaire, was amazed that he had come so far so fast. Cooter was becoming a good friend. Until they came together in Nam, he hadn't been around anyone quite like him, or many of the others, who he now depended on to cover his back and keep him alive.

It was dawn on the twelfth day of the fighting after Riggs's arrival. There was a strange lull in the chaos that had become everyday life for the men of the infantry, the grunts who remained, those still walking in Echo 2/4. They were the same 2/4 that was known as the Magnificent Bastards in World War II and again in Vietnam. They didn't feel so "magnificent" today. Every Marine, to the man, knew all too well the eerie silence of Christmas Eve morning wouldn't last long.

"Well Riggsy, we're still standing this morning so we're the winners," Cooter offered with an air of authority and confidence Riggs hadn't come to feel just yet.

"Cooter, it's hard to think about being winners right now," Riggs replied with a heavy dose of resignation.

It was a group of survivors and those barely surviving. The survivors were a scary mix of baby-faced teenagers with a twelve-day growth of beard and an eight hundred yard stare on the way to a thousand. They were the walking wounded, the tough and the crazy who refused evacuation.

Then there were the poor unfortunate bastards who'd bought the big one. Some would never walk again, or worse, while many more spent the trip home clothed in M1-A1 green plastic body bags.

After twelve days of fighting the NVA day and night, this group looked like the cast from your worst nightmare. One look in their eyes and you knew they had seen things you may never want to know about and they may never want to talk about.

"Riggs … where the hell are you? You trippin' out again? I'm gonna' come over there and give you a good ass kickin'."

Moto wasn't known for cutting anyone any slack, least of all the pig farmer he seemed to be fascinated with. Clayton Riggs was busy on a mental trip wrestling with his life. His life in Nam, his life in the Corps and the life he hoped for with his strawberry blonde beauty back in the world and specifically at school in Bloomington.

For now, though, he knew better. If he wanted to ever see Maggie again, he'd have to focus on Moto and what was left of elements of the NVA's 324th B Division now living in and around Con Thien.

They'd all faced enough killing in the last two weeks to last even the biggest ghoul a lifetime, but it wasn't over. Riggs could feel it in his bones. He was getting like Cooter and the others and could sense when things were going to break.

The 324th B got a serious butt kicking at the hands of the 3rd Battalion 4th Marines in Operation Hastings. That was June '66, and it was now December '67, just over a year later, and they were back for more, directing their evil wrath at Riggs and the rest of 2/4 sitting like toads in the road waiting to get hit.

The thought of fighting them face-to-face and hand-to-hand "one more time" kept Riggs up at night and sent chills down his spine.

I can live a whole lifetime and never hear another scream or bugle blowing in the night, or one more day for that matter. I don't want to face another human wave assault. It was frightening beyond anything I can imagine. I just want to go home. Slopping hogs never looked so good.

The family farm back in Hope hadn't prepared him for the terror spelled w-a-r. He might have come from pioneer stock, people who homesteaded that farm 150 years ago and a long line of Marines who fought for their country and one who even died, but not this stuff. He realized that war really is hell. The boy from Hope High had confirmed that for sure.

Riggs was startled back to his painful reality when the uneasy silence of another soaking monsoon morning was broken with …

"Hey asshole," a gruff growl came from the bunker about 20 yards away. "Let's take odds on what time they're gonna' come screaming out of the jungle." It was Moto again.

He was a five foot seven inch, two hundred and ten pound fireplug of a guy from East St. Louis, Missouri. He looked like a Sumo wrestler on Weight Watchers. He came from the tough side of town. He was a Marine's Marine.

He was the last person Riggs wanted to hear from right now. He might like Moto when he got to know him, but he doubted it. They were worlds apart.

I wonder where Maggie is right now? I wonder what she's doing while I sit on this God forsaken hill a million miles from anywhere, least of all anywhere sane? Oh, if I could just smell her hair and hold her hand and tell her how I really feel. But are we from two different worlds just like Moto and I?

He couldn't help but wonder what life was like back in the world. What would it be like after the war? What would he do? What would he be like? Would he end up with an attitude like Moto and hate everybody? Or would he learn to be like Cooter and take life as it comes and love people along the way?

He pondered those questions hour after hour, yet he found them to be questions with no clear answers right now, maybe with no answers at all, ever. They were answers he sought in his quest for truth. Right now though, truth was nowhere to be found in this part of the world.

"What is truth?"

Maggie asked that question with all sincerity, looking straight into his brown eyes. Neither one of them knew the answer. But that didn't stop her from continuing to ask "her" question over and over.

Truth? Who knows anymore?

Riggs's head was spinning. He realized you couldn't say Vietnam and Maggie O'Reilly in the same breath. They weren't only worlds apart … they were planets apart.

She came from a family of pacifists and his were "hawks," believing in fighting and dying for your country when called upon to do so and even when you weren't asked to serve. The Riggs's were volunteers, thank you. The O'Reilly's, as near as he could tell, loathed the thought of anyone who would support a war.

Moto yelled a string of obscenities at the top of his lungs aimed at whoever was listening and to those who weren't.

"Moto shut up and stop that shit! I am getting out of here alive," Cooter shot back. Cooter's return volley lacked the sarcastic conviction and venom of Moto's outgoing tirade.

"Cooter, you really are a naive, starry-eyed piece of shit. Where the hell have you been for the last two weeks? We're not getting out of here. Replacements aren't coming. We're all going to die here asshole! Let's have fun and go out in a blaze of glory."

It took Riggs more than a little time to realize this was Moto's idea of fun. He loved upsetting people and getting them fired up.

I can't stand that guy. I love having fun but this place and these people aren't fun. I can't stand him. I couldn't have him around someone like Maggie. I never thought I'd be ashamed of a Marine but I couldn't do it with Moto. I could never risk putting her around someone like him. Never!

Moto was someone Riggs couldn't have imagined back in Indiana. Cooter told Riggs to stop worrying over it and to appreciate him for being the man he is when the gooks come blazing in at night.

Riggs was grateful to have him there when the shooting broke out. He just didn't want to put up with him right now or any of the other times when he needed sleep and Moto came calling. Not after what they'd all just been through. It shouldn't be like this.

He didn't want to listen to his perverse humor about not getting out … and then laughing about it. Of all people, Riggs thought Moto would be the one to get out. He was getting a growing feeling of doom about himself but he somehow saw Moto as a survivor regardless of the situation.

"Moto knock it off. I'm getting out of here. I know they'll get the choppers in today with reinforcements and I'll be back in Texas on my rotation date next month, you'll see." Cooter gave an unsure, weak and almost pleading response. Riggs was surprised by what sounded to him like a guy not sure about what his future held. But then who was sure except Moto?

Never one to be outdone, Moto drove the nail in Cooter's coffin when he sneered, "Well Mr. Cooter, sir … look the hell up in the air. You can damn near touch that cloud. Step outside and get your dumb ass drowned. It's the M-1, A-1 monsoon and it's been raining for days or did you forget? Look around my friend. Noah will be here soon to build another ark. The rain ain't quittin' and our little gook friends know we're stuck. They're attacking us because they know we're sitting ducks. That's just in case you haven't 'got it' yet my friend."

Moto ranted on until no one within earshot wanted to hear him anymore, including the gooks that Riggs was sure were moving in all around them. Things seemed to be going from bad to worse at warp speed and he didn't like how he felt.

Clayton Wesley Riggs had stepped in the ring to participate in a heavyweight fight. It was round twelve and each round was getting worse. Each day was horrible and each night took ugly to a new level. He was looking for sanity in a place where sanity was on extended leave and not due to return anytime soon.

I remember reading Bernard Fall's book about Dien Bien Phu called Hell in a Very Small Place. I hadn't been to hell before so I didn't know what it was ... but this little hill we're holed up on is a very small place. I'm afraid hell may be waiting in the jungle all around us. I don't know if I am ready for what may be coming.

Wesley Riggs, as Momma Riggs was fond of calling him, was running full speed into any place where he could be lost in thought. He wasn't going to play mind games with Moto; he knew he'd lose because Moto didn't have a mind to play with. He also knew he couldn't forget his own family history.

He had a family with a long history of serving their country and being proud of it. Riggs's dad, Homer, had served with the first group of Marines to land on Iwo Jima. He was a survivor who talked about the legacy but not the battle or the war. He was a veteran of the "Big One" and he didn't let you forget it. Daddy Riggs had raised his kids to honor their country and tried to teach them to be brave.

As a kid, each and every Memorial Day, Clayton Riggs was standing front and center offering a poem at the old Moravian cemetery in Hope. The ladies of the DAR put on their "Patriotic Dog and Pony Show" every year since he could remember.

Man I was so happy when I turned 12 and didn't have to go back to that old cemetery anymore. Right about now I'd volunteer for twenty poems for the ladies if I could get out of here. I am scared about Christmas Day. I don't know why but I am scared.

As Riggs sat waterlogged in his poor excuse for a foxhole, Cooter sat soaked and quiet nearby. He had a strange, fearful feeling that things were about to get worse, far worse than he could imagine,

Riggs had decided early on, in grade school, to be a Marine. Most people in his family and his school, including himself, didn't think he'd follow through and do it. He had a barrel chest and was athletic and fit but not aggressive... "Too kind," many said, to be a Marine.

In spite of the skeptics, and after a year at IU, he was on his way to Parris Island. He soon realized he'd made the decision to join the Corps out of duty, not desire. When he was honest with himself, he really wasn't sure he wanted to carry on the family legacy. It was a legacy that seemed to carry him on the words of preceding generations.

His cousin served in the Corps during the Cuban Missile Crisis and Grandpa Riggs, although Clayton never knew him, served in World War I. His Uncle Ben was a Marine in Korea's "Frozen Chosin" under Chesty Puller. He died and was buried during Puller's famous "advance to the rear." With a legacy like that, Clayton often thought, "*do I have a choice in this?*"

Parris Island was as tough as he'd been told. It was a trip made tougher after his chance meeting with a girl named Maggie O'Reilly. Meeting Maggie made him regret his decision to join the Corps.

He was young, had never really dated and didn't want to leave when it came time to "ship out." Maggie, as it turned out, was something special to him. He felt it from their first "chance" meeting and didn't want to leave when the time came. He began to feel things for her that he didn't understand, things he'd never felt before.

What if I hadn't volunteered for the Corps? What if I had stayed and been with Maggie at Bloomington and finished my studies at IU? What if, What if, What if? I don't know what I feel right now but I do wonder what would have happened if I had taken a different route.

His mind was beginning to play games on him. Moto provided enough mind games for both of them. Riggs needed to get back to earth, back to Nam and back to keeping his head screwed on right. He needed to gut it out through the tough times, fulfill his legacy and return home and find Maggie.

Riggs woke from his midday stupor when he heard running. His heart instantly shot straight from his chest to the top of his head. Riggs grabbed frantically for his M-14, with blood about to blow his head up like a pop flare from a mortar. The blood was pounding so hard he thought his temples would explode. He spun around; pointing his locked and loaded rifle right square in the chest of a Marine they called Zip.

"What the hell are you doing?" Zip grumbled, pushing the barrel of the 14 away as if it were the toy gun his brother used to point at him in the back yard battles of yesterday back home in Hamilton, Montana, where they all wished they were right now.

Zip sat on the edge of the watery hole Riggs and Cooter had dug a foot deeper just a few hours before. His untimely and belligerent arrival woke Cooter from his mid-morning nap.

They were like the Three Musketeers, but not like the honorable ones of old. These were camouflaged and unsure of the honor they were defending but sure they were going to fight like hell defending it.

Zip was one more survivor of the siege on Con Thien.

"Screw it. Just screw it!" he would profanely proclaim as his patented greeting.

He and Riggs met in a briefing just a few days ago. He was a former biker who was raised in the Hell's Angels and looked every inch the part. Cooter told Riggs that Moto had named him "Zip" after Eric Von Zipper, the infamous villain of the beach movies popular back in the world at the time.

"You mean the ones with Annette Funicello and Frankie Avalon?" Riggs had asked in disbelief.

The answer was yes. This tough, gnarly, obscene Marine with an attitude as strong as a big swig of kerosene and as big as his home state of Montana was named after someone straight out of a Disney movie. What was more amazing was that Moto knew someone from one of Annette's beach movies.

The book on Zip was, as everyone said, *"He'll stare the NVA in the eye and never back down."* But Riggs didn't feel like he needed him right now. He really wanted to be alone. He wanted to be "all" alone.

Zip layback in the mud, unaware of how Riggs felt and oblivious to the cesspool he was lying in. He was out of it, totally fried from twelve straight days of fighting and bombing. Fighting first to gain ground ... only to give it back again a few weeks or sometimes days later.

Where is truth? I haven't seen it yet. It must be AWOL.

It had been days on end of mortar attacks. It was mortars all day and firefights all night interspersed with screaming people running and jumping and crying in the night as they stampeded the lines. It was more than most could imagine or most would want ... except Moto, and he didn't count... he was mad.

Riggs slipped off into his own world, as Cooter and Zip caught up on old times. For them, it was all etched in stone … we were done and as Zip said, "Screw it, just screw it, and let's go out in a blaze of glory."

I wonder if they're right. Twelve days... how on earth have we lived through twelve days and fifty percent casualties? Will we make it? We have to ... I have to by damned. I have to get out of here and go home. I have to see Maggie.

He overheard Zip and Cooter talking about last night's hand-to-hand fighting. Riggs was having trouble getting his mind around the raw violence of a human assault.

Riggs floated along, lost in thought. The morning mist, still clinging to life at midday, turned to a light glow. The sun crept into day, like a cat ready to pounce from its hidden perch above. For a brief moment, the barren, mortar-pocked landscape of the DMZ northwest of Con Thien came to life with a ray of rare sunlight.

Deep in his own world, trying to make sense of the senseless, trying with all his might to get his mind off the girl he loved, Riggs was miles from the matter at hand; he was in a living hell on a dirt hill deep in the DMZ.

Riggs suddenly felt the urge to tell her, tell her what he felt. He hadn't written a letter home since he arrived in country. He hadn't had time to write and didn't even know if mail was going in and out … but he knew it was time to make his feelings known.

I have to tell her... that is my Christmas Present for her. She has to know how I feel. She won't get it for Christmas but she'll know how I feel about her someday soon. She has to know, she just has to.

Riggs grabbed a muddy 5 x 8 tablet he was issued in Da Nang when he arrived in Nam. It was standard issue with the 3rd Marine Division triangle logo prominently positioned at the top. It would have to do … the message was more important than the paper. Maggie would understand.

I just have to tell her how I feel... she has to know ... Riggs began to write to his love amidst the carnage of war. His mind reflected upon each precious moment, each conversation, each event that gave meaning and focus to their times together. If only he could put into words how much she meant to him. If only…

Clayton Wesley Riggs, the farm boy from Hope, Indiana, gently folded the letter and slid it into the envelope that would carry the letter of love to his bestest friend, the one person who knew him better than anyone else upon the earth. She would understand the words that he had written. Maggie O'Reilly would know his innermost feelings. He hurriedly wrote her address on the envelope:

Maggie O'Reilly
121 Fourth Avenue
Apartment 15A

Clayton picked up Maggie's twelfth letter of Christmas and opened it.

I have to read her last letter. It's the last letter in her wonderful, thoughtful gift of twelve letters. I have to read it now while I still can. I don't think there's going to be a cease-fire and I don't know what the future holds for me. But right now I have to get more of Maggie O'Reilly, the girl I love.

November 29, 1967
Bloomington, Indiana

Dear Clayton,

The morning light is coming in my window where I sit alone at my desk, looking out at the trees that are now almost bare. The light of my mind is starting to illuminate some of the shadows of my thoughts, revealing their true nature.

Didn't I just say in my letter to you last night that I did not feel lonely for you? Don't believe a word of it my bestest friend. It's not that I was lying, but I was certainly fooling myself, or I am having trouble saying what I really mean. I am lonely for you every day of the week and that's the truth of it. Though I can feel you *here next to me in some trick of quantum mechanics or other magic of invisibility, I feel you are very distinctly not here enough. For you being here in my mind is not enough.*

Riggs was touched in a way that sent ripples of warmth deep inside his soul. He had always wanted to believe that Maggie cared for him but now he knew for sure. She is lonely for me. She misses me.

He carefully and hopefully picked up the sweet smelling stationery that carried a slight scent of the girl he loved.

As independent and happy as I have always been, sitting in this quiet space, doing my work or enjoying my play, not too concerned about the future or how these pieces of my life might fit together, a path is forming in front of me to meet my feet as I walk it. I walk on one side of it, to the left, for this path is wide enough for two. In some way that is new and inexplicable, the way seems as set in stone as any of the other red bricks we walked on in the IU woods.

For my mind keeps going back there, to the Well House where I first saw you sitting on the bench that colorful October day with the maples and tulip trees and all the other trees behind you in those woods letting loose of their leaves. I see the first smile you gave to me and I hear your first words after I asked if you didn't mind being in my drawing.

But when I see myself explaining to you how landscapes sometimes need people to make them more interesting, I also think about the things I didn't say to you. Your presence would make my art more interesting, and, also, more beautiful. Your form in my picture might make it too beautiful, and it is good you were looking away in my picture, for if I were to put your eyes into it, the way they looked at me, and no one would see the forest for those eyes. Your warm brown eyes seemed to make so much room for me and my drawing and my day or whatever it might be that I asked of you. I knew instinctively I could count on you for anything I might need of you, even your life, if I were to ask for it.

These were my thoughts at the time that I first came to know you—that you were the most generous and considerate boy I knew. Not just because you were feeding your lunch to the animals gathering around your bench, or because you would throw your coat onto puddles for the sake of a lady's shoes, or because you never pried into my private affairs or teased me about my weaknesses and faults, but gave advice and comfort as a brother and protector with no expectations in return.

And though we both know you could have gone with a dozen girls who would be happy to make themselves available to you, you were happy to be in my company even though I never gave you even one kiss on the cheek. But you were sensitive to feel the kisses I did give you, weren't you? You could feel them all the same as I have felt yours.

Kisses? I wish I could feel them now. I wish I could share with you the same feelings I have every minute I get to feel them. I wish I could hold your hand and tell you how lonely I am for you. I wish this damn war was over and people weren't dying and I was back at IU.

So I knew from the start you would be my friend, but I didn't expect you to become my bestest friend, the one who listens and understands without judgment, the one who knows when and what to say, or when words don't have any use at all, the one who reveals and shares with humor and sincerity, with no guile or hiding, no blame of others, no whining, no bitterness on what life has given you. And it dawned on me that you were all these things, and how rare they are found in one person, and if I were to let you go I might never have these precious things again.

Of course I was hurt when you let me go, left the world we had formed together in ten short months. Even if it was for the sake of your parents, your family lineage, your country, even as much as we disagree about what serving our country means, I now see that these are the very qualities about you that I admire. I would respect you even if you ran off to Canada, but I know you would not respect yourself, and this is the clue to your character, isn't it?

So this letter is about you, Clayton Wesley Riggs, the man that I love with all my heart, the man that I wait for knowing you are waiting for me, waiting to join me on that path so that we might continue our saunter into the Hoosier woodlands or wherever it takes us. The next drawing I do of you will have you walking back into my life—for keeps, if you will have me. Do not doubt that you will be here again, for I have seen you here, just as Grandmother with the second sight has told me that you would return one day, even if it is not as soon as we might hope.

So my darling, as you sit down to read my 12th note of this seasonal gift, you may hear the twelve drummers drumming as you announce to yourself or your friends or to the whole world if it pleases you: On the 12th day of Christmas my true love gave to me . . . everything!

Yours, Forever and Always,
Always and Forever,

Maggie

Riggs sat mesmerized by the girl he loved a half a world away. He felt like he was glowing, a shining light sitting amidst a pile of garbage he called home. More importantly, he was glowing from the girl who had just told him she loved him.

Clayton Wesley Riggs was in love with a girl from Chicago's Gold Coast. In love with an "anti-war" girl, from an "anti-war" family … no one would believe it, least of all the kid from Hope.

Nothing could pry his mind off Maggie.

The letters. What a beautiful gift, her beautiful letters. Her words came though the page like her perfume penetrating the summer night air of the IU campus. The campus they shared like the real love they both felt and just now admitted to feeling.

It was so like her to come up with the "twelve days of Christmas." So like her. The twelve days of Christmas and Maggie O'Reilly and me. I can't believe it. I can't believe she loves me.

When Riggs arrived in country he got one package from Maggie and was grateful for it. The surprise was his when he opened his package and found not one but twelve letters, one for each of the twelve days. He didn't tell anyone in the outfit for fear the grizzled "grunts" wouldn't understand. They would make fun of him.

Can you imagine Moto? He would kill me. He would humiliate me for sure.

Right now he wasn't thinking of Moto, he was thinking of Maggie, back in Chicago, or wherever she might be right now.

Today was the most incredible of all the days of my life. She loves me! Finally she said what I was afraid to say ... to ask ... I'm just not good at this love thing. I don't know what to do except I know whom I want to spend my life with. The twelfth letter ... it's so beautiful and full of love. I sit here in the midst of hell. She's so incredible. I love her. She lifts me from a half a world away and carries me to a better place. Now I know I must carry myself home to her.

Riggs felt as if an electric current was running through him and back to the world, to Maggie O'Reilly. This was the magnetic force Riggs needed to survive, to return to the world and match up with the most beautiful girl he'd ever imagined…

21

December 24, 1967
Riggs Home – Christmas Eve
Hope, Indiana

"Lucy, get in here, we're ready to trim the tree," Homer called to the kitchen after getting the little tree he'd just cut from out back on the farm.

"I don't know it's just not the same without Clayton here. Oh, I'm coming but I just don't feel the same this year".

The Riggs family was serious about tradition and none more so than Christmas Eve. Everyone gathered in the family home to trim the tree and sing carols. It would be the first year that Clayton wouldn't be home.

The house was full of aunts, uncles and cousins from all sides. Beth, Clayton's sister, felt out of place without her big brother around. Homer was now the Patriarch with Grandpa gone from the scene. He took his duties seriously, the way most things were done around the Riggs home.

"I think I almost got the tree ready dear," Homer said from under the scrawny limbs of the tree he was getting in place for the trimming. It had been a few years since he had cut down a tree. Clayton usually did that with Beth's help, she loved tagging along with her brother.

"Oh my," Lucy said, walking into the room. You can sure tell who cut this tree."

Clayton was sorely missed around the Riggs homestead. It wasn't just the annual cutting of the tree either. He walked with an air of difference. He was first to stand up and say *'I'll take care of it'* and Momma Riggs missed him dearly.

"Ah Mom it's not that bad … is it?" Homer asked cautiously, looking her way.

She was off to the kitchen to fill a pan with water to *give "the tree a drink,"* as she was fond of saying. But not before she shot back over her shoulder, "maybe you should ask the rest."

He didn't have to ask; the room was hooting and hollering about the ugly little tree Daddy Riggs had brought in for trimming. Even Beth thought it looked "different."

Mom and Dad Riggs had met in high school and had been friends since the sixth grade. Kids in Hope, Indiana didn't date young like they do today, so the Senior Prom was their first official get together. They'd been together ever since, and were pillars of strength for their local community.

Lucy made it through the tough years when Homer was in the Islands. He was determined to serve in the Marine Corps like his family had done for years, even with little Clayton and Mom at home.

Those were lean years and when Homer returned they got even leaner. Life on the family farm was tough but both he and Lucy would agree, rewarding. It was times like tonight that made it all worthwhile. Family was everything.

"Well there it is," Homer proudly proclaimed for all to see.

"There it 'is' is right!" Lucy's brother Frank retorted. Why that thing is like a piece of Swiss cheese, you can see right through it."

"If Clay was here he'd a picked a good one," chimed in Homer's own brother Donnie.

That was all that Lucy needed to retreat back into the kitchen. She felt bad enough that Clay was over there in that Godforsaken place and bad enough that he wasn't here with them, she didn't need to hear everyone's jokes about what he may or may not have done if he were here where he should be.

Oh I know they're just kidding and they love that boy but I miss him so. I miss him right now and don't want to even think about what he might be doing about now. Oh God watch over that boy he is so precious to me.

The laughter and noise rang sweet throughout the family farmhouse. They all took a step back in time when Lucy put on an old Fred Waring Christmas Album. Then she broke out the eggnog.

Homer caught a glimpse of the love of his life hustling out of the room back in to the kitchen. He knew instinctively the problem was the mere mention of Clayton's absence. Rushing to the kitchen he found her standing, sobbing in the corner.

"Lucy, you know I love you more than life. Things will be okay. You made it through Iwo Jima with me and we'll both make it through Vietnam with Clayton."

As he talked, Homer wrapped his arms around Lucy like they were two kids having their first spat." I know what you're feeling because I'm feeling it too," Homer consoled her lovingly, hugging her tight.

Until Clay left for the Marine Corps the strong one in the family was Mom. She stood tall during their first and second babies' births, the lean years of farming and the car wreck that nearly took their lives.

Now she'd have to get a stiff upper lip and do what needed done again. Her only son needed her and she couldn't let him down or her soul mate, Homer.

"Homer, I know you're right dear, but I don't know what's happening to me. Since Clayton left I have had trouble when I even hear his name. I don't know what I will do if anything happens to him."

Homer stood frozen, holding her like a first date. They stood like two pillars in the corner of the kitchen clinging to one another like a summer vine wrapped around the porch. They held on tight as if afraid to let go and return to the celebration.

"Come on you two lovebirds, its time to trim the tree," yelled Lucy's sister Oleta, from a crack in the kitchen door. "Get out here!"

Homer reached down and took Lucy with one hand and started for the door. Lucy followed, wiping her tear stained face with her apron in the other hand. They stopped, as if on cue just before going through the door into the festivities.

"Homer Allen Riggs … I love you. Promise me, promise me, Clayton is coming home."

Lucy looked into those big brown eyes she had loved since the sixth grade pleading for assurance that it was okay to go in and have fun again.

The door swung open before Homer had a chance to do anything more than smile at Lucy adoringly as he had done everyday of their lives together.

"Get in here! Do you need an invitation?" The door nearly hit them both as Donnie reached in and pulled them into the dining room and on to main stage.

The family knew that Homer and Lucy were struggling this Christmas. Oleta had all the decorations laid out so trimming the tree would be smooth. She even had the star for the tree topper sitting on the rocker, waiting for Homer to crown this year's tree to start the festivities.

The next hour and a half was a festive affair, an annual party of family and friends gathering to celebrate friendship, love and the birth of the Savior. It was an evening of tradition in a house well worn by tradition and a family bond that was bound by it.

Tink, tink, tink.

"Can I get everyone's attention? It's time for our family tradition to continue. We have a beautiful tree here and I will now crown it with our star." Homer was doing what Homer did … each and every year.

The star had been handed down through the Riggs family for three generations. It was bent, torn and tattered but it was tradition … as was the speech he was about to give.

"Family and friends … I have never been prouder nor happier than I am standing with you now. It is a joyous time of year and to be with all of you and once again having you in our home … makes Lucy and me complete."

Homer was serious, maybe more serious than most had seen him and that was saying something. Lucy stood at his side, holding his hand, staring at an imaginary spot on the floor as if it offered a window to the other side of the world.

"We just want you to know with Clayton gone this year that having you all over means the world to us. We also wanted to thank you for your prayers and support during this difficult time."

Lucy squeezed his hand tight; trying to hold back the tears welling up inside her tired eyes and at the same time put her arm around Beth who was struggling too. She had been keeping it from Homer but she was barely sleeping since her only son went to war.

"Now if we could all join in singing our traditional carol by forming the Riggs Family Choir." Daddy Riggs stood in the middle with his arms outstretched in either direction, with the others forming a giant semi-circle in the great room of the family home.

Lucy stood front and center before the assembled family. With her right hand raised, ready to lead the music, she looked to her right to the piano commanded by Oleta. Oleta smiled and Lucy looked back towards her family … "ready?"

She swallowed hard and began … "Silent night, holy night, all is calm, all is bright …"

22

December 24, 1967
Christmas Eve – Con Thien, Vietnam

Zip broke into Riggs's dreamy eyed adventure, a dazed world of love and hate. He had just finished reading his letter from Maggie when reality took a deep bite from his psyche.

"Hey new man, we're in deep shit and you can't just trip out. If you got some serious weed here then share the shit with us man. Otherwise don't ignore the obvious, we gotta' kick some serious ass today and tonight."

Zip gave "cynical" a new meaning. He didn't see any silver lining in the constant cloud cover of their home in the DMZ.

Everyone knew Riggs didn't have any weed, he didn't even know what it was. He didn't even drink, let alone smoke marijuana. He was just a 19 year-old kid like all the rest and just wanted to serve his country, fight communism and go home. That's it! It's not complicated. That's really all there was to him, with the exception of having just poured his heart out and admitted his love for a girl a world away.

"Hey assholes! They're movin' in!" With those prophetic words from Moto, the frightening world of the little band of Marines on Con Thien became more frightening. It was about to change … forever.

"Right there at ten o'clock!" Moto yelled pointing north and west into what had become 'no man's land'. "See those little bastards, there must be fifty or sixty going through there … broad damned daylight!"

Fear swelled like a quick rising loaf of Mom's bread, right in the pit of Clayton Riggs stomach, jerking him from the arms of Maggie and back to a painful and filthy reality called war in Vietnam.

This was war, not just a really shitty place to find yourself daydreaming. This is what his family had been doing for generations. But family history be damned, he wasn't ending up like Uncle Ben in Korea. He wasn't dying on some stinking dot on a map of a place called Vietnam. No, he was going home. He would be with Maggie O'Reilly … she loved him and he loved her.

Moto's ravenous verbal abuse woke Riggs from his love induced stupor long enough to grab a nearby pair of 7 x 50's and press them to his eyes. What he saw sent a tremor of fear up his spine and through his filthy body like he just took a good swift kick to the groin. He wanted to puke but knew it wouldn't help.

Oh my God, they really are out there in broad daylight. There's a ton of them and it's daylight. What will happen after dark?

Riggs was injected with a huge dose of reality, reality he could have gone a whole lifetime without. It was a dose the size of his dad's big green John Deere tractor back in Hope. He was now full of fear and uncertainty.

"Aw man … this is it, they're comin' for us tonight. This is the night. Man … it's the big one this time. I can feel it in my Texas bones." Cooter's pronouncements made him the unofficial interpreter for the coming disaster he was sure was about to happen. He went from a solid Texas citizen patting everyone on the back and infusing them with hope to chairman of the pity party.

Man I counted on him. He's the closest thing I've got to a friend here. Why is he losing faith and turning us into losers full of fear? Why is he doing this? We need him. I need him. I have to get home and I don't know if I can do it alone!

Anyone with a pair of 7 x 50's could follow the movement of a growing column of bad guys, "gooks" as they were affectionately called, slithering in the mist, a mist so thick you couldn't be sure what you saw. As quickly as they came, they disappeared into a tree line about 400 meters away. The brief appearance of the sun was long gone, chased away by more monsoon clouds and rains and thoughts of the coming battle.

"Riggs, Zip, Cooter, Moto," they were startled by the voice of Lieutenant Vance, breaking the fragile silence of what had become the afternoon of Christmas Eve 1967. "Get over here right away!"

With a few words, Lt. Vance called the four Marines front and center in the driving rain. Of the four, Riggs was the only one not wounded at least once. He wasn't sure how he'd escaped his very own Purple Heart; he had defied gravity but he wasn't about to complain about it.

The four Marines, wearied by days of fighting, were about to be asked the impossible. Riggs took off with the rest, about to get acquainted with his fate in the new world order of the few Marines still upright and breathing on a fog-shrouded hill known as Con Thien.

Twelve days of fighting, living in the muck, mud and death of hell, had come down to this ... but what the hell is this? Gooks on the move around us in broad daylight can't be a good thing.

What am I doing being called over with these guys? They always lead everything. I don't even have a Fire Team. I am a follower! Maybe he's calling us in to announce the cease-fire. I know that's it, it has to be.

Riggs's mind was jumbled as the possibilities bounced around in his fear-filled head. He bobbed and weaved his way to the Lieutenant, praying to God that there were no snipers nearby and that he was going to hear about a newly agreed upon cease-fire.

"Get over here …we don't have much time," Lt. Vance exclaimed.

There might be more truth to that statement than anyone realizes. Truth! Oh God, give me truth to all of this.

As he arrived at the LT's area, Riggs was getting bad vibes about today, even if it was Christmas Eve. There was supposed to be a cease-fire, at least that's what the scuttlebutt was around the company area. Maybe that's why they were summoned to the LT.

I want to be back with Maggie O'Reilly in Bloomington, Indiana, not with Lieutenant Vance, here in Vietnam with water coming out and in every orifice of my young, skinny body. She loves me, I know that now and I love her. That may be the only truth that is ever important.

"Marines … we've been in the shit now for twelve straight days. Welcome to our very own cesspool. You're about to be honey dippers."

Honey dippers? That's what Dad called the guys who came and cleaned out our cesspool! Oh man, this can't be good!

Today, the Lieutenant had no hint of humor or caring, he was straight as an arrow. "In case you're wondering, there is supposed to be a cease-fire for the holidays. These people say one thing and do another. They're still saying they'll observe it but we can't take a chance. If they hit us here at the base with all they got and against what we have left … they will overrun us."

Riggs didn't find the LT too reassuring. It scared him to death and destroyed the fragile confidence he'd been building since his arrival.

"The four of you are going to lead squads out to the northwest. We have to go after them and engage them before they surround us. If we don't … and there is no cease-fire, or worse, they don't observe the cease-fire, our lives will be no better than shit in the outhouse."

Most of what the Lieutenant was saying everyone knew or felt. They knew the NVA had been trying to surround them. They knew there was a major offensive on the horizon. But they didn't know the plan of attack.

What they did know would crack the nerves of all but Moto. Riggs actually thought he looked excited. It was the eyes. Looking in the eyes always told the truth of the wearer. The truth is that they were both present and accounted for or they were out in space, fried from being in the shit too long.

"Things have been pretty damned rough, we've taken heavy casualties. We must do something right now. If we don't, we're all gonna' fall in the shitter head first … and there's no support to get our asses out."

Riggs hadn't been here long enough to figure out where this was going but he knew it wasn't going in the direction he wanted. Squatting in the damp, cold squalor of the LT's command bunker, listening to the worst news he'd ever heard in his young life, he could only think and trip out in his mind to another place and time. He seemed to do a lot of that lately.

This can't be true. I really don't want to be here. I don't want to leave here. I don't want to be out there on Christmas Eve ... or any other time for that matter.

The Lieutenant didn't enjoy delivering the news any more than the four Marines liked hearing it. Riggs was listening but he wasn't about to believe and couldn't believe something so outrageous to him. He was deathly afraid this patrol would be as screwed up as much as everything else since he'd arrived here. It all had an uncertain ring to it.

Oh how I wish I could have Christmas alone, a cease-fire, a time of calm and reflection. A time to reread all the letters from a wonderful friend, a girlfriend who loves me, a friend who taught me so much about life, mostly how to enjoy and live it. She showed me how to feel good about myself and think about what might lie ahead.

The Lieutenant calmly explained there were no reinforcements, no resupply choppers and no more Medevacs coming for the next 48 hours. The COC, the 4th Marine command center at Dong Ha, didn't feel that Con Thien was at risk.

Listening to his first briefing, Riggs felt like it was the equivalent of attending a wake for your recently deceased family, you included. He couldn't believe that they were left to hang out to dry, alone in the DMZ, betting that a vile enemy would keep a cease-fire when we knew they wouldn't. Whom were they listening to?

What a horrid proposition. This is like listening to your own eulogy ... its like you know you've been killed but the pain of your death is still alive and well and you are staring at it in the mirror.

Riggs hadn't been in the Corps long but he was used to Lieutenants being more positive and upbeat than Vance. Twelve straight days of fighting did strange things to people and the LT was pretty strange today. It was now getting to everyone. The beginning of his watery lecture was depressing, the end sounded downright suicidal.

Riggs wanted to escape. He knew he could always escape in thought.

It's what I remember hearing about Uncle Ben in Korea ... an advance to the rear that brought an end to his young life. I never knew him; just heard the stories. The stories made little sense until now. Maybe this is my fate, to end it like Uncle Ben?

Am I better than Uncle Ben? Better? Well, not better but luckier, maybe. I just know I don't want to end up like him. Will the next generation be sitting around the dinner table at home talking incessantly about what had happened to me? You know ole' Uncle Clayton ...he was a good kid and he died in Con Thien during a cease-fire with the North Vietnamese.

The LT was short and to the point. Silence reigned supreme. Four nervous young men were dismissed to go play in the rain. Vance asked for a volunteer to lead the point squad. Riggs reluctantly raised his hand. He'd volunteered again. He couldn't believe it himself.

I did it again. I can't believe I did it again. I could be in college right now with Maggie at IU but no, I wanted to keep the Riggs tradition and join the Corps. I meet the girl of my dreams, the sweetest kindest person on earth and here I am walking point. I just couldn't tell Dad I held back. I had to do it. If I'm here I have to do what I can even if I don't want to.

"A Marine was a grunt" and he'd heard that all the years of his young life. Now, standing in a driving rain, Riggs just turned and walked away to get his troops and his gear. He hadn't even noticed his own hand raising, coming up beside his body, when Lieutenant Vance had asked for a volunteer to lead the point squad. Everyone was surprised but no one more than Clayton Riggs.

Why? Why do I do this? Why do I risk everything?

Volunteering was always followed by remorse when he did something wrong or stupid but at no time was he more remorseful than right now.

Why did I join the Marines? Why did I leave Maggie? Yea, I wanted to follow in my Dad's footsteps, keep the family traditions alive. But this? Is this what war is about? Is this what defending America is about? What about Maggie? What about my family?

Walking in the rain Riggs realized if he ever wanted to see Maggie again he couldn't think about her right now. He had to take control of his mind.

I have to make it out of here. I have to see her. I have to meet her at the Well House and I have to look into those beautiful eyes, smell that sweet smell of love and hope and tell her with my own words how much she means to me.

He knew he had to take control but he was losing that battle right now.

In all my family life, which was good, I never felt like Maggie makes me feel. Even her letters lift me out of the hell and insanity of combat into the goodness of a kind heart. I cannot imagine life without her. I can't imagine what's about to happen, I only know I now live for her and I must win the game we are playing even if I don't know what it's all about.

There was no time left to daydream, there was only time for preparing. The four Marines and their reluctant squads methodically went about packing gear, loading magazines with ammo, checking radios and checking and rechecking everyone and everything that was going on this run into a night of potential madness while the rest of the world praised the Prince of Peace.

I wish I could be in my old Moravian Church back in Hope. I wish I were there thanking my Savior and God for getting me home alive. I just realized I haven't done anything with my letter to Maggie. I have to be sure it gets mailed. What do I do?

It was 1400 hours before the downtrodden crew was ready to lock, load and move out. The rains were worse, the fog and mist looked inches thicker than the day before and the fear of the impending mission was driving everyone's gonads well up into their bodies.

Moto. Yea, he'll make it back. He always does. I have a strange feeling right now, one I have never felt before. I have to give it to him. I am scared to ask but I have to give it to him to mail.

Moto and Cooter walked up to the staging area with their squads trailing behind.

"Hey pig farmer, you better have your head tied on for this one. We're goin' out there and getting' in some real shit for sure Sherlock."

How on earth do I ask him?

Cooter walked off to get another case of grenades to hand out to the mud-soaked crew lining up for the "party," as Moto called it.

"Moto I need to ask you a favor," Riggs said with a cracking voice.

"A favor? I don't do favors asshole."

"Moto, it's important. I need you to mail a letter for me," Riggs pleaded, which fueled every fire Moto harbored in his warped personality.

"Important my ass, we got a patrol to run … shut the hell up!" Moto took his gear and began to saddle up.

Riggs mustered up courage he was surprised he had. "Moto, I mean it, I'm scared to death and don't know what's going to happen out there. I have a letter here that has to be mailed and I know you will come back. Please mail it for me."

Moto didn't want to do favors. He didn't want to be nice to anyone. He looked at Riggs and for the first time in his life he stood, surprised at the words that came out of his mouth. "Riggs you're coming back asshole; we all are. Stop that shit."

Riggs persisted, surprised at his courage to stand with Moto. "I don't know about anything, Moto, I just want this letter mailed and I know if you say you will … you will. I know you can't stand me but do this one thing for me … please Moto."

"Stop saying please to me asshole. You're crazy, but if it will keep you quiet then go put it in my tent and shut the hell up."

Riggs ran off in the mud with his fully laden pack like he was running naked through the girl's locker room. He was determined to make sure his letter to Maggie would make it to the girl he loved.

The goal was to make the presence of the Marines visible the day before the cease-fire. The NVA soldiers Moto first discovered were also making their presence known. It would be a test of wills or one of stupidity; the reality remained to be seen.

"We need to test the waters," the LT said matter of factly.

Riggs was out of breath and left to think about that statement.

Test the waters huh? The only question here is which one of us is the more stupid? The LT just might win this one. I can't believe he is taking this chance. I can't believe I am here fighting for what I don't know. We take ground and give it up and then I hear back home people are in the streets protesting. I don't know what to think!

The Lieutenant had tried to explain his reasoning. "If we don't get out there and let them know we will fight, they'll bring more troops and with the cease-fire they will be dug in when it lifts."

It was 1440 when Lieutenant Vance gave the word. "Its time to go and do what needs done. Move it out and good luck Marines!"

Riggs walked behind his point man, Huffer, a good Baptist kid from Kentucky, a kid who just wanted to go home to his small town outside Louisville and the blue shrouded hills that made him feel safe and secure.

The remaining 9 Marines that made up Riggs's new squad trailed behind, walking with 80 pounds of gear and a thousand pounds of fear etched on their now aging faces, each step bringing them closer to the fear that now occupied their young minds.

From the back of the column Riggs could hear Moto loud and clear. "Asshole, when you get back I am giving that 'favor' back to you. Get your head in the game and watch where you lead us. You're mailing it!"

Everyone heard the mad man's pronouncement, only Cooter understood. He walked along with a wry smile, "*Could the man Moto be doing something kind? I knew he liked the kid.*"

It was an odd group assembled to lure the bad guys out but it was all the LT had to work with. The only squad that remained in tact was Moto's, the rest, headed by Riggs, Cooter and Zip were all assembled on the fly after the LT's fearful briefing. Riggs ended up with the point squad when the LT insisted that Moto take control of the entire operation and stay in the middle of the advancing Marines.

Nearly half of what remained of Echo 2/4 walked into the misty afternoon in search of an elusive opponent in what looked to Riggs like a perverse game of chicken.

Where is this going? Who will give in first? I have a bad feeling about everything. Moto had better mail that letter for me, he just better.

It was day twelve of a nasty, dirty, evil street fight … but there were no streets to be found, only a treacherous jungle trail that loomed eerily ahead and swallowed the column of some forty Marines with each step.

Huffer, then Riggs were far out in front of the squad of his not so friendly nemesis, Moto. Moto was upset about Riggs expecting anything of him other than to cover his ass but he was furious that the LT allowed Riggs to lead the point squad. It just blew his mind; first, that Riggs held up his hand and second that the LT let him do it.

Cooter was shocked too. On the one hand he was glad he didn't have to do it himself, but sad on the other hand that Riggs, a way "too" nice farm kid from somewhere back in the world, would take the first hit when the shit hit the fan. He knew time would tell if he was right or wrong and time was about to speak.

Riggs didn't have a lot of options so he trusted Huffer and followed every step he took. The pair of young Marines moved forward. Wired like a robot, Riggs mimicked every sight and sound of his trusted point man. These were frightening times but the kid from Hope still couldn't keep his mind where it belonged.

This is insane. Leave our defensive positions and come out here ... late in the afternoon ... trying to find whom ... Charlie? No way ... no way I'm doing this and on top of that walking with the point squad. I really can't believe I am here!

I know I need to do this but I sure don't want to. I want to be home with Maggie. I want her to know how I feel. Moto better mail that letter I wrote. I know he'll make it out of here. I don't know about me, that's for sure?

Reality hit Riggs right, square between the eyes when he saw Huffer freeze. He hustled forward, crouching, heart beating up through his throat, kneeling next to Huffer. Huffer's eyes were huge, like they would pop right out onto the jungle floor any second.

The patrol was a couple of grid squares north of Con Thien. It was after 1600 hours with heavy rain and heavier mist draping their lives more with each step. Riggs could feel nightfall closing in. He was scared out of his mind but bound by years of tradition not to show it. He knew he needed to get control.

"This is where we go west," Huffer said, after exhaling all the air from his lungs to stay quiet in a place where quiet was the difference between life and death.

In the bush, they couldn't afford even a "wisp" coming from their lips unless you begged for a shot in the jibs at close range.

"Huffer ... if this is it, then let's go. We need to move through there before dark. Sitting here will get us killed." Riggs was lost to understand Huffer's reluctance.

It's not like him. If we sit here we're inviting an ambush from all sides. We have to move. We have to move now!

Huffer remained kneeling, looking, listening and searching the thick darkness of the black, smelly jungle that peered back like it would eat them alive. Behind them was a column of dazed, tired Marines, all kneeling, facing to either side of the small trail. They were a group of young men about to be consumed by fear, or a wicked jungle, whichever came first.

Riggs knew they had to move it out. He didn't need Moto coming up but then he didn't need any of this shit either. He didn't want any of Moto's "I can feel them." He never believed any of them ... but he might become a believer now.

"Huffer, we gotta' go," Riggs said as reassuringly as he could, trying to convince himself and Huffer of the wisdom of his words. Riggs new they had to move and they had to move now.

Why is he hesitating? I don't know him real well but I have never seen him hesitate before. He can't hesitate now. We gotta go.

Huffer turned to Riggs with fear dripping from his face.

"If we go in there ...we're going down in that ravine," Huffer said, pointing to a dark, ominous, covered area to their west. It looked like they were about to walk into the jaws of a Venus flytrap.

"I don't like it Riggsy. I like the high ground. Something doesn't feel right about this."

They both knew there was no turning back. Huffer relented and took the lead again with Riggs and his squad falling in closely behind. It was like walking inside a leafy, dark, damp and humid tomb. The jungle swallowed the Marines one by one as they headed down into the crypt-like ravine. There was a small creek running slowly in its bottom. The walls of the ravine narrowed like a vise tightening around them. Riggs began to freak.

God. God. I know you're there. Be with me. Be with us!

Tall, slim, sharp blades of elephant grass sliced their skin with every move as it hid the Marines and everyone else lurking nearby. Moving was slow, painfully slow, but not as painful as the swarm of mosquitoes now mauling the newly arrived meat in the way of young Marines creeping into the unknown.

How insane is this? How crazy insane is this? How could Vance decide to send us in here and offer us up as bait? Cease-fire. What cease-fire? We'll see about all that if we get through here without being attacked and destroyed. God be with us. Please!

All Riggs could do was wonder if this plan, this unbelievably stupid plan, was crazy enough that it might work. Huffer led the way like a cat on the attack. Riggs wandered his way behind him. It was a nightmarish dream as they weaved their way deeper into the depths of a jungle hell in search of hope that they would get out alive. Riggs wanted something to hang on to, something to get him home to Maggie O'Reilly.

Maybe this will work. Maybe we'll get through this creepy ravine and back up to the high ground. Maybe there is a cease-fire.

Huffer slipped, falling backwards into a sitting position. Riggs thought he heard a sound, a whoosh and a thud.

What the hell was it? I heard something. I know it's not Huffer he slipped and fell backwards. He's leaning back on his pack in a sitting position. He's okay I know he is.

Riggs quietly slip up behind him, glancing at his marine green Recon watch with the luminous dial. It was almost 1800 hours and just a couple clicks shy of dark.

It's not time for another Huffer brain fart. He can't sit here and be freaked by another "turn" in the creek bed. We're dead meat if we do. I have to get him up and moving.

"Huffer, get the hell up man. We gotta' go!" Riggs whispered, nearly out of breath from over two hours of intense, nerve racking hiking in bad man's country. Huffer just sat there and didn't move.

Irritated and impatient, Riggs reached down and grabbed him by the shoulder.

"Huffer … oh holy shit!"

Riggs grabbed his point man's shoulder and Huffer's head rolled back, eyes wide-open, blood flowing a frightening stream from his mouth. He was dead. An arrow from a cross bow was sticking out of his chest between the wings of his flak jacket, left open to get air and relief from the searing jungle heat.

"Corpsman! Corpsman!" Riggs screamed like he'd never screamed before as he slid down on the ground next to Huffer.

Almighty God you can't let this happen. No!

Time stood still and life burst into full Technicolor as seconds turned into hours and hours into days as he sat in the middle of nowhere pleading for their lives.

Riggs ordered one of his two Fire Teams to the front to provide cover. The Corpsman was within ten feet of reaching Huffer when the world changed forever.

A wall of AK-47's roared down from both sides of the ravine. Daylight was dying and so were Riggs and his point squad. This was hell in a very small place all over again; only there was no one to write about it.

Sanity was drowned by the cries of the dead and dying. Riggs instinctively jumped on top of Huffer, covering his already dead body with his own. He looked up just as bullets riddled Doc Whitney as he ran to their aid. Doc landed in a motionless heap about three feet from Riggs.

BOOM!

Corporal Hightower, one of Riggs's Fire Team leaders and yet another member of his team were knocked to the ground by a grenade. What was left of Hightower landed near Huffer's feet. He took the full blast from the Chicom tossed from above. He was now raw meat in a green uniform.

I've gotta' get up. I've gotta' get some firepower up the walls of this death trap. I've gotta' get us out of here. I've gotta' get us home!

Riggs rolled over, M-14 at the ready and inched towards two Marines nearby. The two were what was left of Hightower's Fire Team. His squad was strung out behind him and returning fire, but were being overwhelmed by an orange wall of lead raining down from above.

Oh my God! We're sitting in the small end of a funnel with scalding hot water pouring in all around us. If we don't get out of this ravine we're all dead. God help us!

Cries of grief, anguish and anger rained in from all sides. The evil sounds of NVA soldiers yelling orders, taunting and directing more killing on the Marines trapped in the creek below echoed and served as a frightening warning of who was in charge.

Firing, crawling as he'd last done in boot camp, Riggs reached his radio, strapped to the back of a young Marine radioman who was rasping and rattling his last breathes of squalid air, trying to wrestle it from the hot jungle where it belonged.

My God this is it, this is Uncle Ben all over again. I am going to die in this ravine. I can't die. I won't die, I won't. I have to see Maggie. I have to!

Brrrrp! Brrrrp! Brrrrp!

Riggs unleashed his M14 towards an unseen enemy firing from the heights above. Out of ammunition, he clicked the magazine loose and quickly inserted another.

Brrrrp! Brr ... BOOM!

An ear splitting grenade exploded somewhere just above Riggs's head, knocking him to the ground. Now motionless, he tried to figure out if he was still in one piece.

God this is it. I hurt all over. I don't know if I'm injured. I have to get up and do something. My people are all dying. I'm dying. I can't!

Riggs crawled back towards Huffer with pain shooting down his right leg. He reached Huffer, and Hightower lay next to him in a heap, they were two statistics, KIA's the folks back home don't know about yet. He positioned himself behind Huffer's body and in front of Hightower's. He swung his 14 up, his right leg burning, and let loose with another blast of rifle fire into an enemy he could hear but could not see in the black of the advancing night.

Cooter was yelling, screaming ...

"Riggsy, Riggsy ... we're pulling back!"

"Riggsy ... come on ... get out."

Orders came down from the LT to pull back now. Moto was arguing over the PRC-25 so loud others could hear over the rumble of the massive ambush. The order was to regroup and then go back in for the dead. Get the wounded out now.

Pull back? What the hell?

Riggs yelled to Cooter like Grandpa did at a hollering contest. He realized he was screaming for his life, "Cooooooter! Cooooter! Don't leave us. We're coming!"

But Riggs wasn't going anywhere. The firepower from elements of the 324th B's massive ambush had pushed the remaining elements of Lieutenant Vance's Echo Company back down the ravine and separated them from their brothers in arms.

We're going to be alone. We can't be alone out here. We can't move ... we're dead.

Riggs and the other Marines were buried in the most withering fire they'd seen yet. During the pullback two other Marines, one Riggs didn't know from Zip's squad and another he knew only as Alphabet, were separated in the ravine and trying to join up with the others.

The fight raged well into the night. The NVA didn't have to see the Marines directly. The gooks knew they were there and just fired down the ravine into the night. If the Marines dared return fire they exposed their own vulnerable position by their muzzle flashes.

Riggs's mind raced. Like a raging fire, he was fried from the unrelenting firepower of the growing elements of the mainline North Vietnamese units. Lt. Vance had screwed up royally and Riggs and the others were paying for it with their lives.

Riggs was sandwiched between the bodies of Huffer and Hightower, both dead and growing cold. The remaining Marines tried to draw closer, whispering as they went ..."Riggsy, we're coming over.

"No*!"* Riggs yelled shrieking knowing that if they moved it was certain death. The NVA were closing in all around. A dark noose was tightening in the night, squeezing the air out of the lives of those trapped and left behind in the pullout. It was too late.

BOOM!

A grenade shattered the wretched night air and riddled shrapnel into the dead and dying. The blast was so close it put two Marines out of their frightened misery. Bodies flew through the night and landed amidst the carnage that was Clayton Wesley Riggs.

One of them, or was it part of them, or was it ...

My God ... something, someone just landed on me. Ugh! Oh God help me! Help me God. I can't breathe. I can't breathe with this on me. My shoulder. Something is on my shoulder.

Riggs spun to full "tilt" when the dead body landed on his back, pinning him to the ground, face first in the monsoon packed mud. Struggling with a mixture of fear, revulsion and disgust, he mustered every ounce of strength he had left and tried to get free.

Is it a Marine? Oh ... NVA ... where is Zip? Someone ... help me.

"Somebody help me! Help me!"

Riggs couldn't move. The night lit up with tracer rounds streaking across the ravine, like so many laser beams on the Fourth of July. But this wasn't the cemetery in Hope and it wasn't the glory Dad talked about at dinner. Things were going very wrong for PFC Clayton Wesley Riggs.

Moto was regrouping the bulk of the patrol about 500 yards south of the ambush. They could hear the fierce fighting.

Moto was furious.

"How the hell could you do this?" he screamed at Vance. That asshole didn't deserve this … I'm going out there and getting him!"

Vance wasn't backing down. He'd made the decision, however stupid it might have been, and he was standing by it.

"Sergeant!" He said sternly, his voice crackling over the radio. Get over it, get control and settle down."

This wasn't the time for a debate and Moto knew it. He knew if he was going to help Riggs and the rest of the survivors he was going to do it at daybreak. He also knew he'd been in Nam a long time … there weren't going to be any survivors, not by a long shot.

"I didn't like that little pig farmer but he had balls. He didn't deserve this," Moto snarled, as he walked away indignant, refusing to talk to the LT anymore.

Riggs and a few survivors were fighting a small battle that raged within earshot of the survivors. They could hear the distinct sound of the AK-47's but what they didn't hear was much return fire from their fellow Marines. The tide was turning and not for the good.

Riggs lay motionless, squeezing out a breath or two when he thought it was safe. He heard Zip and another marine frantically whispering nearby. He heard movement, gunfire and the weight of bodies falling nearby. The fight for their lives was about over.

Scared for his life, terrified that one murmur from him would draw an outpouring of more hot lead aimed into the mound of flesh Riggs now called home, he remained silent.

Why, Why, Why? Why do I have to die like this? Why do I have to die when I know I have so much to live for? Why God why?

Riggs's mind worked overtime. He could feel the blood of the dead that now fully covered him oozing onto his body. His legs felt funny, cold, cramped, pained. He wondered if he was wounded. The shooting pains in his right leg and arm must be something, he just didn't know what.

What's happening? Where am I? Is this real or will I wake up from a nightmare in Con Thien. It's all slowing down. Life is slowing. The shooting is sporadic ... like popcorn when it's almost done.

Riggs was dizzy, sweat or blood was slowly easing down and into his eyes, burning them in the process. His eyes streamed liquid that rolled down his filthy cheeks. Maybe he was crying, he deserved to cry, lying in a garbage heap of what was once full of life.

My head ... I can't lift it. I can't get up. I'm buried. Buried alive ... or am I. I know I'm buried. I can't breathe ... I ...

Silence. Everywhere there was silence. The savagery of a long and frightful night gave way to stone, cold silence.

23

December 25, 1967
Christmas Day – Somewhere in the Republic of Vietnam

Moto sat by himself with the handset from his PRC-25 tightly in his hand. Waiting. Waiting for any sign of life from PFC Riggs, Zip and 10 others missing from the debacle of Christmas Eve.

"Cooter, that little asshole didn't deserve this shit," Moto angrily growled as Cooter walked up from behind at first light. "He shouldn't a been walking point, just because he was stupid or gung ho enough to do it you still don't let him."

"No Mote, and this ain't the same ole' range we're ridin' on either. That was the big cowboys down there last night," Cooter offered to an unrelenting Moto.

The NVA had upped the ante in the game of war being played in the DMZ. They were for real and they wanted the ugly Americans to know it. While Moto waited for word to go back in and get the bodies of his friends, the NVA were picking over the spoils.

A squad of NVA worked their way methodically through the plunders of their victory, inspecting each body to ensure they were dead, killing them if they weren't and ensuring they took the valuables they found …the spoils of war.

In the ravine, the scene of the crime, the carnage stretched for over thirty yards. There were Marine bodies; parts of bodies and evidence of a battle lost that strung from end to end. There were twelve American bodies in all. In the middle of the narrow cut, was a pile of nine bodies perversely stacked in various stages of death and destruction. These Marines had fought in a tight little circle with Huffer being the first to die. He was laying somewhere near the bottom. The other three were mere evidence of loss, lying nearby.

Where am I? What am I? Am I in hell? I hurt. Oh, I hurt. Am I alive? I must be. I can't see. I can't move. Maggie? Where's Maggie?

Riggs's mind raced … wildly out of control. Anxiety smothered his soul while streams of blood dripped from his eyebrows. *What is it?* A vicious battle raged in his mind as he fought for air and anything that made sense. *What am I feeling, anything, anything but pain? I have to move. I have to get out of here ... wherever here is.*

Riggs dug deep, prying inside what was once his soul. The young Marine frantically searched for even an ounce of the strength and endurance he once used to dominate the courts of old Hope High. Right now he needed each ounce of courage that struggled to survive in every dark space of his near dead body.

As he pushed down, his hands sunk, swallowed in cold slime. His arms shook violently as he fought to rise from the dead. He was suffocating, as if death itself was a cold, dark blanket that sucked the life from his every breath. *I've gotta' get up. I've gotta' go! I can't die! I won't die here, far from Maggie, in a war I don't understand.*

He twisted his neck in a vain effort to live. Pain streaked through his body like a hot bullet. With one eye open, Riggs peered into an ugliness disguised as morning. *Light. I can see light but nothing else. Oh my God! The wretched smell of rotting bodies. Where am I? Where is Maggie? Maggie?*

Riggs was at the ass end of a bitter lesson disguised as a new day in Vietnam. *My God! My God! My God! I woke up in hell?* PFC Clayton Wesley Riggs, USMC, farm boy from Hope, Indiana, never imagined a day quite like this.

I'm going to die. I can't. I won't die ten thousand miles from the sweet smell and warm smile of Maggie O'Reilly. She loves me.

Riggs was buried inside a mass of humanity, heavy lifeless pieces that just hours ago were fellow Marines but now covered him with death and the smell of a thousand rotten eggs. As he poked his head free of the stifling mass, he was a lone rose coming to life in a parched desert. The kid from Hope looked around, soaked in misery and dripping in devastation, and began to quietly sob.

Suddenly, ignited by a strange presence, he knew he wasn't alone. Riggs's body quivered as the cold barrel of an AK-47 pressed hard against the side of his head. *This is it ... this is the end.* Closing his eyes, Riggs waited for the earth-shattering boom of the AK.

Goodbye Maggie, I love you ... Forever.

24

December 25, 1967
Christmas Morning – Chicago, Illinois
The O'Reilly Home

The home of Dexter and Bridget O'Reilly was always filled with laughter and early morning music on Christmas Day. The family believed in opulent extravaganzas in all they did and Christmas was one of the biggest and best. Of course, that's when their daughters Maggie and Beverly were home.

Now that the girls were growing up and away at college, Christmas morning was not quite as intense as it once was. Bridget was elated to have the girls come home for the Christmas holiday. The house wouldn't come alive as early as it used to but it would be wonderful to have the family together again.

It was 7 am when Dexter came down the steps to join Bridget in putting presents under the massive 14-foot blue spruce she had ordered for the girls' Christmas reunion.

Maggie and Beverly were both sleeping upstairs in their old rooms when Dexter stepped on the bottom step.

"Ohhhh! Ohhhhh! Nooooo! Nooooo!" Maggie bolted upright, screaming her self-awake from a deep sleep.

"Dexter what is it?" Bridget asked frightened by the intrusion into the Bing Crosby music she had playing on the stereo.

"It's Maggie!" he said, running up the steps and turning down the hall to her room.

Maggie was sitting in the middle of her big Queen bed, the one with the pink and blue comforter hanging over the sides, the one she loved. Her arms were wrapped tight around her body as if she was hugging herself, her head hung low and she rocked back and forth terrified.

"Honey, what on earth is wrong?" Dad asked as he sat on the edge of the bed while Mom and Beverly came running in.

Maggie sat, with her arms frozen around her body, shaking like she had a bad case of malaria. Her eyes were red, her beautiful, rosy cheeks were now dull, grey and scared by something no one else could see and something she was afraid to say.

"Maggie dear what is it … tell us," Mom said, sitting on the opposite side of the bed from Dexter.

"Something awful has happened. Something awful!" Maggie sobbed, as she placed her head in her hands.

"What dear what?" Bridget said warmly, rubbing Maggie's back and leaning forward in a vain attempt to look in to her eyes.

I hope this doesn't have anything to do with that farm boy over there. I didn't want her going down to Indiana to school. I was afraid of this. She deserved to be at Berkeley not some second-rate school in Indiana.

Bridget came from blue blood and she wanted to make sure she passed it on untainted from the world around her she detested. She couldn't believe her daughter went away and came back thinking crazy like this.

"Mom something has happened to Clay, I know it. Something terrible has happened to him!" Maggie was distraught and with those words, and so was her Dad. He quickly got up and left the room, leaving the "girls" to deal with, in his mind, their own creation.

"My dear, you just had a nightmare," Bridget offered with an air of authority to a daughter struggling to find herself in a time where everyone was lost.

The O'Reilly family was close but not open. They were the upper crust of Chicago society and expected to stay that way. They would marry their own kind, no crossing socio-economic boundaries.

Maggie had to use every ounce of influence she had to be allowed to attend Indiana University. She never felt comfortable or a part of the circles her family ran in. She wanted to be normal and get away from all the things that made her uncomfortable and abnormal.

"Mother, Beverly, I'm telling you something happened and I have to know," Maggie moaned, pulling the rumpled covers in front of her wet and sobbing face. "Mother, listen to me!"

"I am listening honey but this is Christmas Day. Your Dad made arrangements to be here with us and we cannot ruin it for him. You know how he feels about family and Christmas."

Yes Mother, I know how he feels about Christmas. He can "make" one day for us each year. One day we can count on that he won't leave us and have you make excuses why he's "doing it for us." One day where we all have to smile and do what he wants us to do. Ugh Mom.

"Now Maggie ... get yourself together and come downstairs before we upset your Father more than you have already done."

Bridget loved her daughters, she loved them very much but even love had its limits. Loyalty was important in her life and she stood up, straightened her designer apron and walked out and down the spiral staircase to her waiting husband.

Maggie began to quietly sob. Her face was buried in her now wet hands, hands shaking from the mental lightning that jarred her from her deep and much needed sleep. She rolled onto her side as Beverly climbed on the bed and cuddled up next to her.

They had been close since ... forever. There were differences all right, but in the end, there was a love that was safe; safe to talk about and ponder the divides that life would bring. A love that was safe enough to conquer the unconquerable. Beverly and Maggie were soul mates on a journey where only sisters could go and stay close in the end.

"Girls, girls ... time to come down for your Christmas breakfast." Mom was consistent even at the most inappropriate times. She was consistent on pleasing Dad at all costs and in her perfect delivery of guilt. Maggie looked at Beverly and they broke into a quiet chuckle knowing how things were at their house. Beverly's face said more than her words could ever say.

Come on Sis, let's do what we must and we'll talk all night when we're done.

25

December 27, 1967
Con Thien, Vietnam

The Marines of 2nd Battalion 4th Marines had not seen a day quite like this one. There were days, then there were ugly days and then, well, there were days that made you were wish you were blind.

The last of the three Medevac choppers lifted off, heading into the evening mist to the makeshift morgue at Dong Ha. Their fallen comrades would be cleaned and dressed for the ten-thousand mile ride home to their soon to be miserable loved ones.

"Cooter, that damned Vance let this happen. Asshole!"

"Moto … you're a good friend and a great Marine. Let it go man, just let it go." Cooter was packing up, knowing he had only a week left in country. He was done in the bush. Barring his chopper dropping out of the sky he was returning stateside … back to "the world."

"Let it go, damn it. I didn't like him, hell I didn't like any of 'em, but Riggs was a nice kid. If somebody was going to get the shit like that let it be me." Moto was showing the first signs of being human.

"Mote, you never ask a barber if you need a haircut and you don't ask me if you should drop it. Give it up my man."

"Cooter, don't let this go to your head, you're still an asshole but I'm gonna' miss your Texas bullshit." It was the first smile, just a slight grin but the first anyone had seen on Moto's face.

"Well, flattery will get ya' nowhere with me Mote … the biggest liar you'll ever have to face is lookin' at ya' in the mirror every morning when yur' a shavin'." Cooter was going to miss the guy who'd saved his life more than a couple times.

"What the hell does that mean?" Moto growled, quickly becoming the guy they all loved to hate.

He wasn't a guy with a lot of friends. He was a guy who kept things moving and a guy you wanted standing next to you when the shooting started. Moto was housed in a five foot seven inch two hundred and ten pound frame that didn't back down from anyone … good guy or bad he was in your face.

The Marine Corps was a wonderful place if you came from Moto's hometown. He hailed from the heart of Appalachia, far from the eyes of decency. It was in the Pennsylvania hill country. His town was a place cruel to many but downright tough for the kids growing up amidst the poverty of Appalachia shadowed by the Allegheny Mountains of the northeast.

Moto didn't have a clue about love and kindness. They were as scarce as food on his table. He grew up in Renovo, Pennsylvania, a mountain town with no jobs, fewer morals and a dim view of what the future held. He was carrying on the tradition because that's all he knew how to do.

He joined the Marine Corps after barely graduating from high school. The prospects for life in Renovo looked bleak and the local judges encouraged Michael Murray Mason to find a way out of town. The Marines seemed like a way out of what he saw as local misery.

He got "way" out of town and landed in Parris Island just two weeks after the high school graduation he had skipped in favor of getting drunk with a couple of undesirable girls in the neighborhood. When he came home from his bus trip to Philadelphia for his physical, Moto would never forget his Dad's response when he grunted "good riddance." His Dad provided the fuel for much of the anger that was Mike Mason.

His Mom wasn't much better when she said, "I don't know why you have to run away, 'you'll be no good for nothin' whatever you do so you might just as well do it here. You've always been trouble fur' us."

With a Dad who spent most of his time at one of the three bars in town and a Mom who was always leaving with a new man, nobody expected much of Murray, as he was reluctantly known around town.

Rumors ran the Renovo streets more than Murray and his cohorts. Rumor had it that the dilapidated house on 1st Street was the scene of abuse and maybe worse. No one knew for sure and that was something you didn't ask in Pennsylvania hill towns, it was just something you lived with.

When the Corps said okay to him with his "skin of the teeth" graduation, he was gone. Behind him were the bad days of Renovo, a Mom and Dad who were hardly worthy of the name and three sisters who … well Moto didn't want to think about them. He just wanted to leave and start over.

His life in the Corps moved fast. Boot camp, Infantry training at Camp Geiger and a brief stint in the 2nd Mar Div in LeJeune and he had his hand up volunteering for Nam. He came into Da Nang and was assigned as a replacement with 2/4. That is where he and Cooter hitched up and became tight. Cooter was the first, and only person Moto could really call a friend.

He wasn't sure he knew what that was … a friend. Deep down, Moto longed for the missing link in his life, a feeling that he really was worth something more than the legacy he carried like a heavy pack in the monsoon rain. He wanted to belong and be accepted.

The Marines, Vietnam and his growing relationship with Cooter gave meaning to Murray he could never have imagined before. The anger he buried from childhood could erupt during a firefight and that meant people loved having him around.

"Man … you look like one'a them sumo rassler guys from Japan … hell, I'm gonna' call you Moto." That was it, the day Cooter named Corporal Mason … Moto.

The name stuck and Moto grew into the role of his name. He backed down from no one. He stood tall in firefights when the most seasoned combat vet's covered their heads. Many thought Moto had a death wish but Cooter sensed he wanted to be somebody.

After the disastrous battle that cost so much in human life, Moto and Cooter spent a quiet day enjoying a cease-fire that was holding a tenuous reign over the northern I Corp in the DMZ. It had been two days since the guns and bombs stopped. Two days of peace and quiet Riggs would have loved. Time to reflect on the past and generate hope for a better future … if you lived to have a better future that is.

"Cooter we've been side by side now for nearly a year, right?" Moto queried.

"Right on man," Cooter replied with an air of a short timer. He would soon be heading back to the world and out of the hell of Nam.

"Have you seen anything like the mess we cleaned up out there today?"

Cooter sat for a long time, staring out into the rolling hills to the north of the base camp. He took a long drag on his C-rat Camel cigarette, the kind he was sure would put hair on his hairless chest.

He turned to Moto, "I don't want to think about it Mote. I have two heads on here," he said pointing to his head adorned with matted, filthy hair, pasted on from weeks without a touch of soap.

"I'm placing what I lived the last year in one of them and locking it up. When I get home to the world I'll use the other one. It's been a year for me, that's plenty long enough for this country boy."

"Ah don't give me that shit,' Moto exclaimed, 'you're normal and you think about it. It's a mess. When we couldn't get back in to get the bodies out because of those little gook bastards, Vance went and called in Arty. Blew everything to bits. That's what the mess was all about. You saw it dude so don't give me shit about locking it up."

Moto was frustrated; his anger was smoldering like a coal fire back in his Pennsylvania hills; a deep fire that goes on for years. It was an anger that could be as fatal as a direct hit from a 140 rocket. He wasn't one to hold to anything for too long.

"Cooter, all we got was pieces of some of those guys. Riggs is one of'em. Hell, I got one of his dog tags but we don't know what's his or Zip's or any of the others ... I mean what do they do back there with all those parts?" Moto asked, pleading in a vain attempt at reason.

"Drop it good buddy. The guys in graves registration take it from here, not us," Cooter replied with an air of indifference, locking his vault, as he looked his good friend straight in the eye. "Leave it here buddy, leave it here."

Moto stood up, staring down at the only friend he had in the world, "I can leave it here my friend but the little asshole gave me this letter to mail to that broad back home. What the hell am I supposed to do with it?" Moto said holding a tattered 3rd Mar Div standard issue envelope in his hand.

Cooter looked at him with a sly grin and a wry smile twisting to one side. "Well, Mr. Moto, back home in Texas we'd put a stamp on one'a those and drop it in the mail. But here in Nam that shit is free so … now this isn't a tough one good buddy … just write *Free* in the upper right corner and mail it."

Cooter might have been his only friend but Moto's anger didn't discriminate between friend and foe.

"Asshole, we don't need a stamp or to write *Free* here but we sure as hell do need a damned good address," Moto retorted with a gush of anger, pushing the envelope into Cooter's face for him to see.

He read …

Maggie O'Reilly
121 Fourth Avenue
Apartment 15A

"Like ya' think I should just send it and let the Post Office figure out where the broad lived?" Moto shot back, getting hotter by the minute.

"Mote, my main man, I do believe you are showin' the first signs of givin' a shit."

"Kiss off!" Moto spewed, storming away to see Lieutenant Vance who had just called him on the PRC-25 lying next to Cooter.

"Hey man, don't go away mad … just go away," Cooter called after him, laughing as he did.

The Marines of Echo 2/4 were still in shock, suffering the reality of a brutal encounter with the NVA. Con Thien was always a dismal place, but none worse than today.

The numbness lingered for days after gathering up their comrades, some whole, some in pieces and some worse. Enemy and friendly fire had taken a terrible toll on the Marines in the pile of dead in Riggs's point squad.

The cease-fire held as planned and in a week Cooter rotated home to Clyde, Texas. He grew to like Moto more than most and would have loved to see him again, back in the world, but doubted he ever would.

He gave him his info, name, address and phone number just in case.

"Moto, you can't forget a place like Clyde and you can't forget a bar like The Long Branch. Been in the family for three generations … they can always find me. You take care my friend and get that 'piss off' out of your life, you'll do just fine".

It was the end of a strange era.

26

January 1, 1968
Hope, Indiana
The Riggs Home place

"Oh Homer I just hope this is a good year for us. Christmas was really hard on me."

Lucy was working feverishly to get the family dinner ready.

"Momma, that boy is a Riggs. He is strong. He will survive that mess of a war they call Vietnam."

Homer was as steadfast as ever but growing disillusioned with the media, the protests and one Democrat named Lyndon Johnson.

New Year's Day was a strong tradition for starting the year on the Riggs' farm. It was only one of two days that it was acceptable to "not work." If you were farmers and a Riggs … you worked. That was a practice ingrained for generations in the Indiana farm country.

"I hope you're right; I just don't know what I feel anymore. I just worry about that boy. He isn't like the rest of you."

Lucy was close to her only son. She missed him more than she ever imagined.

"What's that supposed to mean?" Dad responded to the nerve the love of his life struck with the "*he isn't like you*" comment.

Homer knew better than to pursue Lucy with questions, especially on a day as special as New Years. Both sides of the family always came for Christmas Eve and New Year's Day and today would be no different.

Lucy hadn't been herself since Clayton joined the Corps. Things had only gotten worse when he shipped out right away for Vietnam. Homer was proud of his boy and didn't mind talking about it down at the barbershop or anywhere else that anyone would listen. But when Lucy was with him he knew better than to say a word.

"Don't ask me what I mean, get me those potatoes and start peeling!" Lucy was in no mood for a debate. The family would be arriving any minute and she would be ready like she was on every New Years since she was married.

"Yes, dear, you're right," Homer dutifully replied as he picked up a paring knife and began his annual chore of peeling thirty pounds of spuds Lucy and he had stored from the family garden.

Peeling away, Homer watched out the side window at a site he'd grown downright comfortable seeing. Clayton's dog, Bob, walked across the yard and rolled upside down in the snow, wiggling on his back, the only one happy when it was cold and snowy.

The big yellow lab was full of energy and followed Clayton everywhere like a shadow on a late summer day; that is until his friend went off to war. Now the poor dog just lay on the porch waiting for Clay to come home and toss the old softball the dog still slept with.

Homer couldn't help but think that the dog hadn't barked since they took Clayton to the airport. That's what made it so odd when he started barking just like he did when Clay would come home. The dog suddenly ran off the porch, scratching as he ran and disappeared.

"That's strange, it must be sis coming," Lucy said to Homer, who was busy with the mountain of slicing.

"Ouch!" Homer shouted, as he cut a slice too close and nicked one of his fingers.

"Oh you do that every year. You're a tough old Marine, get out there and greet our guests." Lucy wasn't one for sympathy when it came to Homer. She always felt he was hard on Clay so she wasn't going to make it easy on him.

Homer sucked on his bleeding finger as he crossed the kitchen and opened the door. It was a blustery January day, gray skies, blowing winds and a light covering of snow that had fallen over night.

He stood staring outside, door ajar, with a cold breeze sweeping into the kitchen and giving Lucy a chill. She stood with her back to him, working on the turkey she had just strained to get from the oven to the counter.

"For goodness sake close that door, I'm about to freeze over here," Lucy exclaimed.

But Homer wasn't feeling any cold or pain and he wasn't able to smell the incredible aroma of Momma's dinner cooking right behind him. He wasn't seeing or hearing anything but the car that could only be bearing bad news.

He stood, frozen, not from the cold, but from what he knew was about to ruin his life. He stood at attention, staring out at their long driveway as Bob, Clay's yellow lab, danced around the green car, a Marine Corps green car with small yellow letters on the front side doors that read simply … *Property of USMC.*

He stood oblivious to Lucy's warning to "*shut the gosh darn door.*" He was entranced as two Marines, dressed in full blues, climbed out of the car on either side. They looked all the part of a recruiting poster. But Homer knew all too well this wasn't a social visit, it was as official a visit as there is. He was glad that Beth had spent the night with her friends down the road.

They were tall, fit and stern-looking young men who stepped out into the white snow of a New Year's Day on the Riggs's farm. Each in turn reached, as if rehearsed, to put their white dress covers firmly on their heads. The mid-morning wind blew hard as Bob danced at their glistening polished shoes.

Homer Riggs stood in a cold doorway, ten thousand miles and a lifetime away from the reality of war he once knew. He was oblivious to Lucy's curt calls for a closed door and he missed her slipping in front of him to close it.

Daddy Riggs ricocheted between his life in the island war so long ago and his son's fate in another, newer war … the war called Vietnam. He was frozen solid not from the cold of an Indiana winter but from the news he knew these Marine Officers were about to deliver.

"Oh no … no … nooooo," Momma Riggs was sure it was someone else saying those words. The numbness of the site of Marines in her yard sucked the life out of a worried mother, frightened by the suddenness of the invasion into her quiet farm life and frozen by the possibilities their presence represented.

Homer hesitated, gasping at the sight of his wife collapsing next to him.

"Lucy!" Homer squeaked, stunned by the sudden collapse of his world. He reached to catch his wife before she hit the floor and added to the damage about to be revealed by the unwelcome visitors running in the snow to help.

One of the bearers of the bad news, Captain Roberts, reached down and scooped up Mrs. Riggs in one sweeping motion. He picked her up, all one hundred pounds and five feet of her and bounded over to the living room couch.

"Mr. Riggs let us help you, let's get you over here to sit down too." Major Scott was right off the recruiting poster that took Clayton to his fate. He took charge of the situation unfolding in the farmhouse, home of PFC Clayton Wesley Riggs. When he spoke you listened, whether you wanted to or not ... and Homer Riggs didn't want to hear what was coming.

Captain Roberts went to the kitchen and brought back a glass of water for Lucy. Major Scott was about to speak when the kitchen door opened again, and again the cold of winter rushed in like a bad dream.

"What's going on? Did something happen to Clayton?" Homer's not so subtle sister Libby and her entourage had arrived. She was a lady who wouldn't use a hammer if a sledgehammer would do.

Major Scott was on his feet erecting a personal barrier between the grieving parents and their newly arrived family. The Riggs's house was filling up fast.

"Folks, we have a situation here. Who are you?" Marine Majors were used to getting their own way and Homer realized this guy was a match for Libby, who was caught off guard by his advance. She stood, mouth open, aghast at the chaos she had entered.

Major Scott quickly ushered the growing guest list into the parlor in the back of the 80-year-old house the Riggs called home. Homer was shocked at the Major's efficiency and aloofness in the face of what was obviously horrible news.

Captain Roberts stood behind the couch Lucy was now sitting on, head in her hands and quietly sobbing.

"Sir, please tell us what you came to tell us. It's our son isn't it?" Homer asked dejectedly, as he slid next to his wife on the aging couch she had wanted to replace for years. Before either of the gentlemen could speak, Homer placed his arm around his love and reached over and took her hand in his with the other.

Major Scott sat across from the two targets of his message. He reached into his pocket and pulled out a neatly folded yellow piece of paper.

Lucy was lost in anticipation, horror bouncing about her head in fear of the news she was about to hear.

He's dead. My beloved son is dead. I will never see him again. He left and is gone. I cannot live. I cannot get over this. I can't.

Homer's arm quivered around her hunched, skinny shoulders, their hands clenched, sweat dripping down his wrist, the pair of special friends awaited the words that would impact the rest of their lives.

"Mr. and Mrs. Riggs, I am here concerning your son … PFC Clayton Wesley Riggs. I have here a telegram from the Commandant of the Marine Corps, General Wallace Green."

Opening the four-fold paper, Homer recognized the Western Union memo. It looked exactly like the one he'd seen so often in his Grandpa's things. A rush of feelings came back, he could see Grandpa and Grandma and the pain they felt when talking about Uncle Ben.

"Let me read …"

December 31, 1967

From: Commandant, Headquarters,
United States Marine Corps

To: Mr. & Mrs. Homer Riggs
We regret to inform you that your son PFC Clayton Riggs, Service number 2064139 is missing and presumed dead as a result of enemy action in I Corp, Quang Tri Province of the Republic of Vietnam on December 25, 1967.

PFC Riggs was part of a forward patrol that was overrun by enemy soldiers. They were recovered in a later action.

More information will be provided as it becomes available. Details of the return of his effects will be provided at a later date.

Regretfully,

Wallace M. Green

Commandant,
United States Marine Corps

Homer Riggs sat stunned, in silent disbelief of what had just been read to him. He remembered all too well the confusion and fog of war. He just never believed it would happen to his son and intrude on his home on the first day of a New Year.

So many questions stood unasked and unanswered. When would his body come home?

We don't know.

When would they know more?

We don't know.

When will you get the hell out of here? Homer wanted to say, but respect for his fellow Marines and the Riggs tradition kept his growing anger in check, simmering like a stew long forgotten.

The two Marine Officers, after delivering their verbal bomb, walked out vowing to *keep everyone updated.* Libby and Lucy's sister Oleta filled the void of leadership and took charge of the house.

"I'm calling Doc Jones," Libby snorted over her shoulder as she marched to the phone, expecting protests from all corners.

No one would protest. Homer and Lucy lay sideways on the couch miles away from the goings on in their own home. They were lost in each other's arms, seeking comfort, order and sanity in a home void of feelings of all but the misery of the loss of a dear loved one.

The day slipped away like no other in Riggs tradition. There were no kids laughing or screaming and fun was nowhere to be found. There were no ladies doing what ladies do on days when their husbands make them football widows. And there was no hope anywhere to be found in Hope, Indiana.

Doc Jones came and consoled Lucy and kept his stiff upper lip with Homer. The shot that Doc gave Lucy allowed her to slip into a place where pain couldn't go, if all but for a brief time. Homer was left to deal with the pain that dominated his every thought.

Libby and Oleta decided to spend the night to be close to Homer, Lucy and Beth. The men took the kids home, some in the hope they could catch the Rose Bowl between Southern Cal and Indiana. The Hoosiers, the family's favorite team, were finally in the big game but life might interfere even with such an event.

Homer crawled in bed beside his sweetheart, took his hanky from the bed stand and dabbed her tear stained face. The last time he could remember doing that was … well … when Clayton was born nineteen years ago.

He placed his arm around her and listened to her gentle breathing as she fell off to sleep. Lucy was still beautiful and she didn't deserve this … no one did. It was a day when time stopped and so did the soul of the Riggs family.

Homer and Lucy were sound asleep as the final score of the Rose Bowl game was announced on the old Philips radio in the adjoining room… Southern Cal 14, Indiana 3.

27

January 3, 1968
Chicago, Illinois

"Hello, O'Reilly residence," Maggie was ingrained in the formality of her father's life.

"Hello?" Maggie asked again to a seemingly empty line.

She hung up the phone and started across her spacious room, striving to put her newly bought clothes away. The day spent shopping with Mother and her sister Beverly had reaped big rewards.

I can't believe it ... it's ringing again.

Dropping a cache of clothes with the tags still on from Marshall Fields, she stalked over to the phone.

"Hello, O'Reilly residence, Maggie speaking," she said with some authority and a dose of irritation.

"M, Mm ... Maggie?" a shaky, weak and familiar voice asked from the other end.

A chill went up her spine and wiped the good time she was having out of her evening like a flash of light in the night.

"Lucy? Is that you Lucy?"

Maggie hadn't heard from her for some time. She knew that Homer wasn't too fond of Maggie's political views so she didn't want to put her in a bad position.

"Yes, honey it's me. Can you talk?"

Lucy didn't bother Maggie because she knew how her parents felt about Marines and the military. She was afraid to call her home in Chicago even after Maggie told her it was okay. She hung up on the first call, afraid that it might be her mother who had answered.

"Lucy, of course I can talk to you anytime. I told you that. What's wrong, you sound awful." The words sprang fresh from her lips and Maggie was suddenly transported back to her frightening dream on Christmas morning.

Oh Mary, Mother and Joseph it just can't be. It can't be dear Lord, tell me it can't be.

Maggie's legs gave way and she sat straight down on the floor, dropping, back against the wall. Maggie sat dejectedly, sitting in her room, head in her hands, waiting on words she didn't want to hear, words from the other half of her soul that just couldn't be true.

"Oh my dear Maggie, it's just been terrible, terrible," Lucy forced out the words as she was sobbing uncontrollably.

"Maggie … they came."

"Who came Mrs. Riggs?" Maggie knew the answer but the tricks her mind was playing wouldn't let her face the truth about to invade her perfect life.

"The Marines honey … I had to call you. Homer … well, I had to come down to the library. I love him so … I love you honey, I know how Clay felt about you dear … oh my, I don't know how to say this," Lucy was struggling to find words to describe the indescribable and give hope where none was allowed.

"Noooo … Mrs. Riggs … nooo, please tell me no," Maggie begged, fighting the ghosts of a war no one wanted, least of all Margaret Erin O'Reilly. Her dreams were racing away, flaming up like a campfire caught in a wicked wind.

Time stood still as Maggie lay, collapsed on the floor crying for hours, tormented by the words of a grieving mother. The house was hers all day, as the rest of the family was off visiting relatives. She had stayed home to prepare for a going away party they were hosting for her cousin Cortney.

Maggie didn't get ready for her dinner party; in fact she didn't get up from the floor where she rolled over into a fetal position when Lucy uttered those dreaded words.

He's dead Maggie. Clayton is dead.

He's dead Maggie. Clayton is dead.

He's dead Maggie. Clayton is dead.

Lucy's words echoed a staccato of vibration, etching the brutal reality deep inside of Maggie's head. Clayton Wesley Riggs, the love of her life, the man she planned to spend eternity with was dead. He wasn't coming home.

The floor where she lay was sopping wet from the agony of defeat as she cried herself to sleep. Love didn't triumph over all and Clayton Riggs was dead. Where does that leave truth?

The doorbell rang its melodic tune and frightened her from the agony of death. The death of the love of her life destroyed the fiber of her being.

It can't be ... he just can't be gone. He just can't be gone from me. No way. I know Clay and he is alive. He has to be alive.

"Hello, anyone home?"

It was Aunt Gloria, Cortney's Mom coming by to check on preparations for the party.

Maggie lay in a heap on the other side of the world, one she'd never visited before and one from which she might never return. She didn't want to see Aunt Gloria or Cortney or anyone but Clayton Wesley Riggs. She curled up tighter than ever, putting her arms over he tear stained face trying desperately to keep life out.

Oh what did she say? She said the Marines came and brought a telegram. She said they didn't know the details. She said that he was "missing and presumed dead" ... did that mean he was dead? It couldn't mean he was dead.

Oh, no he can't be dead. He's missing ... he's missing and he can't be dead. He's just missing and they'll find him. She said Homer was in Indianapolis at the Recruiting Office looking for information.

Oh Homer ... Poor Homer, he didn't want her to call me, Maggie the Evil Protester. That poor thing lost a son and had to sneak to the Hope Library to use a phone to call me. I love that woman, I really love her and I know between her faith and mine we will bring Clayton home.

I love that family ... I love people who are real. I love real people who don't have anything to prove and who just love you. I love Clayton Riggs and Clayton you just can't be gone. You are too real to be gone ... maybe that is the truth we sought ... maybe truth is seeing things as they really are and finding out that love does conquer all.

Maybe ...

"Maggie! My God what happened? Call Emergency!

Aunt Gloria found her way to the strange noises coming from Maggie's room. Noises drifting from a lost soul crumpled on the floor of life.

28

January 5, 1968
Chicago, Illinois

"Beverly … tell me the truth right now. We have been playing this nonsense long enough. We have things to do. Tell me what's going on?"

Bridget O'Reilly was used to getting her way. Dexter was a tycoon but he was no match for Bridget when she zoomed in. If Dexter couldn't hold up, big sister Beverly didn't stand a chance. She was amazed she'd held out for nearly two days.

"Mom please don't insist that I tell you. Please! I promised Maggie I wouldn't … she can tell you," Beverly nearly begged her mother like when she wanted another Barbie when she was small.

"Beverly … that's it, you tell me now!" Bridget knew it had something to do with the farm boy she'd met at that school in Bloomington.

If she had only gone to Berkeley like Dexter and I did and wanted her to do. Those were our kind of people at Berkeley. Dexter was right, he said if we let her go down there with all the normal people she'd come home with a boy not worthy to carry her bag. And that's just what that farm boy is … raising pigs for God's sake.

"Maggie you get up and get downstairs, we have a meeting to go to and you're going!" Bridget ordered with all the authority she could muster which would overpower even the strongest adversary.

"Mommmm," Maggie moaned disgustedly.

"Young lady you don't talk to me that way. It is time to get up and on your feet … now! You just need to put that boy behind you." Bridget didn't mention what Beverly had told her. She didn't mention that she knew Mrs. Riggs had called with the news of the farm boy's demise.

By the time Maggie came downstairs they were late for the organizing meeting about to take place downtown. Dexter worked long and hard for the opportunity to lead an entire citywide protest.

He had dreamed of "his" protest for years and this was it. This was his meeting.

"Maggie get the lead out, quit moping and get in the car. Your Dad is going to be furious." Bridget was heading out the door calling over her shoulder in the direction of her youngest daughter as she walked.

Bridget didn't want to ruin her husband's day in the spotlight. She didn't want to appear to her social group like some "riff raff" who had a daughter dating some crazed baby killer from Vietnam. She also didn't want to get the Chicago protest planned for the Tet Offensive off to a bad start.

"Can you believe your sister? I have never seen her go out of the house looking like that." Bridget was incredulous as Maggie haltingly walked to the family Mercedes.

Maggie opened the front door and slid in, looking the other way from her Mother. She slammed the door. Beverly reached up and rubbed her shoulder. They were inseparable.

I don't want to be here. I don't want to listen to her. I can't believe she hasn't once told me she is sorry or put her arm around me. If it wasn't for Beverly I would leave here and never come back.

"Maggie. Maggie. Maggie!" Mom was becoming uncharacteristically out of control.

Maggie, turned away from her mother, looked over her left shoulder and exclaimed, "Mother, you haven't as much as said one thing about why I am completely out of it. Not one thing!"

Bridget sat blue blood upright, stern faced and raced the engine of her luxury car in the driveway of a neighborhood not used to racing engines.

"So Mother, who isn't talking now? The man I love and want to marry is missing and presumed dead somewhere ten thousand miles from here in a dirty, filthy stinking jungle and all you can worry about is what people will think!" Maggie burst into tears as Beverly once again leaned over the seat to touch and put her arms around her little sister.

"Mother, for goodness sake can't you 'say' something?" Maggie cried.

Beverly pleaded and begged that sanity would return to their otherwise well planned and stable life.

Bridget was regaining control and putting starch back in her stiff upper lip. "You want me to say something? I will tell you both something. You are not marrying any commoner like a farmer. You are not!"

"Mother … you are incredible! Always worried about how you'll look. You never cease to amaze me." Maggie had never responded to her Mom like that before.

Bridget's mouth flew open as she gasped in disbelief. Her head flew back and she covered her mouth muffling a whimper of the hurt she felt that her daughter was betraying her and the family.

"You only worry about what you want Mother; it's never about what we might want." Maggie let the anger boiling inside flow out like hot lava spewing down a distant mountainside smothering life in its path.

"Don't you ever call him a farmer again, don't you ever refer to him as a baby killer or crazy or … and you understand something. He might be dead but I will never give up on him. Never! I will never give up my love for him."

Maggie wasn't crying now; she was getting stronger as the anger and bitterness overflowed with venom that was poisoning the family outing Dexter and Bridget lived their whole lives for.

"Margaret Erin … don't say another word. We are now late and your Dad will be totally embarrassed with us walking in like this on his special day. You are a very ungrateful, uncaring daughter. You should be ashamed."

The kids were no strangers to the firmness and tactlessness of their Mom. She loved them and they knew it. But when it came to her "appearance" in public … they knew they came in second place. It was always "Do as Mother says and look as Mother wants you to look or don't say anything and don't look at all."

Maggie turned and glared through eyes that looked like they'd been darkened by a bad storm, the same eyes that Clayton Wesley Riggs loved to look into and dream about. Right now he'd be surprised to see the love of his life in a heated exchange with her Mother.

Bridget put the big Mercedes into reverse and turned to back out of the four-car garage. Outside she swung the big rig into drive and started forward around the long, shrub lined circular drive that led out onto Michigan Avenue.

"Stop the car!" Maggie screamed at her Mom.

Shocked by the aggression streaming from her youngest daughter, she slammed on the brakes realizing she was halfway into the street.

"Thank you!" Maggie screamed, opening the door and running from the car.

"Where on earth are you going? What are you doing?" Mom called out, standing in the street, door open, next to her idling car.

Beverly was sitting in the backseat; head in her hands, listening to her world disintegrate before her very eyes.

Maggie was halfway up the cobblestone walk that wound around the finely pruned rose garden when she stopped and turned, facing her Mother in the street.

"Mom, I am not going to a protest rally when men are dying so that we can have the right to protest. I am not. I am not listening to you worry about how 'we might look' going in late. I don't give a damn. I am not going with you now and I may never go with you again!"

Bridget stood in the street, speechless for the first time in her life. She was torn between two worlds, that of motherhood and that of "The Cause." The O'Reilly home was feeling the impact of Vietnam. It was a protest…it was reality coming home from ten thousand miles away.

As Bridget stood in the street next to the car, part of her saw a young Bridget. She saw herself and what she often wanted to do but didn't. She saw the spirit in Maggie she once had until she'd sold out to the world of reality and money beyond belief. She was caught up in the world of her Father and the one Dexter showered her in every day of their lives.

Standing, staring back in time, a hint of a tear forming in the corner of each well painted eye … Bridget couldn't believe what she was hearing.

"Mom … I won't be here when you get back. I need to go back to school early and get away from here. Beverly … I'll call you. I love you." Maggie was standing on the ornate front porch of the house she never felt comfortable in. She disappeared into the double doors with a behind the back wave and nothing more. She was entering a world she wished she wasn't part of, a world that didn't include her love … Clayton Wesley Riggs.

Bridget's dreams disappeared with Maggie's slam of the front door to her dream home. She slid back into her beautiful car, regained her composure and sat back behind the wheel, pulled the shift lever into drive and took off hastily for downtown.

Beverly, sat stunned, staring back at the door her sister entered until it quickly disappeared from site as Mother was off speeding to the meeting, not wanting to disappoint Father.

29

January 30, 1968
Bloomington, Indiana

Maggie O'Reilly woke up for the third week in a row harboring a secret. Never one to lie, she was struggling now with what truth might be. She thought she had it but then everyone around her seemed to be doing things they didn't believe anymore.

I haven't told Mom and Dad I'm not going back to school. I haven't told them. I must discover for myself the meaning of truth no matter where it takes me.

What is happening to me? What is happening to us? Mrs. Riggs left her home to call me without telling her husband. I am leaving IU to discover for myself the meaning of truth without telling my parents. Neither of us have ever done anything like this before. I had it all and don't know where it's all going!

Why am I so desperately in need of discovering what truth really is? Yet, it seems to me that truth is seeing things as they really are. And this is how things really are right now ... robbing life of love is a lie. It can't happen and therefore it cannot be true. I know that love is truth but it sure doesn't feel like it lately.

Bags packed, car loaded, Maggie descended the stairs of 121 4th Avenue, Apartment 15A for the last time. She decided school and mourning didn't mix. She decided she needed a change of direction and a change of scenery.

Turning the key of her loaded Volvo, the engine hummed to life. All that she owned was packed inside the present her Father and Mother gave her for being the Valedictorian of Preston Prep School. It was now all she felt like she had left. A Volvo loaded with her entire life.

As she drove away from the only home she loved, her thoughts were of the endless hours talking with a young man who quietly stole her heart and who maybe, just maybe, had read her twelve letters of Christmas and discovered her love for him.

She pulled the Volvo out of her drive onto the street and headed north towards Indianapolis. Suddenly she felt a breeze … her windows weren't down. What was it? She felt it again … a warm feeling, a feeling she'd felt before. She wasn't sure what was happening but she knew it was something special.

She reversed her direction and a short drive later Maggie O'Reilly was sitting in her Volvo in front of The Gables on Indiana Avenue staring at the walkway leading to the Well House, the place where it all began. She knew what she felt and she needed to be here, right now.

Without knowing why or even what she was doing, Maggie was digging through her things, looking for a piece of paper. Grabbing an old legal pad with notes from a class long ago, she made her way up the old sidewalk to the Well House and sat down near where she first met Clayton Wesley Riggs.

She owed him one more letter…

January 30, 1968
Bloomington, Indiana
"Tears for my love"

My beloved Clayton,

As I sit here at the Well House looking at that special place where I first beheld the man who would become my friend, then my bestest friend and the man I have come to love with every fiber of my being, I feel an emptiness, an aching, a longing, I have never before experienced. My eyes are filled with tears pouring down my face like the monsoon rains that you must have experienced in Vietnam.

Your parents received notification that you were missing in action and presumed dead. Write to me and tell me that it is not so, my darling. It would be unbearable to imagine that I might not hear your voice or see you once again to seal my love with that singular kiss at the midnight hour in the Well House.

I am writing this letter, hoping and praying that you are not dead, but alive, and that by some miraculous intervention you have been spared the cruel fate of your friends. And yet, who am I to be considered exempt from this tragedy of life that is being played out so cruelly in that far away land called Vietnam. I have no such right.

But if, per chance, your eyes fall upon the words of this epistle, then let each letter, and every syllable be a testament of my love for you, dearest Clayton. As the sun greets each and every morning may I be the light that warms your lonely heart. May each sunset be a testimony of the glory of that God that loves you and me. As you gaze upon our moon, know that my hand will be there touching your hand connecting us across these invisible miles and bringing us together once again.

If perchance you have been taken to that sphere beyond this existence where there is no pain and suffering but happiness and joy, know that someday I shall be there to be home in your arms again. I shall seal this letter with a kiss and let you know that I shall be waiting for you to return to me, my beloved. I love you, darling.

Maggie

Maggie took the letter, and stared at it as if the ink might reveal his whereabouts. Giving into reality she walked back to the car and rummaging through her bags, found an envelope.

Leaning over the hood of her import, she carefully wrote an address, surprising herself in the process.

Clayton Wesley Riggs - POW
PFC United States Marine Corps
C/o Ho Chi Mihn, President
Country of North Vietnam
Hanoi

Please Deliver

Maggie took one last look toward the Well House, eased into her car and drove to the Post Office.

Truth ... the way things really are. I must see truth or it will never see me.

30

May 21, 1968
Renovo, Pennsylvania

"Hell … you made it home. Well I'll be damned." Moto's Dad could've cared less if he made it home or not. He cared more about the steady flow of booze he needed to help him cope with his wasted life.

When Moto stepped off the bus after the thirty-six hour ride from Pittsburg, via Chicago and then Bloomington, Indiana, he was struck by how badly he wanted to climb back aboard and return directly to Viet 'damned' Nam. He didn't want to pass go or collect his $200 … he just wanted to go back where life was simple. As the bus drove out of sight he knew he was home and would be back in trouble, big trouble real soon.

The house was even more run down and dilapidated than when he'd left over two years ago. The last person he wanted to see first was his old man. He wasn't taking any of his shit anymore.

"Hell boy … ain't you gonna' give me a big hug?" With that Boots, as the gang down at the bar knew him as, gave out a huge, evil belly laugh. It was a laugh Moto associated with all that was bad about life at home in Renovo.

Dropping his sea bag in the dirt and clutter that was once a living room, he turned to his father and said, "Don't give me no shit no more … where's Mom?"

His Dad came out of the chair like he had years before, teeth glaring, slobbering all over his chin and anyone else within spitting distance, making a bee line for his only son.

Moto squared up and growled right in Daddy's face, "Don't do it ole' man I ain't your whippin' boy no more"

They stared each other down until Dad backed off, laughingly calling out … "Your Mom … hell she left me a year ago. I don't know where the hell she is."

Boots walked back over to the torn and tattered recliner he spent most of his waking hours in and sat back to watch what was left of the TV Moto once loved to spend hours dreaming in front of.

"Where the hell are the girls?" Moto queried with a scowl he was used to wearing.

"What the hell do you care?"

The look Michael Murray Mason gave his Dad made it official.

Don't screw with me.

"Ah, they took off with your Mom, I don't know where the hell they are." With that he got up and left the room. He knew better than to stay with an angry Marine even it was his own son.

Alone ... Michael Mason was alone. The house where he grew up, miserable and cramped was now empty. Home from a war he grew to love to a place he grew up hating.

What the hell do I do now? Back to this shit hole, no one here ... my friends are in Nam ... dead and alive. What the hell do I do? Nam is better than this place. I wish to hell I could go back.

He grabbed his sea bag, a three-foot long green cylinder of canvas packed full of his whole life. It was filled to the brim with two years worth of life in a bad place, but not as bad as home looked to him right now. He ran up the stairs to his room. Turning the corner, he crashed head first into eighteen years of memories that weren't getting better with age.

My hooch in Nam was better. I haven't had these feelings since I left this hole. Paper falling off the wall, floors rotting and the smell ... Cooter where the hell are you when I need you?

Once you left Renovo, you could see the difference. And coming back was worse than never leaving.

That's it ... I need to call Cooter, I need to talk to someone ... a friend. I don't know if I can take it here.

Moto tossed his belongings on the bed and it let out an old, tired creak at the invasion of weight it hadn't seen in years. He bounded down the steps, racing around the house in a vain search for a phone. But Pennsylvania Bell had long ago tired of not receiving payment from Boots or anyone else at the residence of Fred Mason. There was no phone and when the cold came, if Michael came back in the fall after his discharge from the Corps he'd find out there wasn't any heat either.

Out the front door and down the street, the recently returned Nam Marine, sporting clean clothes and a serious attitude, charged off in search of the nearest pay phone. He found it by the 4 Star Café … his old watering hole. It was late in the afternoon by the time he spied the phone booth standing on the corner.

I'm calling Cooter. I need to talk with him again. But right after a beer or two ...

"It's 2:30 am Mikey and we need to close."

Where the hell did the day go? After midnight, what the hell am I doing? I can't start this all over again.

The bartender, a veteran of the Big One, World War II, had heard enough. He hadn't seen Mike Mason for two years or more and he didn't need him messing the place up again right now. He didn't need a no good Vietnam vet coming into his bar anyway. He knew Michael Mason before he left for Vietnam and as far as he was concerned he wasn't any better now than when he was at home.

Walking around the bar, he put his hand on Moto's shoulder.

"Don't you touch me asshole!" Moto growled as he jerked his shoulder away from the bartender. "This ain't like it used to be old man."

Mr. Carson knew a lot about this town. Right now he knew not to mess with Fred Mason's son, not anymore.

Moto walked outside into the cool mountain air of the Appalachians. He long forgot about the call he was going to make to Cooter. He stumbled home and fell asleep, passed out on the glider still sitting on the back porch.

An early sun startled him awake as he heard cars driving down the alley nearby. With a head the size of Alaska he stood and straightened his clothes. Still used to Marine Corps discipline he wanted to look decent … it felt good.

I gotta' call Cooter.

Moto bounded down the street to the 4 Star Café, only this time he went straight to the phone. Fumbling for change, he negotiated through the operator and experienced a miracle … the phone was ringing at The Long Branch in Clyde, Texas.

Come on man answer the damned phone.

In Pennsylvania it was 0600 … in Texas it was 0500. After a ring that went on forever, a groggy voice came alive on the other end.

"Yep, whatdya want this time of the mornin'?"

It' about damned time someone got up.

"I'm trying to reach Cooter," Moto offered as gentle as an elephant at a ladies tea.

"Cooter? This is a helluva' time of day for a wrong number fella," the voice on the other end mumbled in a sleep-powered drone that further irritated the mountain man on the other end.

Time of day? Hell, it's morning.

"Wait a minute. I'm looking for Cooter. Is this the Long Branch in Clyde, Texas?" Moto questioned like his life depended on it.

There was a long pause on the line and then an agitated, yet sleep filled voice replied, "Fella … it's 5 in the mornin' here. We ain't open and there ain't' no Cooter 'round here."

"The hell there ain't, I talked to him a couple a weeks ago. I was in the Marines with him," Moto growled into the phone from the Appalachian street he was looking at from his phone booth.

"Well, hell why didn't ya' say so. I'll go and get'em outta' bed."

Man I go through this shit every time I call that worthless piece of crap. Get his ugly butt outta' bed. I can't be waiting all day on this guy.

"Do you know I'm not in the Corps anymore? What the heck are you getting' me outta' bed at this time of the morning for? Do you know I run a bar and am up half the night?"

Cooter knew there was only one guy calling asking for "Cooter" and only one guy calling that wanted him up at O dark early. "Moto … how the hell are ya?"

"Cooter I ain't worth a shit," Moto blurted out like it was something unexpected. "I just got home to PA and it sucks worse than I thought. But worse, I took the bus down to Bloomington, that university town where Riggs's honey was supposed to be."

Cooter was trying to wake up from a short night when he heard the words 'supposed to be' coming from Moto in a barrage of words that made little sense at 0 dark early.

"Whatdya mean, s'posed to be?' Cooter drawled, shaking the cobwebs from his dreary mind.

"I mean supposed to be. The broad wasn't there. She's gone. What the hell am I supposed to do with this letter from Riggs?" Moto was disgusted, frustrated and sounded like he wanted to crawl through the lines to Texas.

Here were two warriors from a time shortly passed, caught up in the early hours of a slow morning in Pennsylvania. A few days earlier Moto had called Cooter from Chicago and surprised him when he wanted to know in what town "that" university was located in.

Of all people, Cooter couldn't believe his friend Moto was going to follow through and do something nice for a change.

"Did you go to the right address?' Cooter asked, doubting Moto could carry out the assignment or would even want to.

"You told me to go to Bloomington, Indiana so I did," Moto shot back.

"I know you went to Bloomington but did you go to the right address … the right apartment man?" Cooter was waking up and as he did he realized this might just be the first really nice thing he'd ever seen his friend try to do. He wasn't ready to tell him that for fear of his life but it was strangely nice to even think about.

"I went to 121 4th Avenue, Apartment 15A just like his letter said. They said she dropped out of school. Went home." Moto was factual and getting more frustrated every minute he had to talk about it.

"Well home is somewhere on Chicago's North side. The rich part of town according to Riggsy," Cooter chimed in.

The rich part of town? Chicago? The north side? Who gives a big ...

"Were you in Chicago?" Cooter asked the question attached to the fuse Moto wore inside his newly shaved head.

"Chicago? Hell yes I was in Chicago. Before I went to Bloomington and before I got thirty-six hours out here on a damned bus I was in Chicago. I called you from there asshole!"

Moto had talked all he wanted to talk for one day. He stormed off down the street, heading home with the phone dangling from its flexible, metal cord. He had done a lot of things in the two years he'd been gone but gaining patience wasn't one of them.

"Moto … Moto … where the hell are ya' man?" Cooter was left dangling in the morning air yelling into the phone at the young man who'd saved his life many times. He turned and headed back to bed. Clyde, Texas was a long way from Renovo, and for Michael Murray Mason it was a long way from where he wanted to be.

31

September 1968
Boulder, Colorado
Campus of Colorado University

"Hi Maggie, welcome back. I'm glad you decided to come and finish school with us".

It was Maggie's new roommate, Cameron Melton. Cami as she was called, was a friend of Maggie's from high school who had gone west to school at the same time Maggie had gone to IU in Bloomington.

Her choice to meet up with Cami and move to Colorado had been an unpopular decision back in the O'Reilly home in North Chicago.

"One bad choice after another," her Dad had said, as she walked out the door to Big Sis' car and her ride to O'Hare.

"Hi Cami, glad to be here. It's nice out here in the mountains and I needed to get away."

Maggie was being as nice as she could to someone she couldn't stand in high school. But she needed to get away, away from home and away from memories of the past, a past that included the unknown whereabouts of the love of her life.

She wasn't ready to talk relationships or anything other than school right now were forbidden topics. What she didn't need was Cami to start in about her brother Richard. While he wasn't anything like Cami, Maggie just wasn't ready for another "boy" discussion.

"I'm just going to drop my things here and take a walk," Maggie said unconvincingly. "I love the mountains and want to soak it all in.".

Oh what I really want is to be left alone, alone from you, alone from phone calls, from TV, from everyone and everything. I just want to be alone.

"Hey, I know what you mean. I know some great spots we can go and see. It'll be great, just like high school," Cami squealed in her high pitched, extremely fake, cheerleader voice that Maggie loved to hate back in school and right now.

Oh great, now I have to deal with her again. Well, this isn't high school and your Mom isn't next door to make sure her little girl doesn't get left out. I am not taking you with me. Period.

Maggie turned at the door in time to see her lifelong nemesis reaching for her purse. "No Cami, I'm just going to take a ride. I need to be alone and do some thinking. I know you have things to do so we'll go out together another time."

Cami stopped in her tracks, a deer in the headlights, frozen by her bedroom door, not used to being put off and not getting her way at every turn. "Oh, I see Mom was right, you're not over that Vietnam guy are you?"

The words cut through Maggie like a cold stiletto plunging deep into her tight, fit, stomach. The anger of years of not being what "Cami was" came bursting to the surface. She felt herself fighting for control of a part of her that could easily be uncontrollable.

She turned with a glare that would strain the best of relationships as she said ..."Cami, that is something you and I will never discuss. We're roommates because I respect my Mother and she wants me to be here. Period."

Cami's mouth flew open like she was ready to belt out a cheer, but the shock on her face was worth all the pain Maggie had endured over the years. She was speechless.

Maggie reached for the door and the wall phone began ringing. "I'm not here," she said with a wave and motion spewing forth with an angry, newfound authority.

"Hello, Cami and Maggie's place."

Oh my God ... we're not playing house, I just got here and I can't believe it. I can't believe I agreed to this arrangement. I can't live with that person for a year. I couldn't stand her when she slept over and Mom was always throwing us together.

Why can't you be more involved like Cami? Why can't you be a cheerleader? Why can't you this ... why can't you that ... Cami, Cami, Cam ...

"Maggie ... it's for you. Yes, Mrs. O'Reilly, it's great having her here; we were just going for a walk in the mountains out here by the campus. It's gorgeous … can't wait for you to come out. Here she is … bye."

Maggie stood, eyes blazing hate so strong it might melt the toothy smile and prissy nose of her new roommate.

She hasn't grown up a bit. She wouldn't even be here if she wasn't a cheerleader on the university football team. This girl hasn't changed since I can remember. She ...

"Hi Mother. Yes I'm here. I got here okay … yes we'll get along fine … I know … I know … Mother, the fact is I'm tired from the flight and need to get going. I will call you tomorrow."

Maggie was never that abrupt with her Mother. That was not something you did in the O'Reilly family. But these days Maggie was beginning to do things that weren't in keeping with the O'Reilly way.

She hung up the phone with a bang, turned without a word and vanished out the door. Cami quickly grabbed the phone to call Bridget and report her concerns about her new, old roommate.

Outside, Maggie stopped and took a deep breath to gather her thoughts and her composure. The last thing she needed was to run into someone looking like she must have after her encounter with her lifelong nemesis. Her face was flushed and tears poured down her rosy cheeks as she slipped back to times so soon gone by.

Clayton, Clayton, Clayton. You cannot be dead. You cannot be dead. I need you. I have never felt a part of this family and now I am lost. I need you to create our family and get away from people like this. You must be coming home.

She began walking; almost running away from her new apartment and a girl she'd known her whole life and couldn't stand to be near. She was running from life and the truth it dealt her in the last hand.

Ooooh Clayton, dearest Clayton, you cannot be gone from my life. I have never felt I belonged until I met you and now you're gone forever.

Maggie wasn't sure where she was going but she knew it had to be away; away from Cami and away from all that she represented.

Oh I hurt so much. If I could just talk with you Clay I would be better. You always made my hurts go away. I just knew we were meant to be. We were born into families that drove us to become only what they could see as possible and not what we might be together. We have parents driven by the past while we live with the hope of the future.

Nearly out of breath and at the top of a lone street near the edge of town, Maggie turned and started up a small hill, quickly disappearing into a small family of tall pine trees. After a few steps she found herself surrounded by the comfort, warmth and the sweet smell of pine all around. A gentle breeze nipped at her neck and she sat down, wrapped in privacy and draped in the sorrow of what might have been.

Clay? Clay? I know you're there. I can feel you. You brought me here. Even if you're dead I know you're there. I know you wouldn't leave me alone. I don't know if I can make it without you. I know you're there for me even in your loss. I just know you have to be there. Oh dear what am I saying ... what am I doing?

The tears gushed down Maggie's cheeks as she wept uncontrollably. The strawberry blonde hair Clay so loved was soon full of scratchy, dry, pine needles as Maggie O'Reilly rubbed her hands on her head as she bent over, holding her head between her legs, sobbing wildly for her missing loved one, gone, the price of a war no one understood.

32

December 24, 1968
Hope, Indiana

"Mrs. Riggs, thank you so much for inviting me here this Christmas. I know it is hard on your family … that is, having me here."

Maggie knew what a strain life had been since the news of Clay's situation in Vietnam. She knew that Homer was taking the tough Marine route and was convinced it was over. No one touched by Clay had come to grips with the reality of it all.

"Maggie …" the words came hard for Lucy. It had been nearly a year since news came of Clay's death.

"Maggie, that boy loved you," Lucy warmly held Maggie's hand as she stated what only a mother knew in her heart.

"Oh, Mrs. Riggs we were just friends. Good friends for sure. He was so sweet." Maggie wanted desperately to blurt out "did he say it, did he say it Mrs. Riggs" … she wanted to know with every inch of her being but had no right to question a grieving mother about her pronouncements of a missing son. She had no right but oh how she wanted to know.

Grabbing Maggie's other hand, the same hand her son had held so tightly when he left the airport over a year ago, Lucy tugged, looking straight into Maggie's beautiful brown eyes and said, "Young lady, he loved you. He loved you and don't you ever forget it."

Maggie nearly collapsed, falling forward with her head bumping down on Lucy's thin, frail shoulder. Lucy had once been known to be "stout" as the farm fraternity was fond of calling someone who had put on more than a few pounds.

"Oh Mrs. Riggs I loved Clay, I loved him so very much," Maggie whispered under her breath as she cried quietly into a caring shoulder of one lady who was grieving more than anyone would ever know.

"Call me Lucy, dear. We're closer than anyone imagines … you were the one for him. I just wanted you to know that … I know how you felt and I know how he felt. You were the one … we'd better get over there, it looks like they're ready."

The two walked arm in arm across the historic cemetery in Hope. They approached the growing number of people gathering for the Memorial Service Homer insisted on having. He said it was closure and for Lucy, barely fifty years old, it seemed like the end.

Homer came over and forced a smile on Maggie that was as cold as the December day, as he took his ailing wife by her free arm. He quickly escorted Lucy to the front row of the graveside service.

It was quite a debate in the Riggs household, the decision to hold a Memorial Service, let alone one in the graveyard where there wasn't even a body to honor. But Homer insisted on closure, accepting the unacceptable and burying his only son with military honors.

Life on the family farm was never the same after the first telegram detailing the "incident" involving the love of their lives. It was a tough year since the obscure battle in a place faraway in a war that no one wanted and fewer understood.

It was Halloween eve when news came from Washington that Clayton Wesley Riggs's status was changed from missing presumed dead to killed in action … things got worse in a hurry.

Homer and Lucy, lovebirds since high school had barely spoken a word, at least not a civil word since reality kicked the door in like a goblin in the night. The numbness they felt had consumed their souls, souls once in love and happy beyond belief.

The Riggs family was a large crew and when they all sat down at the five rows of chairs graveside, there was no room for anyone else. A crowd of a hundred or more stood, surrounding the family and facing an empty casket as six strong, proud young Marines, in full dress blues faced the music for a missing comrade, fallen at arms in a dirty and distant land.

Maggie slid from view, taking her place at the edge of a throng of well-wishers. She stood, shaking, her face cold and raw from the winter wind cutting across her wet cheeks, damp with warm tears, fallen like the man she loved.

Oh I hate sermons, especially sermons that tell us all is well when we stand alone, lost and hurting more than life itself.

"Life serves us lessons that are available for the taking. Some are easy and obvious. Others are painful and the meaning is only to be found by those who truly seek it."

This guy must be the minister that Clay talked about. He sounds like he knew him, like he cared ... Oh God he can't be gone, he can't be gone.

"My good brothers and sisters, I want you to know something very important about what is taking place today. I want you to seek after the answers in this tragedy."

Well I need to know something important. I seek after the answers. God I seek after the answers.

Maggie was lost in her own world, deep in thought much like the man she longed for, Clayton Wesley Riggs used to do. She stood among the onlookers, those that cared and those that didn't, all surrounding the man of God as he offered words they hoped might drain some of the pain from an extremely painful day.

"I want all of you to know one important thing. Just because this US government of ours has declared this young man dead … doesn't make it so."

Oh my ... what does he know? He knows something ... I'm right, Clay is alive, and he has to be alive!

"I want you to know that God lives and Jesus is the Christ. I want you to know that Christ died that we all might have life Eternal. The government doesn't make someone dead … he lives my good friends."

Oh what am I thinking? He's talking about ...

"I have known Homer and Lucy Riggs for many, many years. They are good people. I knew Clayton most of his young life. He was a good young man. He didn't deserve this end to his young life. They don't deserve this tragedy. They don't deserve this pain. Their son didn't deserve to die."

A chill went shooting up Maggie's spine, giving her a jolt worse than what she felt from the needle of her spinal tap when she was hospitalized while still in high school.

He is dead. I am standing here at his funeral and he is dead. The only person to make me feel like I could fly and he's dead. He just can't be dead. Not now, not this young, not without me ... us.

Tears welled up, pushing against the dam she'd built to hold back the emotion she knew would draw the attention of the man who could have been her father-in-law if she broke down and let her flood of pain crash into the open. She had to be strong.

Reverend Ingram continued with an air of authority, speaking like he knew something the gathered group of sad friends didn't know.

"But the lessons our Lord offers us are not based on deserve." He paused, looking at the crowd of friends bundled on the outside to keep the late December chill out, while their hearts were bursting on the inside with the love they owed a young man they'd never see again.

His words ... his hope ... it is so beautiful. Does Christ live? I think he does. Is that the truth Clay and I so desperately wanted? Is there truth in fighting in a land where no one knows why you're fighting? Is Christ there? How could I lose someone so sweet as Clay? How could there be a God that allows such misery?

Maggie was lost inside her own world and deeply engaged at the same time. She fought for control of the uncontrollable and to make sense of the senseless.

"As I conclude my remarks honoring this young man who gave his life for the freedoms we enjoy, I want to share with you a story. It's a story that will help you see where Clay is at this time. It will help you see the hope Christ offers each of us."

Hope? What hope is there at a time like this? There is none that I can see.

"Imagine with me we are all standing on a shore; a shore watching a boat about to depart on a long journey. On that boat, among others, is Clayton Wesley Riggs.

We are all standing, together, waving at Clayton as he departs on a long journey, a journey where we won't be seeing him again for some time."

Oh, I stood bidding him farewell one other time. I stood as he boarded a plane that took him away for a long time just like you say. I already stood there and I don't know if I can do it again.

"I want you to watch with me as Clayton sails away and as you watch and wave, he is getting smaller and smaller. You watch, it's a beautiful day, and as you watch the ship sail off towards the horizon. It is a small block, dark and unclear and then it's a speck … and then … it's gone."

Maggie stood silent, frozen not from the cold but from the fear that all he said was true. She could hear quiet sobs break out among the friends and family, knowing it was true … their friend was gone.

Oh yes, I have stood there on that shore ... and I watched him board a plane and now you see they have told us he isn't coming home. He isn't coming home Sir ...

"But now, you know this," he spoke with clarity and conviction. He stood looking straight at the family, seated, sobbing in the front row.

"You know that what I tell you is true. For on another shore, a distant shore in the next life another group of people are standing, waiting, knowing that Clayton is on his way. They know that he lives.

"As they wait, suddenly someone exclaims 'there he is' and as they look they first see a speck, then a small dot and then a block and suddenly an outline of a ship, arriving as all of us do."

Oh how I want to believe that ... I want this to be true... I want to know he is okay. I want to know that our love is alive and well and I will in fact see him one day. I want to believe.

"On that distant shore, my Brothers and Sisters, stands Uncle Ben, Grandma and Grandpa Riggs and many others who have gone before. They stand waiting for the first glimpse of a loved one, Clayton Wesley Riggs, waving and awaiting the greeting of special people who have gone before to prepare the way."

Oh how it must be true ... it must be ... he does live ... I must have faith that I too will one day see my dear Clayton ... one day we will be one again and I will hold him in my arms and tell him face to face how I feel ... one day.

Maggie was in a stupor as the Marine Color Guard carefully folded the beautiful American flag that had draped the coffin. It was a symbol of love of country and Corps, an outpouring of freedom that the daughter of second-generation anti-war protestors had never seen before. She was moved beyond anything she had ever imagined in her young and perfect life.

Maybe that flag is truth. Maybe truth is to know things as they really are and seeing them clearly for the first time. Maybe we will find our elusive truth where we least expect it; on Christmas Eve ... Clay's special day, the day he loved above all others. Oh how fitting that we would remember him today ... the day before Christ's birth ... the hope he brought to all of us is the hope Clay gave me ... Oh my I can't take it anymore ... I have to get out of here before I have to face anyone ... Oh this hurts so very much ... Oh!

B-B-B-B-B-Boooom!

The firing squad blasted the crisp morning air with their six M-14's, simultaneously barking a salute to a fallen comrade.

Maggie ran sobbing uncontrollably, hand over her mouth for fear of others hearing her moans of pain and heartbreak. She jumped into her car, barely able to see as tears flooded her eyes and ran into her open mouth, crying out for sanity in the midst of an insane crash of life and death. Maggie O'Reilly raced off into the early afternoon of a special Christmas Eve, a day she would replay for many a night in her uncertain future.

33

February 12, 1973
New Kensington, PA

"I'm tired of it and I want you out," Shawna Mason had been married to Mike for three and a half years and that was long enough for anyone. I put up with your whining after Kent State. I put up with all of it since then and I'm done."

Moto sat on the couch glaring at his wife, sipping on his seventh Carling Black label, the beginning of his second six pack of the early morning.

"These damned prisoners come home and you're sitting here at the boob tube tripped out. You've been up all night waiting on word. You're supposed to be down at the union hall trying to get your blasted job back."

His wife of longer than anyone would have imagined, refused to call him Moto. Calling him "that" was acknowledging his past and she was the future, not the past. He was Mike and that was that. They were an odd couple and the fact they lasted three years was odder still.

"Mike!" Shawna yelled at him as he sat staring at the TV.

He turned and glared back, eyes glazed on the outside and thick with booze on the inside.

"Do you hear me? Are you in there?"

Mike Mason was in there all right, but he was in so deep that nobody was going to dig him out. He felt trapped, alone and tired of all the crap society dealt the Vet's after Nam.

"I've had it Mike. I've had it!" Shawna stomped over and stood between him and the TV.

"Are you going to talk to me?" She pleaded, voice quivering, tears creeping inside the anger rising deep in the girl who was sure she could change a tough Marine just home from the war.

Moto sat unmoved, staring a hole right through Shawna's midsection where the TV would be if she hadn't blocked it. As if staring at a group of NVA sneaking up on his position, he didn't blink and all emotion was long drained from his swamp.

"Mike!" Shawna screamed again at the comatose man sitting in front of her, the man she loved but couldn't penetrate. She wanted to get a rise out of him, to make a difference in the lonely man she met at work but who always led a double life.

The young, tough, fireplug of a guy, a stud, came swaggering into the office at the J & L Steel Plant in New Kensington. The muscle shirt, the "Mr. T' voice and the "take no prisoners" approach fit Shawna, daughter of a long time plant supervisor and former United Steel Worker to a "T".

Without a word Moto stood, picked up his newly opened 16-ounce bottle of Carling and downed it in one swig. Shawna hated it when he chugged his booze and went to his "bad place." He'd trip out. She'd lose him for hours on end as he visited places and people from a time most wanted to forget.

I need out of here. I need to keep moving. I can't live with this life, this pressure ... this bullshit.

As he turned his back on his bluffing wife, Moto was lost in thought, the most peaceful place he knew.

Cooter. Where are you man when I need you? Life made more sense in Nam than it does here. I can't stand people in my face... people expecting things at every turn and the constant demands to change. I'm not changing.

I can't stand her constant nagging ... change this and change that ... I ain't changin' ... I'll get out of here and things will just be fine. I'll find Cooter and maybe Vance. Hell, that worthless LT is better than this.

Moto stood in the upstairs bedroom of the row house they were renting in town. It was small and cozy, a lifetime better than his home in Renova. But it wasn't good enough for Shawna who was always pushing him to buy "their own place" and put down roots.

Life was simple in Nam. It was life so simple and now I have this ... I just want to be alone. I need to keep moving. I can't take all the petty bullshit people give me. I won't go down with those losers at the union hall and beg for my job. Screw 'em. I don't need this shit!

He grabbed a small gym bag lying in the back of the tiny closet he shared with the woman he could no longer stand. Picking it up to pack his things, he couldn't stop his mind from racing full speed ahead, about to crash with his painful past.

I can't believe Riggs ain't released with those guys. Damned flyboys all get out but where the hell are the grunts. They always suck wind. Damn it. He didn't deserve it. He didn't deserve to die. Why the hell did he give me that letter? I don't want that responsibility. I don't want anything other than to be with my Marines. That's all that ever made sense.

He threw his "health and comfort gear" as the Corps taught him to refer to it, his toothbrush, toothpaste, deodorant, razor, shaving cream and mouthwash in the little bag followed by a pair of jeans, a couple pair of socks, a shirt and a handful of underwear and "*the letter.*"

Standing at the bottom of the steps was Shawna, tissue wrapped around her nose in one hand and wiping her eyes with the other.

"Mike please don't leave, I didn't mean it. Don't go ... Please?"

She pleaded for what seemed like the hundredth time. Each time Vietnam receded from the horizon of their lives another wave would come out of nowhere like a human wave assault and destroy the little chemistry Shawna had built.

Moto bounded down the steps; head down, on a mission straight from the ghosts that called the shots inside his newly shaved head. He was walking out one more time, just like his first marriage that ended in just four months.

He stopped on the bottom step. Shawna was standing still, eyes pleading for mercy from the man she couldn't change. Without a word, she stepped back, resigned that this time was the last time she'd ask him to leave.

In the kitchen Moto stopped, looked around until he spotted the pencil and pad Shawna always had laid out near the phone. He walked over, grabbing both in one sweep of the area and stood, writing a note at the table.

She couldn't believe what was happening … what was he writing? Was it over? It was all strange behavior even for Moto; he hadn't said even one word.

Three and a half years and it all came down to this … a note, a small bag of clothes, and silence. Shawna crept into the kitchen, on guard for an outbreak of "Nam" any minute. The volcano she expected walked out the door. She didn't get a wisp of trouble, just a dejected, angry look and a finger pointing to the note he'd written now laying on the table.

"That's it. That's it? After three years that's it?"

Shawna stood crying, sobbing, her face in her hands, she looked up just in time to watch her husband disappear from the kitchen door of their cramped but cute little house, the house she never wanted to live in anyway.

She sat at the table, picked up the note and read the words that made it all final.

To Who It Might Concern:

I Michael Murray Mason give all that I have to my wife Shawna Ellen Mason. All that I have and I mean everything except my Harley that I'm driving out of here. The rest is hers and a divorce is what I expect.

Willingly,

Michael Murray Mason Feb 12, 73.

The roar of his Harley riding off in the winds of a February night drowned out the sobs of a broken heart, crying out in anguish, fueled by the reality that love doesn't conquer all after all.

34

September 14, 1974
Hope, IN

"Frank, you're her brother … can't you help her come to her senses? She has to get out of this stupor she's been in since the word of Clay's situation came down," Homer pleaded, hoping upon hope that someone or something would bring his bride back to him.

"I've tried Homer, I don't know what on earth to do. The Doctor has talked with her. Oleta took her in last week and they say there's nothing wrong."

The two men, brought together by marriage, had their friendship sealed on the dusty fields of the family farms in Bartholomew County. But all the challenges of making a living on a farm in the Midwest was nothing compared to the puzzle they had been trying to solve since Clayton died in Vietnam.

"Frank, it's been nearly seven years since we lost that boy. I still lay awake at night thinking about it but we can't just stop living." Homer worked hard to convince himself that things would be all right again.

He had tried everything to snap Lucy out of her "funk" as he called it. He tried being loving and kind and he tried being tough and directive. Nothing moved her from her old rocker by the window, the one where she spent Clay's early years sitting, watching him play.

"For goodness sake I've still got that old Edsel out there in the barn. She won't even let me sell it. I can't sell it Frank, did you hear me … I've still got his car." Homer didn't even convince himself anymore, but he did seem to feel better after sitting on the porch pouring out his pity on his brother-in-law.

"Homer, Doc says she's depressed and you and I don't know nothin' about that stuff. You should consider doin' what he says, Homer." Frank had been trying to convince his good family friend to reconsider his stance on letting his wife take medication for the thing they called "depression." But Homer survived World War II, droughts and long winters and he'd put his arm around his dear wife and survive this too. He just didn't know how.

"Frank, I just don't believe in it. I don't believe that's anything more than a way for those doctors to get in cahoots with those drug store guys and make money. I can't do it."

Frank put his arm around his best friend as they sat quietly on the porch. Libby and Oleta were inside doing what they could to get rid of her "blues."

"It's worse at these times of year. You know his birthday was yesterday and boy does she get down about that. Frank I feel like I lost her in Vietnam along with my son. Gosh darn it; it's just not right. What on earth is wrong about that war? It destroys everything and everyone it touches."

All Frank could do was listen; listen like he'd done for over six years. Listen while they walked, while they worked and all the while know there wasn't a thing he could do.

Lucy was once a vibrant, fit woman with a cheerful smile and a radiant bounce in her step. She was always the first to help anyone who needed it and always the one to have everything "just right" for her "Prince Charming" … Homer Riggs.

She never missed church down at the Moravian Church in Hope. Reverend Ingram knew he could always count on Lucy for a dinner, or a prayer or to take care of families in need. Since the death of her son, he could hardly count on her to show up. With each passing Sunday her ties to her Lord and Savior seemed to be suffering as much as she was.

"I don't know how much more I can take Frank. I mean the clothes are never clean and dinner is barely edible half the time. I love that woman but I don't know how to help her anymore."

Homer went through his primary list of complaints every time the two men sat down. Frank patiently sat nearby, always consoling his sad, dear friend, who remained faithful in spite of the distance growing like a field of dandelions between him and the love of his life.

"Homer, as your friend … can I tell you something?" Frank was venturing into the field of advice, which didn't comfort the suffering man sitting next to him.

"What do you mean 'can you tell me something' … of course you can, you know that," Homer responded with more energy and surprise than Frank liked.

The entire goings on had put a strain on the lifelong friendship of the two Hope farmers. He took a deep breath and decided it was time to take a risk and confront his friend.

"Homer you're going to have to do some things you don't want to do. We're both from the old school and some of the things going on don't make no sense." Frank gained strength with each word he shared in love with his dear friend. "You need to do something you don't want to do. You need to look this in the eye. You need to …"

His long time friend interrupted his painful words when he shot upright and turned to face Frank square on.

"Of all people you know better. I am not letting them fill my Lucy full of those God-forsaken drugs. She just needs to buck it up and be her old self … you'll see."

Homer turned quickly, dropping his head and looking at the flower beds near the porch that were once beautiful from Lucy's constant care. They now stood barren, weeds winning the day.

Frank wasn't big on face-to-face confrontation but something told him to keep going for the sake of his ailing sister. He got up off the swing they'd shared and stood next to Homer. His friend now gazed out across the acreage they'd farmed together for nearly half a century.

Placing his big, strong arm on Homer's shoulder, Frank tried to touch his friend's strong heart with words he had to find.

"Homer, my friend, you really need to do something different for that girl."

"Something different huh? Well I did something different this afternoon. She begged me to call that draft dodger girl from Chicago. She still talks to her. That girl killed him I'm telling you Frank. So I did something different today … okay?"

Homer took off down the four front steps, skipping halfway, defying the arthritis that plagued all his attempts to do the physical things he once did with ease. He began walking around the side of his house, Frank knew, on his way to sit down and talk with Bob, Clay's big yellow lab that spent every day lying on the back porch staring at the highway. He swore that dog was still looking for his son to return from the war.

Frank had heard it all, all of Homer's theories about how Clay died. He couldn't believe the man who told everyone to accept the death of his son, still couldn't let go of the fact he liked a girl who protested the war he died fighting. Somehow he couldn't accept what his son had accepted long ago.

Many a night Frank sat up sipping coffee listening to how Clay died, at least the "Homer" version. According to Homer "that girl" messed up his son's mind with that anti-war talk and he was questioning himself and not paying attention to what he should and "they" got him.

It was clear to Homer. Nothing else made sense to him. Frank realized that Lucy and Homer both suffered the same thing inside but on the outside they had a different way of showing it.

Frank walked off the porch and around the house and down the sidewalk enough to see where Homer went. He didn't want to disturb him and interrupt his private time that seemed so precious to a lonely man. He seemed to spend a lot of hours with Bob, Clay's beloved dog.

Oleta and Libby, opened the front door, spotted him at the end of the walk near the car and quietly walked to join him. There was something different, something strange about the way they approached, and Frank could feel it.

"How is she?" he asked, almost afraid to hear the answer.

"Well," Oleta said, "we got her to go to sleep and we tucked her in … but …"

Frank stood up from leaning on the 1963 Chrysler with 135,000 miles and counting. "But what … is she okay?" he asked, worried for Lucy, for Homer and for himself.

Oleta looked up and with the soft demeanor she'd come to be known for said, "I am more worried about her than ever before. The light in those eyes is growing dimmer everyday I see her. She's down to 90 pounds and barely eats enough to feed one of her parakeets."

"But the Doc said she didn't have anything wrong, what do you mean?" Frank searched for something more than "women's intuition." He had an obligation to help his friend sitting on the porch talking with an old dog and who didn't believe in any "intuition from women."

"Well, let's get home, it's getting late but I tell you we have to stay close. That good lady has lost her light. Oleta had a way of making things crystal clear.

The three distraught friends got in the family car that had taken them everywhere they'd found a need to go since he'd bought it new eleven years ago. He turned the key and the engine hummed to life, sounding as good as it ever did.

The evening was swallowed by the dark of night, invading the family farm as the west sun dropped into the horizon. Frank turned the big Chrysler to the left and his lights slowly panned across the silhouette of a man and his dog.

Homer sat on his behind, framed as a silhouette, dark figure in the night, with Clay's dog, Bob, sitting between his legs kissing his face … as the trio drove off.

I know you loved him like I did boy. You're loyal to him. You're always here for me ... at least you never changed. I know you know what I mean.

The sun sat on a quietly sobbing man, fighting for life and happiness where all seemed lost in his once happy home.

35

April 30, 1975
Chicago, IL

Breaking News - - -

The headline flashed across the screen of Maggie O'Reilly's new apartment in downtown Chicago. She'd landed her dream job at the Chicago Tribune.

Maggie rushed across the room and turned up the volume on the new TV she'd just bought to outfit her new life at the Trib.

Walter Cronkite was front and center and this was a big story.

"The North Vietnamese have taken South Vietnam. We have live images of the fall of Saigon and the dramatic rescue of the last supporters of the fallen regime by U. S. Marine helicopters."

She sat down on her new white couch to watch the news that would pull the curtain down on a play that wouldn't end, a play that had drowned the life out of Maggie O'Reilly.

Rrrrrring. Rrrrrrring. Rrr …

Maggie sprang to life, and quickly crossed the pristine Italian white tile floor of her dream kitchen to pick up the phone before she missed the details of her distant past being played out on TV.

"Hello, Maggie here." She sang without taking her eyes off the news cascading through the room.

"Maggie … turn off the TV right now." It was Beverly, her ever-faithful sister calling to keep her focused and recovering from her obsession with Vietnam.

"What … Beverly … is that you calling?" Maggie replied with a twist of mystery in her voice. She knew all too well the call would be coming, only surprised that it came before she had time to think about it.

Beverly had called her little sis' when the Kent State shootings happened; when the prisoners came home and whenever her husband Ben yelled at her and said, *"all hands on board if you want to get your sister married."*

"Yea Sis, that's me … turns off the TV right now."

Beverly knew the drill and had three kids to get ready for school. "Maggie…"

"Come on Beverly, I just want to watch the report. I'm in the business, you know that and …"

"Maggie you write in the community section of the Trib Dear, don't give me that nonsense. I'm your sister … remember?"

"I know but I have to stay informed if I'm going to get anywhere in this new job. I know they'll …".

"They'll what my dear … give it up. It's over and you're doing great. Don't scratch that wound open again. Turn off the TV."

"Oh Beverly I am over that … I," it was hard for Maggie to finish a sentence anymore. Beverly and Ben were her shadow ever since she got engaged to Richard.

"I know you're over it, Maggie, and Ben and I are going to make sure you stay over it. You've got your dream job, your dream apartment, and your dream guy and in another few months you'll have your dream marriage. Now … my love, turn off the TV, stay focused and get to work."

Beverly listened as Maggie went over her "life" as was the custom in the O'Reilly home. Also as was the custom, Maggie did what she was told and turned off the TV. She needed to get to work and Beverly bid her usual "cheery eyed" adieu and was gone.

Maggie sat down in her newly outfitted living room to catch her breath before taking the L to work.

Beverly is right, I'm so glad she called. I do have everything in my life falling into place right now. Finally, I have put that terrible chapter behind me. Finally.

She looked across the room at the new decorations, wall hangings and boxes of memories, stacked, waiting to give new life to a new place. There was one box, distinctive by its aging cardboard skin, screaming from the past.

I should get rid of that box with Clay's and my mementos. I really should, Beverly will really give it to me if she comes this weekend and finds it. I need to take care of that but … I can't do it. I really don't think I can do it. I just know I can't.

Clayton Wesley Riggs, long ago lost in a war in the minds and memories of loved ones and strangers, left an unknown trail of kindness and caring in a box in the new apartment of Maggie O'Reilly.

Clay would never believe I kept that picture I was drawing when I first saw him at the Well House. He'd never believe I kept the napkin from our first date when we had a hamburg over at the Commons in the Union Building, or the straw from our first malt at Mamma Bears on Third Street. How about the pressed rose I have in my bible ... the one he sent me to say he was sorry for going in the Corps.

Shaken, with tears rolling down her cheeks like butter melting in the noon sun, Maggie knew there was a place deep in her soul with a wound still unhealed. She knew Clayton Riggs was still alive, if only in the warmth of her tender heart. She knew she had never buried him and couldn't do it now.

Standing upright, reaching inside her purse for her handkerchief, one of the embroidered set Clayton had given her as a "just because" gift so long ago, she wiped her face dry, attempting to leave her perfect makeup untouched.

Maggie was startled, chills streaking through her petite five- foot-one inch frame, as a knock came to her apartment door. She could barely hear the voice breaking the silence from the other side.

"Maggie my love. I'm here dear," it was Richard, her fiancé.

He was coming by perfectly on schedule to accompany her to the Chicago Symphony Orchestra fundraiser she was covering tonight for the Trib.

"My love ... open up dear, it's time to go."

His voice still grates on me ... the way he talks to me ... he is nice and kind ... but he's, he's not Clay. Sometimes he is very condescending.

"Coming dear ..."

36

November10, 1978
U. S. Steel Compound
Gary, Indiana

"Mason, you screwed up guy. I'm here to give you a break". Moto was sitting in a police squad car in lot 14 of the massive U.S. Steel plant on the dirty shores of Lake Michigan in smoke-filled Gary, Indiana.

"You gonna' talk to me Marine or am I gonna' let these "blues" take you to a place you ain't gonna' like; a place where everyone's as tough as you Mason!"

"What the hell are you doin' callin' me Marine?" Moto wasn't into telling anyone about his past or his future. He wasn't sure about either one at this point.

"I'll call you what the hell I want. Put it here," the six-foot five two hundred fifty plus pounder reached a ham sized hand out as he spoke. "Names Carmine Conti, United Steel Workers Union. I'm your Business Agent. I'm also a former Marine. Is that good enough for you?"

"What do ya' want?" Moto snarled up at the mountain of a man towering into the back door where two cops had wrestled him into position.

"What do I want? You better wake up. Your sittin' in a cop car with your arms behind your back in handcuffs for bustin' up a white shirt in there, not that he didn't deserve it, and you're askin' me what I want?" Conti laughed a huge laugh that could be heard deep inside the sprawling steel complex, aging since the big war. He turned like the world was watching, swinging an arm like he was playing to an audience of thousands.

"Get a load of this piece of work." Just as fast as he'd have you laughing Conti would turn like lightning in the night and hand you your head.

"Do you want help … Maaareeene … or do you want me to let them take you where you'll be a piece of meat? Your choice?" Conti was fuming.

Moto wasn't used to being intimidated and he wasn't used to being told what to do … he also wasn't used to Carmine Conti.

"Yea, I want your help."

Conti cut a deal with management and took Moto to the union hall in downtown Gary. The black caddy made Moto feel uncomfortable. He wasn't used to luxury and he didn't want to get used to it.

"So you clocked this guy because he smart mouthed to your wife? Is that it?" Conti never shut up and the questions weren't making Moto any more civilized.

"Yea, that's about it," Moto grumbled with an attitude that said …

… *It's none of your damned business.*

"Well that's gonna' get you in serious trouble. You want the truth or you want to sit here and play games?"

The truth? What's true? It's true that I'm in trouble again, my wife asks for trouble and I'm trouble ... always have been. It's in my family. It's true I've never done any good. That's truth.

Carmine Conti wheeled the big boat of a car into the lot of the Union Hall where a senior business agent was God. He pulled to a stop as close to the old brick wall as you could get and not knock it over.

"Mason, go inside and wait on me, I got some business to attend to." Conti unwound his huge body from the statement of authority he was driving and stepped outside. As he did the throng chided …

"Carmine, you da' man, you da' man … what's comin' down … any work?" A dozen bedraggled men, young and old, packed around Conti like autograph seekers at a Cubs' game. He was "the man" … he held the keys to job openings in the Gary steel mills. Without him or someone like him, these people didn't stand a chance of getting inside to the big money.

Moto got out of the limo and wanted to dust off and wash up. He wanted away from Conti. He hated money and the people who pushed it. He made his way to the building and up the cracked brick sidewalk and inside to the dimly lit lobby complete with a receptionist with an attitude the size of six-foot high barbed wire fence.

He glanced at the dark haired, razor eyed girl long enough to dodge a murderous glance that shot his way. He turned and sat in the corner on a World War I leather couch with several fatal cuts running haphazardly across the seat.

Feels like home.

Moto sat down to wait as ordered.

What the hell am I doing here? I'm married to another dirt bag and I need to move on. I don't need his crap. If I wanted to be told what to do I'd have stayed in the Corps. I need the hell out of here.

The door swung open and slammed around and against the wall where Moto sat. He jumped and ducked.

"Well that got ya' Mason, get in here," Carmine Conti always made a grand entrance. He was also always in charge. Moto stood and stomped into an office the size of Renova.

"Come over here and sit down Marine. I got somethin' ta' tell ya ' … now!"

He wasn't used to anyone challenging him and he wasn't going to start getting used to it now.

A reluctant Moto stood, staring … and then moved into position on a chair that was a matched set to the couch in the lobby. The two sat and talked while Conti got to know where his troublesome member came from. Moto wasn't volunteering much but his questioner didn't need much. The Mill was a tough place and he'd seen tough guys before.

"Mason I got a lot of things but one of'em ain't time. So let me give it to you straight. You said you wanted the truth didn't ya?"

"Yea … just give it to me and let me get out of here," Moto gritted out the words like they were ground from glass.

"The truth is that broad you hooked up with has been workin' around this Mill for years and screwin' up guys' lives." Conti didn't blink and he didn't take his steel blue eyes off Moto for a second.

Moto struggled mightily to keep a lid on the anger fighting to erupt into a volcanic response to the man delivering the painful truth to one too well acquainted with pain.

"How many times you been married? This ain't your first screw up," Conti chided the young man he really wanted to help. Moto reminded him of himself shortly after he returned from Korea; hate filled and full of venom that spelled trouble everywhere he went.

Moto took a deep breath … "This is my third marriage."

"My God how old are you Mason," came the startled reply from the big Italian trying to help his alter ego.

"Thirty." Moto aimed a quick and deadly response direct from the tough kid who fought with his old man. He was a kid again and his Dad, if you could call him that, was putting him down for the umpteenth time in his young life.

Conti sat bolt upright so fast it startled Moto who tensed, eyes becoming slits and fear racing to attention like it did so many times ten years ago in the DMZ.

"Here's how it's gonna' be. You get one more chance with me Mason … and you know why?" Conti stared through him and didn't leave room for a wiggle.

"You know why you're getting' a chance with me Mason?" His Italian brogue was thickening as he picked up speed. "Semper Fi Mason that's why. Marines are always faithful. God, country and Corps … you remember that don't you Mason?"

Conti hadn't blinked since he started his speech.

Moto sat deep inside a weathered hole in the old leather chair next to a friend he'd never met. He was seething with anger but a flame deep inside sparked to life with the mention of Semper Fi.

This guy actually cares enough to tell me the truth. He's right ... my wife is a dirt bag. Semper Fi ... always faithful ... I wish I could say that ... I wish I were always faithful. One simple thing and I didn't finish the task. One simple letter to deliver and I failed. Shiiit!

"Mason, it's simple. My word is my bond. You get it? My word is my bond. Yours better damned well be when dealin' with me. You got it?"

Suddenly Conti was the DI at Parris Island giving orders to a young man from Renova, Pennsylvania, that saw the Marine Corps as a way out of the poverty and circumstance that was Appalachia.

"Mason, your word … if you want your job. You will give me your word that there's no more fighting. I can cover you when you screw off, when ya' don't work fast enough or maybe even steal somethin' ya' need but clockin' somebody, let alone a supervisor, man I can't fix that."

Conti was almost pleading for sensibility from an angry young veteran not unlike the one he used to see in the mirror years ago when he returned from Korea.

The pride he'd buried under 10 years of disastrous decisions welled up inside the shaved head of Michael Murray Mason. He sat straight up, almost at attention, just like he was facing Sergeant Chada, his Senior Drill Instructor.

"Mason, your word or your job … now that's the truth my new friend." Conti offered a close to the session as he stood, towering over the guy he hoped would give him his word and go and make a life for himself.

Mason snapped to attention, reaching his hand out and across the massive desk that was cluttered with years of clocks, every kind imaginable, collected by Conti as an unexplainable hobby for a man like him.

"Carmine … I appreciate it. You're fair. I want you to know I can't give you my word that I won't drop the next loser that gets in my way. But I won't give you any trouble either; I'm just going to leave. Semper Fi my friend. Thanks. I have another job to do for a fellow I gave my word to years ago."

Conti was not known to ever be speechless but Moto ripped the words from his mouth like a gator grabbing the neighborhood cat. He turned and headed towards the door and for the first time he noticed the 8 x 10 pictures lining the top of the wall by the ceiling. The entire room was lined with pictures of the man … Carmine Conti.

"Mason … your word is your bond … you gave it to me. Not the way I wanted but you gave it to me. I don't know what the hell your problem is but whatever you do … keep your word my friend. Semper Fi."

Moto smiled for the first time he could remember. He turned and nearly bumped into the life-size cardboard cut out of Carmine Conti guarding the door of the big man's office.

Outside he quickly walked past the line of hopefuls hanging out, waiting for the God of the Union Hall to grace them with work. Only then can they go home to the family with news that will lighten the weight of another day. But that wasn't for Moto; he had work to do that had been chasing him for a lifetime.

Mason's Harley was long gone, lost with the hope of a better tomorrow somewhere between Renova, three wives and Gary, Indiana. He walked down the sidewalk heading eleven long blocks to a home apartment that was no longer his.

Lost in thought, he moved along with a new spring in a hobbled step. His years in Vietnam had taken its toll.

I'm out of here. He opened my eyes. I'm so stupid ... but no more. Her and I are history. I just need my rucksack. I haven't done much right; I guess nothin' right in my life. But that wop's right ... I got a word to keep. I have work to do before they cover me in dirt.

37

April 5, 1981
Chicago, Illinois

"Maggie. Maggie. We need to talk."

Bridget O'Reilly wasn't feeling well to begin with and with this news just in from her younger daughter, she was feeling worse.

"Mom, we can talk but you're not changing my mind. I'm not marrying Richard." There was an air of calm assurance like a warm morning breeze wisping in from the ocean that Maggie and her mother loved so much.

"Maggie, you sit down here at the table and talk to me. I am still your Mother and I want to look you in the eye and know why."

It was the same kitchen table at which she had suffered through many a talk growing up in the O'Reilly household. The same lace table cloth, the same huge chandelier and the same china set was placed around the table like it always was throughout Maggie's life. The table no one ever used.

"Why? It's my business Mother. It is my business!"

Maggie was just now standing up to her Mom. She loved her family dearly but she decided some time ago she had a life to live. A life that made her true to herself and the Creator she knew watched over her every move. A life of peace and love … lived her way.

Bridget O'Reilly, fifty eight year old socialite and matriarch of the O'Reilly good fortune wasn't used to not getting her way. Her way was for her youngest daughter to marry Richard Melton, oldest son of her longtime friend Shannon Melton.

"Maggie, your Dad wanted more than anything to see you finally happy and married to Richard. That man is the perfect husband. He has waited years for you Maggie, years."

Bridget was opening the floodgates and letting out years of frustration and now the recent passing of her husband of nearly 30 years had filled the reservoir of sadness to overflowing. In Maggie's mind it was about time for her mother to understand the anguish she'd been through.

"Mother, I am so sorry. I miss Dad as much as you do. But Mother … I am happy. That's what I realized, I am happy Mother."

Maggie wanted so desperately for her Mother to feel what she was feeling, to know how happy she really was and she wanted her to come and put her arms around her like she once did as a kid, when the storms came blowing across Lake Michigan and she would sit scared in the corner of her room.

But it wasn't to be, as the floodgates broke. The bitter poison of a recent widow came gushing into the kitchen where mother and daughter sought to bring heaven and earth together.

"Maggie … you're not happy. You're not even content. You forget that you're talking to your mother. I brought you into this world and know you better than anyone. You've never been happy since you met that … that … farmer, that …"

"Mother, I know you're hurting from losing Dad, we all are. But …

"Don't you tell me what I'm feeling, I know what I'm feeling, anger. This is about you young lady. It's about you and the anger you're causing me. You haven't been our daughter since you took up with that …"

Maggie had been down this old dirt road many times before. She reached across the family table and took her Mother's aging hands in hers. As she did Bridget pulled back abruptly, covering her face and bursting forth in a wall of tears.

"Mother," Maggie said firmly and lovingly as she stood and walked around the table.

Bridget wasn't used to losing control and she wasn't used to being on the receiving end of sympathy from anyone, let alone one of her own breed. Her body tightened as her baby stood behind her, hands resting on her neck, caressing her as she did during her bout with breast cancer just two years ago.

"Mother … I love you. I love you!" Maggie leaned down and placed her head on her shoulder, wrapping her arms around her quivering, frail body.

"Mother, please … we can never let our differences get in the way of the fact we love each other."

The two soul mates were often gladiators in the game of life. The game that was often played by families so deeply in love they missed the smell of sweet friendship that only years of bumps and bruises could deliver. Mother and Daughter were frozen in a grip that words could not unravel.

Their silence gave way to a private meditation that only a mother and daughter could endure; two lives intertwined into one life full of empathy and clothed in misunderstanding only generations could explain.

"Mother, let's go in and sit on the couch like we used to."

The two women, one aging faster than she'd like and one feeling older by the minute walked into the living room they'd shared for untold years. Years that were filled with an unspoken love; yet, love all the same for family, God, country and the movement.

Minutes became hours, and it was dark when Maggie woke up. Sitting on the couch with her Mother's head on her lap, she realized the tables were turned. They had fallen asleep together, only this time Daughter was gently stroking Mother's hair, consoling her in the tragic loss of her life mate who was stolen out from under her by a heart attack in the night.

"Mother," Maggie said, gently pushing the hair from her Mother's peaceful face sleeping quietly beside her.

"Oh, Dear, I'm sorry," Bridget said, sitting up next to her daughter.

The roles were now reversed and life came around full circle.

"Mother, I love you. I am happy. I have the job of my dreams, I just got a promotion, and I have a wonderful apartment. I have you. You're so right about Richard, he would make a perfect husband but it won't work for me. I'm okay Mother. Believe me. I want what you and Father had but it just hasn't happened and I'm okay with it. Please understand me, please?"

Life paired a loving and dedicated daughter struggling for peace and understanding, with a parent who was struggling for the same thing. One heading up the mountain of life, the other descending a difficult cliff on the back end of happiness.

"Maggie, thank you so much for understanding me. Since your Father died, I am so lost, and I wanted you to be as happy as we have been. I finally understand that you are special, just not in the way we intended."

The two embraced in a way that said, ..."*I understand and everything is okay.*"

Maggie stood and walked to the door, stopped and turned to face her Mother who spoke with wisdom that only a mother could understand, "Maggie, it's okay. I will handle it. Richard will find someone he deserves ... and you will find the truth you've been searching for all these years."

The daughter who always felt like the white tie at a black tie dinner finally felt the peace she always sought from the family she loved more than life.

A tear escaped from the corner of her right eye, sliding slowly down her rosy cheek, pulling her mascara in a short dark pattern. A smile slowly lit up the thirty-four year old face of the beauty still in love with a dusty past, long buried in the memories of a nation unwilling to forget and unable to forgive.

"Mother, we'll all be okay and Richard too."

Bridget stood, regaining the strength that carried her through the "movement", a lifetime in the limelight of the expected, two daughters and all that came with raising them, breast cancer and the loss of her husband.

Maggie turned and nearly disappeared from view out the cranberry hued front door when her Mother called out ... "Maggie?"

"Yes Mother," she said turning, silhouetted in the front door.

"Maggie, I know you loved that young man ... Clayton. I want you to know that it's okay with me. I understand. Just make your peace with it someday soon. I love you dear."

"Thanks, Mother."

Maggie ran to her beloved Volvo, jumped inside and cried tears of joy, the tears she hadn't cried in 14 years.

38

November 13, 1982
The Wall
Washington, D.C.

"Moto, you're still whinin' about that letter. That was … hell … that was a lifetime ago man. I'd give you a stamp man but the price went way up since we were in Con Thien."

Cooter hadn't changed a bit. He was still thin and he still looked like Jerry Reed about to belt out a country western song in The Long Branch back in Clyde.

"Don't give me that man; you know it's drivin' me to drink."

Moto had lived with the ghosts of that night long ago since it happened. He was haunted by the ghosts of a guy he couldn't stand but wished with all his heart he was exactly like. He saw in Riggs all that he wished he were.

"My good man it would be a short drive to get you a drinkin' … come on let's take in these ceremonies." Cooter tried to get up but Moto grabbed him by the shoulder pulling him back down next to him.

This pair of special friends sat below Abraham Lincoln and pondered a life gone by. They were brothers of war, bound by the blood of fallen friends. They sat in the afternoon sun, talking, trying to sort out a lifetime of memories that were measured by the time between nightmares. Moto wasn't leaving without a resolution to the nightmare that haunted him the most.

"Look out there, Cooter," he said calmly, pointing towards the Capitol. "See that pond out there with that big tall building reflecting in it?"

Moto leaned against the monument of one of America's greatest, sitting with the one true friend he had in the world. It was the first time since he returned to the world that he felt whole, alive and important. It was the first time since Vietnam he felt he might make a difference in the world.

"That pond? That building? Moto did you just get here? Have you been lost between Nam and PA?"

Cooter hadn't changed in the 15 years since they'd spent hours solving world hunger, debating the issues of the day and killing gooks.

"My friend, you surely know that's the Washington Monument and that pond ... well dude, it's supposed to reflect ... it's the Reflecting Pool."

Cooter gave his lost friend with the bedraggled fu Manchu, shaved head and rock hard air a brief history lesson as the new Vietnam War Memorial swarmed with people preparing for the dedication about to take place. He rolled to his right; leg bent back, intent on getting up and taking on the crowd. Before he could stand, Moto grabbed, reaching up again, this time getting hold of his jungle jacket.

"Not yet," Moto growled like he did so many times before and it brought a grin to the Texan's face, remembering the nature of "Mr. Moto" in days gone by. They'd spent hours on end debating cars, bars, fights and girls.

"Come on man, I wanna' get down there and mix it up," Cooter pleaded.

Moto sat staring straight out into the crowd at the elongated black granite V with the names of over 58,000 lives snuffed out in the prime of their young lives by an evil enemy 10,000 miles from nowhere.

"Cooter, listen to me. I've never done no good in my life. The highlight of my life was being with you and all the guys in the Corps in Nam. I've been miserable ever since. I can't take it no more."

Cooter had long ago buried any demons that followed him home to Clyde in his Nam head like he said before he left. He wasn't about to unlock that closet, but he also couldn't let his friend fall off the cliff of sanity either.

"You're a good man Mike Mason," Cooter surprised Moto with a declaration of an identity he hated.

"Like I told you in Nam, when Vance screwed up and sent Riggsy and the crew in there ... you just gotta' drop it my friend, I put it down a long, long time ago."

As the two lifelong friends sat struggling with the demons of a lifetime ago, a pretty young woman pushing a microphone forward from her tiny tape recorder startled them.

"Pardon me gentlemen, could I disturb you a minute … I'm with the press, I'm from out of town, Chicago actually, and here to cover the dedication for the …"

Before she could finish Moto was on his feet, bounding down the cascade of steps, dodging between the mass of humanity climbing up for their view of the festivities.

"I … I … I'm sorry," the petite strawberry blonde reporter called after the trail of the departing vet disappearing into the crowd.

"Ma'am, you didn't do nuthin' wrong, I assure you. He's just as jumpy as a rattler at the Sweetwater Roundup." Cooter smiled, tipped his black bull rider hat and waddled away in his new Justin boots, chasing his elusive partner and leaving the cutest little lady he'd seen in some time. Standing, Cooter walked into the biggest crowd the man from Clyde, Texas had ever seen.

"Hey … Moto … wait up!" Cooter chased his old patrol leader in, out and around the human bamboo field, not sure if he'd ever see the guy he missed more than he ever admitted to anyone, including the guy in the mirror each morning. He loved that guy to whom he owed his life many times over.

Cooter was out of breath and sure he was out of luck. He walked east along the river. A few yards towards the Washington Monument he noticed Moto sitting at the water's edge, doubled over, hands on the back of his head.

"Hey, where on earth did you go … and why?" Cooter walked closer but the silent figure remained frozen, motionless, lost in time and space. As he neared his side he knew he'd found his friend. He knew from painful experience not to touch the Moto when he was in a "mood." He walked until he was next to his side, sat down, mirroring his friend, and stared out at the water without saying another word.

"Cooter, I got some stuff to say and you're the only one I can say it to." Moto wasn't much for talking and he was even less for caring… but 15 years of misery needed its rightful escape and Cooter, his lifelong friend, was in the crosshairs.

"My friend, when the rattler bites you, you don't chase it man, you stop and get the venom out." Cooter was a Texan with Texas values and a good mom's upbringing. He was all ears; ready to listen to the guy who needed him most.

"Did you ever think we'd be at a place like this Cooter? Did you ever think when we were in the shit out there at Con Thien we'd ever be sittin' here together?"

His friend from Clyde turned to respond but the venom was flowing, the bite was packed full.

"As weird as it is Cooter, this is the best I've felt since I last saw you. The best. I'm just leavin' my 4th wife, I've been homeless for six-months, just gettin' back where I can live inside."

The fleshy wound Moto had been carrying around for over a decade wouldn't close, the poison too powerful for healing in a sentence or two.

"I was ready to give up and end it all when you called and asked me to come here. You know I'll pay you back for that bus ticket up from St. Louis. You know I will. You'll never know what it means to me to sit here with you, my friend."

Cooter turned, looking at his long-lost partner. He couldn't believe that this guy referred to him as "his friend" like he was the only one … or just maybe he was?

"I've thought a lot about suicide. I just can't get my life together. I lost my bike several years ago and hell; I don't even have a driver's license anymore. I can't hold a job. I can't keep a woman. I don't have a lot going Cooter."

Cooter spun sideways, sitting cross-legged, Indian style, chin on his fists and elbows on his knees, ready for a marathon counseling session with a fellow Marine in deep trouble.

"My friend you're hurtin' like you been chasin' cattle til' midnight. Did ya' really think of doin' yourself in?" Cooter inquired with meaning so deep he surprised himself. He was so happy with his life and couldn't relate to someone so far gone he thought of taking his own life.

"Yea Cooter … I could do it. I looked down the barrel of my 45 and just didn't care … bring it on. I didn't want to get up another day. Ever!"

"Moto you don't have that gun over there in that old rucksack of yours now do ya'?"

Cooter grew nervous, knowing that about one more interruption from another fine young lady from the press and there'd be tracers lighting up the sky by the new Memorial.

"Naw, I had to hawk it, gave it to a pawn shop to get money to eat on the way out here."

"Well my good friend, that sure makes your good buddy here breathe just a tad easier. Kinda' like getting' a stone outta' your boot in the middle of a long walk."

Cooter hadn't lightened up on his wisdom one bit with the years that had passed. He loved to pass along his one-liners to anyone in earshot.

"Cooter you might have a stone in your boot but I'm about to put a boulder up your … " Moto turned for the first time with a face looking a lot like he just poured his Mountain Dew all over it. He was sweating like it was August and the day was pretty cool around the Memorial this afternoon.

"Go on good buddy, go on … didn't mean to make light of your pain." Cooter focused in on the eyes, the eyes once made of pure, cold, hard steel were now soft, wet and overflowing with a lifetime of pain he could never imagine. Moto was quietly sobbing as years of pain poured out like a monsoon rain.

It was nearly dark when Moto finished his frightening biography of life in the Mason home. It wasn't a life Cooter could relate to … *why would you treat your children that way, your daughters?* The mere thought of such a history made Cooter want to run home and hug his parents and kiss his lovely wife Sally Jo.

"Cooter, remember the statue over there of the three grunts … the one by the Wall?"

"Of course I do Mote, what about it?"

Cooter wanted to move on, get something to eat and take a break from the avalanche of heartbreak he was trying to dig from the bottom of Moto's life.

"It's their faces man … the guy that did that statue captured the faces … we were just kids. I don't give a shit what you say Cooter about giving it up … I remember that last big deal, the day we lost Riggs, Zip, and all the others. Remember that shit?"

Cooter remembered all too well. But he placed all that in a vault in one of his "heads," locked it in, and threw away the key long, long ago. "Mote, I spent exactly 391 days in country and I decided I wasn't spending 392. I left it there good buddy and you need to leave it here, at the wall … right now."

Moto sat silently, looking at his best and only friend and cried. He sobbed as the sun began to cascade down the western sky. He was crying, tears streaming down the cheeks of the toughest man he knew. It was unnerving to Cooter to think about the weight his old squad leader had been carrying since he saw him last in Nam.

"Remember that kid, Riggsy you called him? He gave me that letter. He gave me that damned letter."

Moto reached inside the tattered side pocket of the Marine rucksack he carried through the battles of Vietnam and the battles he'd fought since then.

"Don't tell me Mote that you actually still have that letter? I was just givin' it to you man, because I just can't believe you still have that letter. I mean let it go man, let it go!"

Moto pulled his hand from inside the pouch and with it came a dirty, crumpled letter from the other side of time. It still had the faded, faint insignia of the 3rd Marine Division in one corner. He handed it to Cooter …

Maggie O'Reilly
121 Fourth Avenue
Apartment 15A

"Well I'll be damned ole' buddy, you can read. I thought you were pullin' one over on me when you said you were still packin' these memories." Cooter sat in total disbelief, mouth open, his Mom would say "catchin'" flies."

He didn't know what to say to his friend about the ancient piece of history he held in his hand. It was plain that this was a major source of torment for his long lost friend.

"Mote, take that damned thing over and leave it at the Wall … you know, beneath Riggsy's name. I saw a bunch of stuff lying' along there. That would be a great thing to do with it. I'll go with you, come on."

Moto sat, staring a hole through his good friend and back at the letter that spanned the bridge of time.

"That's the weanie way out asshole! I don't know why in hell's name I did it but I gave that little turd my word and then he went and died and didn't address it right."

The two veterans, reunited in tribute to fallen comrades, sat, debating into the dark of night like they'd done so many times before. They sat under a lone tree, hours on end and into the night. The fire of hope was rekindled by the breeze of understanding as Cooter tried to console his special friend.

"Good buddy it's gonna' be harder than rasslin' a Brahma bull to find somebody who don't live where she did and you don't even know where that was and on top of it all … my man, its been fifteen years in case you ain't been payin' no attention."

It may have been their greatest debate and it raged past midnight into the dawn of a new day, when only the heartbroken, downtrodden and crazies stayed behind in the area near the Wall.

"Cooter where the hell was this Maggie from?" Moto asked of his learned friend who was trying desperately to stay awake and at attention while he himself was showing no signs of tiring.

"I do remember she was from Chicago but then that's a helluva' big place I understand. Now I haven't been there myself but if it's anything like Dallas you ain't got enough life left to find her. Moto, you don't even know what she looks like."

The 12-pack of Bud the two shared from the trunk of Cooter's 67' Chevy was fueling an unproductive exchange that delivered little in the way of concrete plans and wore the two aging warriors down to ground level. They were shot.

The morning sun rose over the river, Cooter rolled over, cold, pain in every joint as he tried to move. It was then he first realized he'd spent the night on the banks of the Potomac.

"Moto, my main man, this really is like old times. It's a wonder these big city pol-eece didn't kick us outta' here." As he sat up and looked around he realized he'd been talking to himself.

Where in the heck did he go? Man my wife is gonna kill me. I gotta' go n' call her before I lose my happy home. Moto you ...

Standing, looking around, Cooter noticed a thin piece of cardboard nearby with a rock on it. As he walked closer, he saw his name scrawled across the front of the torn piece of wrapper that their beer was so beautifully packed in the night before.

Cooter reached down, tossed the rock aside, picked up the cardboard and began reading the note from his recently departed friend ...

Cooter

Thanks. I want you to know that coming here with you has meant everything to me. I never had family and you and the guys are it, even that turd Riggs.

I don't feel like I ever done no good. I've had more wives than I can count and nothing ever seems to work out when I'm involved. I've had every job you can imagine and got fired from most.

A few years ago an old Marine from the Korean War tried to help me when I got in trouble. He is the first one to ever say 'Semper Fi' to me ... always faithful. It made me feel good but I couldn't tell him. But it meant a lot to me ... it took me back.

Cooter, I don't feel like I've been faithful to no one 'cept you guys in Nam. I don't know nothin' bout God or stuff but a couple times my Mom, when she was sober, made us go to church and for some reason I remember somethin' about penance ... somethin' bout makin' up for all the bad stuff you did ... it was some shit like that and last night it hit me ... do something good before you die.

It came to me last night sittin' here watchin' you sleep ... I was on watch again just like Con Thien. I was still coverin' your Texas ass. I sat there thinkin' about all *we've been through and I realized I got one more patrol I gotta' lead. It's mine.*

That same old Marine gave me some shit about "his word is his bond." I thought it was hokey BS and then I looked at him and I believed what he said ... when all is said and done all we have left is our word. That's the truth my good friend.

Last night I realized that I gotta' do it. I gotta' keep my word to the turd, Cooter. I gotta' do some good and make up for the bad I've done. I gotta' go and keep my word to Riggs and find that broad and deliver this old letter. I just have to.

Thanks my good friend, you're the best. I'm headin' for the bus station downtown. I couldn't sleep so I'll sleep on the bus. I'm changing my ticket from St. Louis to Chicago.

I know you're about to lay some of that Texas sized BS of yours on me. But you know what ... I'm not stateside anymore. I saw the names of my guys over there on that Wall and the thousands of others that got zipped up in body bags and sent home to be heaped on the pile of misery from Johnson and McNamara and I knew I needed one more patrol, I don't care how long it takes either Cooter. I can't sleep until I do what I must.

Well my friend, I've never wrote this much stuff in my life. Always hated to write. Don't know what tomorrow will bring, don't know what'll eat or where I'll sleep or who's gonna' jump outta' the bushes ... just like Nam my friend. I'm home and I feel great again.

Keep your head up, take care a that good lady of yours, they're pretty tough to find, 'course I foundem' then ran'm off. Keep movin' my friend, never quit fightin' the battles worth winnin'.

I've never told a guy this before, not sure I told a woman. But the time here at the Wall made me realize I think I can say I love ya' brother and welcome home.

Don't take it wrong. I mean it in a good way I'm not one of those guys.

Always remember there's a body bag with all our names on it … just a question of who's gonna' zip it up …

Semper Fi
Your friend,
Mote

Cooter sat in the same spot where he'd held the eternal debate with his departed soul mate of war. Dumbfounded. Speechless. He didn't know what he felt other than the pain in his neck, a neck sore from a night on the ground in the nation's Capital. He grinned to himself looking at the note Moto scribbled on the flap of the torn container. He was always crazy but never before was he more right than now.

My main man has a heart after all.

39

November 10, 1985
Hope, Indiana

It was a gorgeous fall day in southern Indiana. The hint of the coming winter danced in the late morning air as Maggie O'Reilly, or as thousands knew her from her growing Chicago Tribune audience, Midge Madigan, raced up and down the rural roads of Hoosier land to a past she had just begun to accept.

Hope was like her memories of Clay, frozen like a winter ice sculpture she would see on her weekend getaways to Wisconsin, in a time when love conquered all. She slowed her new 1986 Volvo Sedan to the lawful thirty-five mile per hour speed limit on Route 9 heading into the village, passing Hauser High School, new since Clay graduated from Hope High the last year before it was closed.

Don't ever speed coming into Hope, Maggie.

Maggie was surprised at the smile creeping across her attractive thirty-eight year old face as she heard Clay telling her to watch out. She laughed out loud hearing him describe the one policeman the town had and his part-time sidekick the kids were fond of calling "Barney Fife."

The years since landing her dream job at the Trib had been difficult ones for Maggie. They were years absent the smiles and laughter that usually filled their home. Maggie still felt the loss of her Dad, dying from a massive heart attack in January of 1981.

The tragic death of Clayton and then the loss of her father made the coverage of the dedication of the Vietnam Wall in Washington very hard.

Maggie slowed at the Moravian Church on Main and eased her pride and joy into downtown Hope. She turned right on Washington Street, wanting to cruise past Hope High, where Clay played on the Red Devil basketball team, and made some memories of his own. The building still stood and she couldn't help but think it was in pretty good shape for being as old as it was.

Doubling back around, Maggie punched the throttle and her Volvo accelerated past the Town Square and took a right on Main Street, Route 9 heading toward the Riggs's farm. It was a Technicolor ride for Maggie, remembering Little Haw Creek and Haw Creek and just where to turn on 800 North and then the short ride to heaven.

I can't wait to see Lucy ... even Homer and Bob, how could I forget Bob. I hope they're all okay? I know it's been awhile.

Maggie had been busy building a new life and putting the old one behind her. Dealing with the loss of her Dad and now her Mom's fate hadn't given her much time to think about what might have been.

Heading out 800 she crossed the rolling hills and the words of Bridget's doctor still echoed in her ears.

"Your Mother has 2 to 3 months to live. We've done all we can."

She could feel the pain of those words cutting like a dull knife into what was left of her heart as she turned right down the dirt road that led across the Haw Creek and up to the tree shrouded house that was the Riggs family farm. Turning left into the dirt driveway, with the barns to her right she noticed Bob didn't come out to greet her as he always did.

I guess it's been so long he might be gone.

Maggie got out of her Volvo, now covered with a thin coat of Indiana dust from the trip out of town and walked the few short steps to the door. The swing Homer and Lucy loved to share still hung on the aging, paint starved porch where she now stood.

After several knocks she could hear someone moving inside. She had a sudden feeling that there was more that was different here than Bob missing, and the place looking like it needed more than a little TLC.

An aging Homer shuffled to the door looking like getting there was a whole day's work. Maggie was struck by the distant, hopeless look he wore like a bad Sunday suit. Homer was in shock when he stared at his painful past. Gaining his composure, he surprised even himself when he took Maggie by the hand and sat on the front porch swing he'd shared with his life mate for nearly forty years.

This unlikely pair sat and rocked away a cold fall day for over an hour. Maggie was touched as the aging country gentleman who was sure this nice young lady killed his only son, placed his hand on her shoulder and comforted her as she struggled to accept that she was losing her mother and she'd already lost the little lady she'd stopped by to see. Lucy had passed away a year before.

Beth was away at school in Bloomington. The home place was quiet, the life it had always known was long gone but the peace and serenity remained as it always would.

Maggie was shaken, numb and deeply touched as she maneuvered her car back on to route 800, reversing her course, heading back into Hope and praying for better times ahead.

Hope? How ironic. It's times like these we don't seem to have any hope and here I am heading into Hope. I only hope that some day I can make sense of my life. Maybe even find hope ... no, truth, in all its splendor. Maybe one day?

Maggie O'Reilly had to hold on to the steering wheel with both hands to keep from shaking as she turned on to Route 9, the road that would take her to Hope for the very last time.

I can't believe she's gone. I can't believe I didn't return his call when he called last year. I remember it now. I remember a note saying 'Homer called'. What an idiot I am. I'm running my life so fast ... what am I running from? Truth? I don't know anymore? Oh, Lucy, I am so sorry I couldn't be there for you. I am so sorry.

Back in town she wheeled slowly past the Norman Funeral Home on Main Street and couldn't help but notice their sign which read 'Established 1880'.

That's truth ... they've been here forever.

Maggie also knew that the truth was that they were the one's who conducted the funeral that wasn't really a funeral. That was the truth Homer still insisted was the case for his only son, Clay. He was sure of it.

Oh I have to let that go. I can't start those thoughts up again.

As she drove along the words of Big Sis' came rushing in ...

Don't go there kid. You know better.

And she did know better. Maggie's life was falling into place, she was comfortable living it as a columnist, living her dream and living in Chicago. She was also comfortable living it alone.

She turned right on Locust Street next to the Moravian Church, easing her pride and joy west towards the oldest cemetery in Indiana.

It's all just the same as I left it. It's exactly like the day when we had the service for Clay. I can feel it. I can feel him. He's here.

She eased the Volvo along the two dirt paths that served as a road in and around the cemetery. This wasn't just history for Maggie and the Riggs family; word had it around town that this cemetery was where John Henry Kluge, the first white child born in Indiana, was buried.

It's so comfortable ... this town ... this place. It's odd to feel that driving in a cemetery. But that is Hope, where even the cemetery is comfortable.

I'm glad I saw Homer and sad I will never see Lucy again. She could have helped me bring closure to my life and my feelings. I have so many feelings anymore with losing Dad, now Lucy and Mom struggling, Beverly and I will have a lot to talk about after this.

Winding her way through the history of hundreds who had gone before her, Maggie couldn't help but think about her own trials. She and Beverly had lost their Dad and now Bridget the wonderful mother she had certainly had her share of struggles with, had challenges she couldn't overcome.

Bridget O'Reilly had breast cancer. It wasn't her first bout with a killer more devastating and far reaching than the killing in Vietnam. They didn't zip the victims in body bags or write about them in the paper but they were ripped from their families early in life in a different kind of war story that came with the same ending.

It's so unfair. It's so hard to lose your parents even when you know it's bound to happen and even when you know it's coming. It's still very hard to cope with.

Maggie pulled along Maidens Creek and turned towards the grave of the man she gave her heart to long ago. She stopped in front of the little rock garden along the creek. She reached up and switched off the engine, the quiet hum gave way to stone cold silence.

I have to sit here. I have to think. I have to soak it all in one more time. I have to think. I have to close this chapter in my life. Oh, how I don't want to close it but I must. I love you Clay.

Maggie sat in the sleek vehicle she'd worked hard to afford. She'd given her all to her job and she traveled far to make a difference by touching people with the columns she wrote. She would soon kneel next to the man who had touched her more than anything she could write or say.

She sat in the car, hands cupping her wet face, head bowed, sharing a piece of history with hundreds she didn't know. Maggie came to pay tribute to a lady who gave birth to the man she loved. She came to give her love to the man whose only existence was now acknowledged by a gravestone and an empty casket.

Okay, I just want to get through this and talk with Clay and get to Cincinnati for my meeting tomorrow. God I know you can get me through this like you have everything else. Please?

Maggie opened the door and stepped out into the crisp autumn air. Leaves blanketed the grass much like the day 16 years ago when she last walked this hallowed ground burying an empty box a government far away swore contained the life of the man the world knew as Clayton Wesley Riggs, Private First Class, United States Marine Corps.

Right up there ... on that little rise above the cave stood six Marines who shattered her young life as they fired a volley of bullets honoring a fallen comrade they'd never met and didn't know. God it still hurts ... I can still hear those shots ... it hurts so very much. My soul hurts and my heart aches once every day and sometimes a thousand times. I can still feel little Beth next to me, under my arm, crying for her big brother.

Maggie shook her head from side to side in what was a lifelong effort to shake the trance that followed her like a pitiful little stray dog that hadn't eaten in days and wanted nothing more than to be saved from uncertainty. Walking around the front of the black sedan that represented her working world, she headed for the headstone that represented the man she loved and lost.

A simple goodbye is all that I want to accomplish. God I know you can get me through this, I know you can. I just want to say one last goodbye to my love.

Maggie O'Reilly stood; staring at the headstone that proclaimed this was the resting place of Clayton Wesley Riggs. It was a simple, white stone flanked by two gray stones on either side. One on the left not yet used, one on the right now filled with the wonderful little lady she'd just found out had passed to the next life, too.

What did it all mean? This is just society's way of saying that a person known by that name had passed this way between these dates as we measure time. It's not their life. It's not them. His body is not in that casket. I don't even know if he's dead.

Maggie O'Reilly had learned to control herself like her Mother did so very well. What she hadn't learned was the answer to the question that plagued her all her life.

Is this truth? Is this all there is? Was Peggy Lee right when she sang 'Is That All There Is?' It can't be. Truth has to be more than this, doesn't it? There's lot's more than this ...

Feeling uncomfortable standing as she was at the foot of an empty grave, Maggie looked nervously around. Time stood perfectly still, the breeze stopped, birds quit singing and Maggie nearly stopped breathing. She stood, a symbol of love and commitment, in the chilly air of November 10, 1985. It was the Marine Corps' Birthday; a date of honor and celebration and a date Maggie O'Reilly never knew existed.

Alone, Maggie knelt first on one knee, then the other, facing the headstone of the man that represented the life she so desperately wanted to spend all of her life with. She took off her gloves, placed her hands together in front of her and began to talk to the only man she allowed into her heart and ever let enter her life.

God I'm not very good at this prayer stuff although you know I try. I don't know what all this means or why I'm here after all these years. But I do know I love the man we both know as Clayton Wesley Riggs. I also loved his Mom. I would give anything for the life of either one but I know that I must give it to you. I must let it go.

God I need to talk with Lucy. Lucy, I am so sorry I got so busy I didn't know you were gone. I am so sorry. I would have been here to honor you the way I know you would be for me. I am so sorry. I live my life with you in my thoughts and with your example of how to love and how to live in my heart. Thank you Lucy.

Maggie O'Reilly was experiencing truth through the man she'd come to know better than any other. He was the man of her life now, the one who never left her and made a lifetime of hurt bearable. It was God. She had come to know God thanks to Lucy Riggs.

Lucy, you are like my other Mom. You always accepted me for who I was, not what I did or who I should be. You always made me feel better just by sitting down and being with me. I will be always grateful for you and all the talks we secretly held on the phone. I wanted to talk with you about my Mom.

Lucy, she has cancer again and they told us it's just months and she'll be gone and I don't know what to do. I still have Beverly but we lost Dad awhile back and ... and ... well Clay, I've never married, Lucy, because of Clay. I know there is no one for me except him.

That is why I knew I had to talk with you ... you would make me feel better. I knew you would make everything okay. I knew if I came to you I would know. I would know the truth.

Maggie knelt on the cold ground of the oldest cemetery in Indiana talking with her best friend for more than over an hour. The day turned from chilly to cold as the afternoon sun dropped slowly in the western sky.

Lucy, I am kneeling before Clay's resting place and I need to have you put your arm around me and tell me it's all going to be okay. Everything will work out ... just like before. That is what you always did for me Lucy and I need you now. That is why I came here today, to talk with you. But I am so sorry that you are gone, I didn't know. I hope you'll forgive me.

Maggie was startled by a warm, gentle breeze that lightly touched her quivering body. Deep in prayer she opened her eyes, looking around. She was alone with a warm breeze on a cold day, connecting with God and the two special people she loved. She bowed her head and closed her eyes one last time.

Lucy ... thank you. Clay, I will always love you, you know that don't you? I know things will work out. I know you got my letters and I only hope that wherever you are you know that I love you ... forever.

Maggie got into her Volvo and turned the key to the car that now meant nothing more than a way to get to her appointment in Cincinnati. She smiled looking at the headstone of the lady that just surrounded her with a warm love she'd never known before. She was a lady who meant more than the world to her through all the years of her trials.

Maggie O'Reilly drove off leaving Hope, Indiana in her rear view mirror yet knowing hope would never leave her. She didn't know what truth was for sure but she did know that Lucy Riggs was part of it.

I know that was her that touched me. I talked with words and she talked with feeling. I know it's okay now. She went ahead to look after Clay and meet my Mom. She is there to take care of her when she arrives. She will be there with Clay to meet me when I arrive, whenever God sees fit to take me from this life.

How silly Beverly would say, just like she said it was silly of me to give that short, little bearded Vietnam Vet outside of work the money I did every time I saw him ... I don't care, it's right to do that. Sure Lucy was a simple, farm lady from a small town who could care less about money. Mom is a sophisticated, educated high society type who loves her money and notoriety but ... where we're going differences won't matter. Maybe that's truth?

"Cincinnati 10 Miles."

The sign read.

Goodness, where have I been?

Maggie drove along lost in a world she visited and needed to leave behind.

Oh my gosh, I didn't spend anytime with Clay? Oh ...

Maggie had a strange feeling, a warm breeze in a car traveling at 50 miles per hour on a rural road. She reached up to turn the heat off and realized she hadn't turned it on. She smiled …

Thanks God ... I know everything will be okay.

40

October 31, 1992
Clyde, Texas

The Church bells rang the usual chimes, at least that's all Cooter ever thought they were. He and his wife Sally Jo walked out of the First Baptist Church at 216 Austin Avenue in Clyde as they had for the past 20 years, arm in arm.

"I love you," Sally Jo said, looking up with the eyes of a newlywed in spite of the twenty-year marriage they had just celebrated with a dinner and night out in Abilene the night before.

Cooter smiled and walked his bride to the pickup truck, opening her door and then walking back around the car for the drive out to the ranch.

Cooter and Sally Jo hadn't changed much in all those years, especially the love part. They were like Clyde, it didn't change much either. They had spent all their days in town and liked it that way.

Legend had it that Clyde, a town of somewhere around 2400 people, was born during the railroad era in the late 1880's. The railroad workers, as the story goes, congregated at Robert Clyde's construction camp and spawned what was now Clyde, Texas.

Clyde sat eight miles east of Abilene and 5 miles west of Baird in the panhandle of Texas, an area known for the extremes. It was either a bitter cold, snow blinding winter or a parched desert, with temperatures that made an egg fry on US 80; a favorite right of passage for the young folks in town with little else to occupy their time.

"Ya' know Sally Jo, I love you too."

Cooter put the big Ford F-100 in gear and turned out of the drive as he'd done for years and headed out on old US 80 to the little ranch they'd called home since cashing out of the Long Branch two years ago.

"Lets go out to Lake Clyde Hon, you love to fish and it's a nice day?" Sally Jo was made for Cooter. She loved whatever he loved and he loved fishing for pan fish and bass. "That'll make a perfect anniversary. Abilene last night and fishing today."

Sally Jo always wanted to be on the run.

Cooter thought it was a little hot, even for this time of year in west Texas but he wasn't about to turn down his 'Hon' and he wasn't about to turn down fishing.

The lovebirds drove along, holding hands and smiling as they often did, passing time together. At the gate to their "gentleman's ranch," Cooter turned and stopped at the cattle guard swing gate crossing the dirt lane heading home.

"Guess we better be checkin' the mail. We've been gone a couple days over there."

Sally Jo got out and walked to the barn size mailbox Cooter installed the day they closed on the house. It had a huge American flag they would put up so Jimmy Sue Taylor, his old friend from high school and long time postman, wouldn't miss the mail when they sent out the monthly bills.

It was the end of the month so Sally Jo had a handful of envelopes and a strange look when she climbed back up in the big truck Cooter loved as much as fishing.

"What's up with the funny face Hon'?" Cooter pried before she could sit her still petite and slim five-foot frame securely in the seat.

"Well, we got a letter here from over at the Long Branch. Looks like Billy sent it on over … says something on here about 'Moto'?"

Before Cooter could say anything Sally Jo was digging deeper into the small stack of mail she'd retrieved from the big box.

"That ain't that guy that kept you out all night in DC is it?" Nervously, she held up the envelope for him to see as they sat in the Ford. Cooter reached out and took the well-worn piece of mail from his wife's hand.

Cooter read the address …

Cooter
C/o the Long Branch
Clyde, Texas
79510

"Well I'll be dogged. That snakes been under that rock for a long, long time."

Cooter couldn't contain himself and neither could Sally Jo who knew what the distant past did to the man she'd spent twenty years trying to keep in line and bury it. Looking at his wife, full of fear and concern, Cooter reached over and gently grabbed her by the neck; giving her the gentle squeeze he'd been reassuring her with for two decades.

"Hon', Sally Jo … we're goin' fishin'. Let's just change clothes, I'll read what the mad man has to say and we're outta' here … this is our day."

Inside their two-bedroom bungalow Sally Jo walked with the bounce once again in her step knowing Cooter was keeping his promise. She dropped her Sunday handbag on the kitchen table and disappeared into the bedroom.

Cooter sat down at the table and carefully opened the letter he never thought he'd get. A letter from Moto was not something anyone expected to receive, least of all him.

October 1992

Cooter,

Bet you never thought you'd hear from me? Me neither. Hope this finds you down there in cowboy land and doin' great. Seems like a lifetime ago we were together at the Wall in DC. Sure hope that little wife of yours forgives you and me both for keeping you out all night.

Well, let's get to it. I've been tryin' to get my shit together since I saw you. Can you believe it? Me? Moto? Tryin' to be better and do somethin' good?

To be truthful, ever since I saw you and that wife and every time I close my eyes I see that turd Riggs, I'm ashamed of who I am. Been married more times than I can remember and don't want to either.

One good thing I did was not have kids. I just knew after my time as a kid I'd never be a good dad so I wasn't about to do that to another kid ... that is what happened to me you know. Just couldn't do it.

When I left you buddy I took that bus to Chicago and been here ever since. I still struggle but things are okay I guess. I'm learnin' can you believe it, me learnin'. Your Texas wisdom is finally sinking in.

Cooter sat in the kitchen he shared with his sweetheart and he couldn't believe what he was reading.

Man alive ... what's this guy up to? What's he talking about. Wonder if he found a damned stamp for that letter yet?

"Ya ready yet Hon'?" Sally Jo called from down the hall.

"Just a second Sweet Pea, I think Moto's gonna' be sealin' this letter with a kiss."

Cooter scooted up to the table and flipped over to the next page.

Where have I been? Well, here in Chicago but doin' all kinds of things. Worked for Pepsi & Coke ... Wrigley's, you know them gum people.

I did okay for a while and never found the broad of Riggs to give the letter to. But Cooter, I still got it. More on that later but I got an idea Buddy.

I don't really have an address, I just move around. It's a tough city but Con Thien got me ready for it. Livin' here in the city, I'm outside but it ain't bad, at least in the summer. Winters are tough though.

I had an apartment for a while but the last year or so has been tough, work is hard to find and I'm 'temping' now, that's what they call it when they screw you out of benefits.

I coulda' used those too, was out on the streets for about 9 months and this guy I knew from Pepsi let me come and clean up every week at his place. Worked out pretty good though.

Anyway, 'bout 3 months back I got these pains in my left arm, man did it hurt, this guy, he said 'get to the hospital'. Don't have any money but guess it don't matter no more cause they took me in. Heart attack.

Nothin' big, they fixed me up and I was on my way. Anyway, wanted to get in touch and bring ya up to speed on your old Buddy. With winter coming don't know how I'll fair this time around so wanted to thank you for changing my life.

Sound funny coming from me? Bet it does. The guy from Renovo gettin' smart. I'm hardly smart. I mean truth is if I had a trailer you could call me trailer trash but ... I don't. Maybe I'm bridge trash? There's one for you Buddy. I live under a bridge in downtown Chicago, not far from the big newspaper building.

Hey man it ain't bad. I found this mattress and a couple of wooden boxes. Got me this little bedroom under there. You know me; I'm mean enough everybody stays away, just like Nam.

Everyone stays away but this one woman. Nice lookin' lady, maybe mid-forties, short hair, business suit type ... works at that newspaper. I was out there one day when I was really down and out and she asked me if I was a vet.

She gave me twenty bucks. Now she always gives me somethin' when I bump into her, which isn't often, but she seems nice anyway. Long way from that day at the Wall huh? Remember when I wanted to clock that newspaper broad. I thought one day it might even look a little like her.

Anyway Buddy, hope you're doin' good and that kid of yours is growin' up good like you. Wanted to say I've had a good life. You changed it Buddy.

I can still hear you tellin us your BS and I finally realized it ain't BS after all. I went in the library to get some stuff to write you and figure out how to get this down to you. They were real nice and I started goin in to *stay warm and started reading. A Mason readin' ... can you imagine?*

Anyway, this is getting way too long for me and you. I know I'm borin' the shit outta you but here goes. Cooter, I really miss ya and wish you the best. I read this book, this guy Og Mandino. It was called The Choice. It's about making 'the choice'.

I realized I did Cooter. I made the choice he was talkin about. The lady at the library told me to read it and I laughed. Then somethin said to me 'read it'. Can't explain it good Buddy and don't think I'm gettin soft on ya either. I just knew I needed to read it.

I still got that damned letter from that kid Riggsy. I came here from DC and didn't know how to find anyone who I don't know anything about. I've carried his damned letter in my old rucksack (still got it) for 25 years now and it's time. I made 'the choice'.

I woke up a couple days back and rolled over to see the newspaper headline and realized that I have to do it now. So you don't think I've gone completely over the edge, I don't read the paper everyday I was just wrapped up in it like I usually do and happen to see this article.

Anyway good Buddy, I see this headline about this delegation that is being sent to Nam from Washington. I don't remember exactly what the hell they're doin' but our government Cooter is sending people over there to look for the dead that didn't come back I guess. They even want to open up relations with those gooks. It hit me like one of those 140 rockets that used to shake our world ... I gotta' do the letter now.

Then I remembered some articles I see in the paper by this woman here at the Tribune newspaper. She writes about Nam. Don't know why a broad is writing about Nam but I see it in there. (I read now you know, ha ha) I also use the Trib to wrap up in good buddy – it's a helluva lot colder here than in Clyde.

Since I'm livin' near the Tribune and I get chased away from there by the Security Guard every time I hang out, I decided I'd give it to him and let him give it to this broad. Her name is Midge Madigan. Ever heard of her? Probably not down there in Clyde. Don't imagine you get much news down there now do ya?

So that's it good Buddy. The choice. Mission will be accomplished even if it took me a damned lifetime. Never got a damned stamp but am going to be 'the postman' myself and then I can rest. I can lie down on my mattress at the bridge and know I done my best ... all because of you good Buddy. I'm finally gonna' do good.

It's been real. It's been good. My life wouldn't be the same without you, without Con Thien. I was sure I was comin' home in a body bag. Zip. But hey ... look at me. Still standin'.

Cooter, you'll always mean a lot to me. This sounds weird and well, I'm sure to you and Sally JO my life seems terrible. Don't you take it that way. Things have been good the last few years since I saw you and all because of you.

I still enjoy bangin' a few heads but a good book at the library on a cold day ain't bad either. You're the best. Don't know what this winter will bring. It's damned cold here and newspapers ain't very good below about 20 degrees so we'll have to see what I can scrape up.

In case we never see each other again, want you to know you're the man. Cooter, you're the man. Give the kid a hug and that little woman of yours too.

Mission accomplished ... soon,

Semper Fi,
Your Bud

Moto

PS: (learned that 'ps' over at the library my friend) Take it in the right way but I do love ya ... and that's the truth.

Sally Jo walked out into the kitchen so see her husband sitting in stunned silence. He looked up, tears streaming down his cheeks, a grin creeping across the face she loved to kiss.

"Sally Jo... come here and sit on my lap. I gotta' hug for you from Moto ... I love you babe ... forever."

41

December 20, 1992
Chicago, Illinois

"Hey … I told you before … get away from here, now!" Screamed the security guard at the Tribune.

It was nearly midnight on a cold, cold Chicago night. The city crews were out trying to clear the streets of the newly fallen snow before the Monday morning rush hour.

"I know, I know … just hear me out." Moto wasn't sure why he was coming to this guy. He always gave him a hard time and had a heart as cold as the winter wind howling the streets of Chicago. He should have tried the guy on days that treated him decent. This guy, the night guard who just came on duty was in no mood for drifters or war wannabes.

"Buddy, I'm calling the police unless you get off my doorstep. Now get out of here. Now!"

There was a day Moto would have taken the guy down but between the years he'd spent on the street, the heart attack and Og Mandino … he wasn't up to a confrontation. He had a mission to complete and that's all that mattered to the tough guy from Renova.

"Man I don't know why I'm coming to you but something tells me you can help and I have a mission to complete. You gotta' help me and I'll go and never come back." Moto fought what was once his nature and pleaded for help, pulling the hood of the old parka he'd been lucky enough to get in the last shelter, off his head so the guy could get a better look.

"Help with what?" The guard replied with a mountain of indignity covered with a lifetime of pain and attitude.

"That woman that writes here, Midge Madigan. Ever see her? Moto inquired, all the while spewing a deep cough that resonated from the painful cold that had settled in his chest.

"I don't talk about people that work here."

Moto was freezing, parka, hood and all. The pain throbbing in his chest was nothing compared to the pain ricocheting around inside his aching head. His fever caused him to sweat like a racehorse at the end of the Derby. Then, in the next minute he'd freeze when the wind whipped around and in and out of the maze of buildings that surrounded him.

"Come on man … it's a mission I've worked a lifetime to complete. You gotta' help me. I gotta' get this letter to her." Moto wasn't used to begging and this guy wasn't used to helping.

"What's this mission stuff?" questioned the security guard.

Moto stood in the wind, snow racing by his head like he was in a wind tunnel by mistake, as he explained his life on Con Thien and his need to deliver his letter, a message from a lifetime ago. Moto had never before spoken of Nam to a single person outside of Cooter.

He reached in his old rucksack and pulled out the tattered letter from a young kid to a young girl back home during the Vietnam War.

"Man, all I'm askin' is you give this to the woman who writes that stuff about Nam. Maybe she can do something with it. I have to deliver it."

"Why her?"

Moto was learning patience but he was suddenly done with twenty questions. He was done with everything. He didn't know why, he just knew something was telling him to do it.

"Look man, just take it to her and you're done, that's all I'm asking. I'm doin' good by keeping my word … now do your part."

Moto was a desperate man and didn't know why but he did know it must be done. He knew he felt worse now than during his heart attack and that was saying something. He stood, arms wrapped around his chest, bare hands under his armpits, waiting for a response from a guy he couldn't stand.

"Were you in Nam, man? Come on I'm freezin' here. Take the damned letter and give it to that Madigan woman, that's all I'm asking you." Moto was getting to the end of his rope for pleading with little tin soldiers. He was feeling worse by the second and needed to lie down soon.

"Look at me … I'm seventy years old. I wasn't in Nam but my kid was and it messed him up."

Moto took a deep breath and took his last shot.

"Then you know about pain and commitment. You might know about love? I made a commitment. Don't ask no questions. Deliver this letter for me and let me have peace. I ain't no damned wannabe' I'm the real thing."

Moto took the tattered envelope, reached out and pushed it towards the Guard.

"Take it" Moto said handing him the treasure he'd carried since that fateful day on Christmas Eve of December 1967.

Turning, Moto walked around the corner before he could hear anymore from the man he'd entrusted to deliver on a promise from forever. The guard was visibly shaken. He came face to face with his past; with a son lost forever in a war that made no sense and now an ugly part of history is resurrected all over again by a drifter with a cause.

He looked down at the envelope.

Maggie O'Reilly
121 Fourth Street
Apartment 15A

What kind of an address is that? What is this ... is this a joke? Naw, can't be it looks real. What harm could it do? Madigan writes that stuff all the time, I'll just give it to her...

Moto had unknowingly helped another man, an aging bitter man, keep his word too and do something good along the way.

Moto walked away as quickly as his condition would allow, hoping upon hope his effort would help warm him up. He wanted to feel strong and young again. He wanted to get away before the cranky guard could change his mind. He wanted to make a difference.

As he walked he felt better than he had in years. Reaching the Michigan Avenue Bridge that provided cover for his home, he climbed down the circular concrete steps to his resting place. He was home. He was careful not to slip on the snow blowing up and under the horizontal 'v' formed by the street above and the cement plates covering the land below the bridge.

Secure in the home of the homeless, Moto crawled up on his mattress and lay on his side, facing the inside of the cement structure. The wind howled at his back, the cold air attacking every open spot on his body. He shivered, teeth chattering and fever shooting through his skull like nails in a coffin.

I did it. I did it. I wish I could see Riggsy again. Say Riggsy, I did it man. Cooter I did it. I wish I could meet that lady that writes that stuff, see her face ... ah ...

Michael Murray Mason had done good. He accomplished the task he set out to do. He was good in Nam, he was a great Marine and he was good in life, finally. He kept his word to another Marine. Semper Fidelis ... *Always Faithful.*

I can see him. I can see his face. He didn't deserve to die. That Lieutenant didn't know his ...

The cold invaded like the NVA on a bad night at Con Thien. The snow swirled around his sick body like a sand storm in a wind swept desert. Moto lay motionless, drifting off to another place and another time and another era.

Riggs. You didn't deserve what you got. Me? I should have got it but you ... truth be known I wish I were you. You were good and I was no good. You wanted to do good and I wanted to make fun of you. You done good ...

The night wore on and so did the early winter taking over the city, draping it with a frozen blanket of misery.

I'm not hurting as bad. I'm not coughing. I, I don't hurt at all. If I stay still I'm not dizzy. The tunnel. The tunnel is back. I feel like I'm drifting down that long tunnel. Oh man here I go. Cooter, Riggsy, Zip ... Vance, you asshole.

It was early for Chicago temperatures to dip this low but ten degrees below zero blared out of the bank clock on the corner above the street leading to the bridge that housed a former Marine clinging to life and the end of a lifelong mission.

I'm okay. Dad ... you were wrong, wrong. The Marines were right. I'm okay. I done good. I made good and I kept my word. Is there a God? I don't know but I'm okay ... I did it. I did it Cooter. I told you I would. I ...

The cold won the battle on this bitter night.

42

December 21, 1992
Chicago, Illinois

"Good Morning Ms. Madigan. How are you today?" Pat Norris the daytime security guard at the Tribune building knew Maggie by her pen name. He also knew her since the day she came to work for the Trib and wasn't the big shot she was today.

Maggie was one of only a couple of people working there who took the time to acknowledge that security guards were human beings. Most of the people there just rushed in and out with no more than a grunt at lowly people like Pat.

"Pat I'm great … except the weather. It's so coooold this morning." Maggie answered politely; smiling and exaggerating her motions to the man she'd come to know as more than a $5 an hour uniform.

Chicago was experiencing an early and bitterly cold winter. The city was blanketed with a new four inches of snow and the morning was just waking up after an ugly and bitter night.

"I feel so bad for the homeless, Pat. I hope there are enough shelters. I hope that guy I often see here is okay. There was something about him, he seemed like a nice man. It seemed as though I knew him or had seen him before."

Pat knew the man she was talking about. He hadn't seen him much but remembered his old camouflaged pack, his scraggly Fu Manchu beard, baldhead and eyes. He remembered the eyes.

"Ms. Madigan, I haven't seen him, but I think the guy on night shift, you know him, the fellow I replace?"

Maggie nodded in agreement.

"He said something this morning about a homeless bum outside here last night. I think the guard's still here."

Maggie smiled.

"Pat you're great. You always know what's going on. I probably can't do much but if you see him and he needs help … let me know, okay? I really feel for him, he's a Vet you know!"

She ran inside just as a siren sounded in the street out in front of the Trib. Pat looked up just in time to see a police car stop and block traffic to one lane of the nearby bridge.

Norris got his backup to fill in and walked down the street to the stairwell of the bridge and saw a small crowd gathered near the edge of the bridge. Pat felt something pulling at him, urging him to witness what was happening at the bridge.

"Hey Pat, what brings you over here?" It was one of Chicago's finest, a cop named Buzanoski. Everyone called him Buz. Pat had known him most of the ten years he'd been guarding the day shift at the Trib.

"I could ask you the same thing," Pat shot back at Buz.

"Ah Pat, it's just a homeless stiff down there. Froze to death last night. Gonna' be a tough year to be outside I'm afraid. I'll see ya', I gotta' get this body bag down there."

Buz was matter of fact about his job of picking up the dead. It happened all the time in Chicago. Pat, feeling uneasy witnessing the whole process, walked back to his post at the Trib, as Buz disappeared around the corner of the bridge.

"Here ya' go." Buz slipped in the snow as he ducked underneath the bridge to give his goods to the bod squad as they prepared to lift the body into the bag before carrying it street side.

"Buz … this guys a Vet. He's got a globe and anchor tattoo on the inside of his wrist."

The chatter coming from the paramedic was matter of fact. Buz was a Vietnam vet too, and a fellow Marine and he wasn't going to have just anyone zipping up a fellow Marine.

"No shit," Buz shot back.

"Then let me do the honors boys. He's one of ours."

The two paramedics stretched out the black body bag on the fresh snow. Buz came close and spread the opening as they lifted the body, frozen sideways, into the bag.

Buz reached down and pulled the sides of the bag up, straightening and stretching. Through his black leather gloves he reached down and grabbed the zipper and pulled.

ZZZZZIIIIIIIIIIIPP!

"Just another number, boys, just another number, Buz sighed. "God Bless and Semper Fi my friend … Semper Fi whoever you are!"

43

December 21, 1992
Chicago, IL

Tribune Headquarters

Inside the Chicago Tribune building Maggie O'Reilly, known to the world as Midge Madigan, straightened her hair and brushed out the snow that had accumulated from her talk with Pat.

She turned to walk to the elevators when she heard her name.

"Ms. Madigan, Ms. Madigan."

It was the deep, gruff voice of the third shift security guard. At seventy years of age, he was all the man he once was and then some. But he never talked with anyone, including Ms. Madigan.

Maggie turned, startled by the urgency in his command for attention, she faced the charge of the guard she rarely talked with.

"Yes, what is it?"

"Well … I … eh … I …"

"What is it sir?"

Maggie was the only one who ever called him "sir." He didn't know why that bothered him but it did.

"Well, Ms. Madigan … one of those homeless fella's out here on the street came by last night and he wanted me to give you this letter. I don't know if it's anything but it looked harmless so I told him I would see that you got it. He talked about a mission he had to finish."

Maggie looked at the aging man and noticed a dirty and tired looking envelope he was holding in his hand.

"I hope you don't mind. I need this job but … well … he really wanted you to have this thing and he handed it to me and left."

"That's fine sir, I'll take it." Maggie reached out and retrieved the envelope from his hand and turned it over. She casually looked down at the newly arrived prize.

"OH My God! OH My God!"

Maggie stood frozen like the edges of Lake Michigan, white as the morning snow, mouth wide … gasping as if fighting for her last breath.

"Ma'm … I'm sorry. Are you okay?"

The guard imagined the worst. What had he done?

"Oh my God!"

Maggie looked down and read her own name on the envelope and her old address a world away in Bloomington, Indiana.

"Oh my God!"

As much as she tried she couldn't mouth the words of anything else but cry out to the only man left in her life.

"Oh …"

She turned and ran to the elevators, brushing passersby from her path as she raced to her office.

On the ride to her tenth floor office she held the crumpled, smudged and yellowing letter to her chest. She didn't need to look at it to know the person who'd written it. She knew the handwriting better than her own. The 3rd Marine Division insignia swept the slightest doubt out into the cold Chicago morning.

The bell rang for her tenth floor stop waking her from her trip back in time, a time recently buried under more than two decades of reality.

"Hi Midge … what's wrong?"

She brushed by one of her assistants in a mad dash to her windowed corner office.

"Hold my calls Molly. Cancel my meetings."

Maggie moved double time, closing the door behind her before Molly, her trusted assistant could respond to her surprising early morning tirade.

Inside, coat still on, Maggie O'Reilly stared at her name on the envelope.

Can this possibly be a letter after all these years? Can this never end? Can this be a letter from my beloved Clay? Can this go on forever? God help me, please?

Maggie sat for an eternity staring at the envelope, holding it in both hands, examining it with the eyes of hope and the pain of faith unreturned. Staring. Afraid, afraid of what this beautiful gift may do to her perfect life.

Should I call Beverly? Oh, I can't. I'll ruin her Christmas. I have to open it. I have to see what it really is ... I know it can't be, but yet I know it is ... a letter from Clay. It was a letter from the other side of time and back home to eternity.

Maggie picked up her ivory handled letter opener, and carefully began to cut the top of the envelope. She knew it was twenty-five years old and she didn't want to disturb it. If it really was Clay's ...

Is it? Can it be Clay's? It's his handwriting I know it. I just know it. But how can it be?

... The top of the envelope had a handwritten *Free*; Maggie's heart raced as she reached inside and gently removed the pages of a letter that took twenty-five years to deliver.

Oh my God it's true. It's true.

Her hands trembled and tears ran down her cheeks, time rolled backwards desperately trying to catch the memories of lost in forever. She unfolded the brittle pages on her mahogany desk. She reached down deep, grasping for all the strength she could muster ...

Christmas Eve, December 24, 1967

My Dear Maggie (My bestest friend),

I received your twelve letters, your gift to me for Christmas and have read one each day as you asked. I have one left to read, and I am prompted, (maybe by that still small voice you always talked about) to make sure I write you before heading out to the bush this time. I wanted to wait until I had read every letter to respond but I know I need to do this.

Each letter has been so perfect. They have been like a salve to caress my wounds each time I return from the fighting. I find it hard to put into words how they make me feel. I have never felt this way before but I sure need to feel that way over here.

I needed to know that someone like you cared. You said so often that I was capable of using both sides of my brain, which, according to you, is rather rare in a man. I don't know about that but I feel like I may be only using one side over here. That is until I think of you, Maggie.

Maggie stopped in a futile attempt to compose herself. She heard the door to her office creak, as Molly opened it and peered in, not knowing what to expect.

"I'm fine Molly. Please hold everything for awhile."

"Everything?"

"Yes, everything and please let me have my peace. I will be fine."

As I write this we are heading out on an operation I don't feel good about. I needed to talk with you, so this is it; you're not here thank God, so this letter must do.

I just realized ... he didn't read my last letter. He hasn't read how I really feel about him. My God this is really happening ... after over two decades of pain the sands of time are talking to me like it was yesterday.

Maggie reached in her drawer and pulled out an embroidered handkerchief that Clayton had given to her the first Christmas they had met. She used these only for occasional colds, she was never sick and she never cried. She gave that up years ago. But today was different as the past launched an avalanche that overwhelmed the present.

I find myself at a difficult time. Ready to go to war but wanting to write of peace. Living in a place of hatred and wanting to write of love. Smothered by lies and deceit and wanting to write about truth. Living in the here and now but wanting to write about forever and you.

In a few minutes we're leaving for a stinking jungle hell but all I can think of is that precious moment I cherish at the Well House when we first met. Me ... Clayton Wesley Riggs, pig farmer extraordinaire and you ... the beautiful, sophisticated girl from the big city.

I was the kid from Hope who once thought of being the mascot for the high school basketball team. Remember me telling you about that? I just wanted to have some fun. Good thing I graduated before the new high school opened.

I chose to play the game instead and felt the thrill of Hoosier Hysteria with each and every dribble, with each pass, with each drive to the hoop. I wish you could have been there Maggie. It was such a high.

I always wondered why someone like you who had everything and probably anyone yet you found me. You chose to sketch me and I have been with you ever since. After all, I was just sitting there on a stone bench looking lost like most freshmen at the great Indiana U.

I sit here in the monsoon. It's been raining since I got here but right now I remember the autumn leaves, radiant and dripping with color in the October sun.

Your first words captivated me but I couldn't say it, not me, the unsure kid from Hope. I'd never had a girl friend to talk with and, yet, from that very first moment we never stopped talking, did we?

You, Maggie O'Reilly, with the strawberry blonde hair, magnetic smile, the eyes that glistened with a zest for life and you wanted to be friends with me? It shouldn't have happened but it did and I'm so glad.

Maggie, I feel as though we lived a whole lifetime in just a few short months. We talked and talked and experienced so much in such a short period of time. We were so very different, our families were different, our expectations of life were different ... yet we're so very much the same and that's what makes us strong.

If you ever reflect and want to know what your "Clay" is thinking ... I wanted to make it clear right now; something is telling me to let you know how I feel about you. Sorry, I guess being a Marine and being in these life and death situations everyday has made me have a sense of urgency about my reality.

I don't have much time to write and I am hopeful that I will finish and have time to read your last letter before we move out. I have an eerie feeling about this one. I don't know what the "truth" will be Maggie but I want you to know "my" truth.

On the one hand I have this warm feeling like "tell her how you feel now and everything will be okay;' and on the other hand I feel like this is it, this is the one with my name on it."

We go to the bush, the jungle, and it stinks; it's musty smelling like old sweaty, wet socks. It's dark, really black out. It's the monsoon. The only time I feel good is the rare time when the moon comes out at night. It's so dark and then when it comes out it's so bright. One night it was a full moon and everything was shiny like the night we were together at the Well House at I.U.

Maggie sat back in her high back executive chair she'd gotten from Beverly for her birthday. She took a deep breath and it was as if Clay was there with her. Clayton Wesley Riggs was talking to her once again. He took the time to tell her about his feelings, about his hopes and his fears and about the last chance he had to pass on forever.

I think about our friendship. What is friendship, Maggie? True friendship is a pearl of great price, a gem of eternal value. Once you possess it, you must treat it with great reverence. Friendship isn't confined by time and doesn't lend itself to foolish definitions. It's a life force that bonds two spirits heart to heart and hip-to-hip.

We're true friends Maggie O'Reilly. I want you to know that no matter what happens over here we really are true friends. We're friends who met at 11 one night at the Pizzaria on Kirkwood for a short chat that lasted for over three hours or how about the time we sat at the Big Wheel

Restaurant and enjoyed and shared one of their famous tenderloin sandwiches.

I sure wish I had one of those tenderloins about now. I sure wish I were there with you to get it. Maggie, I'm afraid. I'm afraid of dying and I'm afraid of losing you. You're my safe harbor in the storms of life and I have a big storm on the horizon. I am worried Maggie, really worried.

Maggie, you are my safe harbor. When I see my buddies, some of whom I've been with for just a little over twenty-four hours being carried away in body bags I retreat into the only safe place that I know, the harbor of your arms and your sweet smile. You're here listening, comforting me whether you know it or not. Maggie, you are, as you said many times, my very "bestest" friend.

As my "bestest" friend, it's time I share my inner most feelings with you. I don't do this well but I feel I must. My time is short and we'll be saddling up in a few minutes. Heading out deep into what they call the DMZ. It means Demilitarized Zone. Now that's something huh? Going out to fight in the Demilitarized Zone.

I just have a feeling, like you used to tell me about. I have a feeling and I want you to get this letter. So I am asking this guy, Moto, you would hate him, to mail this letter for me.

Why would you hate him? He is everything you stand against. He loves this stuff. I don't even know his real name. They call him Moto, everyone goes by nicknames in the military, and mine is Riggsy.

But Maggie he is something else. He is a fireplug of a guy, short, built like a wrestler and meaner than a snake. All he'd have to do is shave his head and he would be right out of a horror movie.

Why have him mail it? Because he is so mean he wont die out there, he'll come back ... I don't know why Maggie and I don't want to worry you but something is telling me to give it to him, so I am. You know what's funny?

He doesn't even like me. He's a miserable guy, already balding with a gravel voice and steely eyes.

Maggie O'Reilly sat straight up in her chair. Her heavy heart was lightened. A warm breeze swept across her tear soaked face. She didn't need to look around for an open door or to see if the heater vent was blowing … she knew Clayton Wesley Riggs was speaking to her. She knew forever was just fine.

The guys Homer talked about so long ago ... they had the letter ... they tried to deliver it. Pat downstairs, he met Moto. He's here in Chicago. Moto might not have liked you Clayton Wesley Riggs ... Riggsy, but he kept his word. He was faithful to the end.

Maggie got to her feet, took her coat off and realized she'd been in her office for over an hour. She straightened her hair and walked to the door, opening it and calling to Molly.

"Molly … make me reservations for Cozumel. Leaving today, this evening … coming home Christmas Eve. My usual place."

"But you have plans Midge … you're going to Beverly's for Christmas."

Molly knew the intimate details of Ms. Madigan's schedule.

"Midge, pardon me for asking … but are you okay?"

"My dear friend … I'm better than I've been since December 24, 1967."

Maggie bounded back into her office leaving her associate and friend standing, mouth wide and dumbfounded. Maggie O'Reilly had a spring in her step she hadn't felt in over two decades. She sat back down and picked up her letter and began where she left off.

Anyway Maggie, that's what's happening here in hell. I would give anything right now to hear your sweet voice, smell your radiant perfume and have you welcome me home. I have such a need to protect you and keep you safe. I have to be honest ... I want us to grow old together.

He really did love me. We really were meant to be. After all these years I knew I was right. I knew he loved me.

Maggie's red eyes began to flow again but this time they were tears of happiness and love. Tears of love that came raining down after a lifetime of wondering, wondering where truth might lay and if the man of her dreams loved her.

I became a better man because of you. I found myself in you, Maggie. I know when I danced each slow dance with you at the President's Christmas Ball, my heart, my mind, my eyes were totally focused on only you. As I held you close to me and smelled the apple blossoms in your hair and felt the warmth and tenderness of your body next to mine I felt stirrings within me that I had never before experienced. You're my Princess, my Cinderella and my Everything. Reading each of your letters gave me the 'why' to endure any 'how' that life brings. I can't explain that any better but I feel it deep inside.

I think of the stone wall next to Beck Chapel overlooking the Jordan River where we stood facing each other in the autumn rain and I wanted so much to hold you in my arms and kiss you. But I was afraid that if I did the magic of our friendship might disappear.

Maggie, what I'm trying to say is that I want to be with you forever. I love you, Maggie O'Reilly. I love you for everything that makes you, you. I love you unconditionally and there are no strings attached.

Maggie began to sob uncontrollably. The man of her dreams had spoken from the grave and he loved her. He loved her just as she thought all this time.

I know no matter what happens, we've experienced what few people ever will in this life. Maggie, it's selfish of me to think that you have the same feelings as I do. I don't know if you do or not but I know I will always cherish the special friendship we have. I know that friendship is love and I know that love must be the elusive truth we so talked about finding.

Maggie, please forgive me for leaving you as I did. In my search for truth it brought me to the Marines and to this place called Vietnam. As I leave to do some more of something I don't understand I do so knowing at last that I have told you of my love.

Let me close and be on my way; it's time. I will read your last letter now. Let me say, "What is truth, Maggie?"

I think of the differences between you and me and our beliefs. I think of your family and their dedication to peace and avoiding war at all costs. Then I think of my family and their willingness, almost eagerness to be "true" Americans and go to war at any time.

Are the Riggs's right with our heritage of Marines, warriors fighting with guns and knives for truth and right in America? Or are the O'Reilly's right in their heritage of fighting for truth and right "in America" by marching in the streets and doing no harm to anyone more than making them mad?

Are the NVA right for wanting to kill us for being in their country or are we right for killing them for exploiting the weak and oppressing the poor and believing in Communism while we are sure that freedom and liberty is right?

In the midst of the carnage we know as daily life in a combat zone, I have learned what truth is Maggie O'Reilly. Truth is that none of this matters. All the differences we have as human beings are what make life valuable.

Somehow, some way this all comes together out there somewhere in time. I'm not sure what I know about religion but I do know this, Maggie O'Reilly; I know the truth is that we can never let our differences get in the way of the fact that we love each other.

I love you Maggie O'Reilly ... I love you forever.

Clay

Maggie O'Reilly laid her head down on the big desk she worked so hard to drive. She turned her head to the side, held the letter from Clayton Wesley Riggs to her heart and cried twenty-five years worth of tears.

44

December 24, 1992
In the air – Flying home from Cozumel

"Ms. Madigan, can I get you anything? This will be the last chance as we're going to button up. We're heading into Indianapolis."

"No thanks, I'm just fine. Best I've been in years." Maggie was at peace for the first time in twenty-five years since she first learned of the death of Clayton Wesley Riggs.

It would be nearly ten o'clock when they landed at the Indianapolis Airport. Maggie called Molly on Tuesday and had her flight routed through Indianapolis. She would drive on to Chicago. Her time on the beach restored a long lost peace … almost. She knew there was one more stop to heal the wound that had festered in her heart for a lifetime.

"I think I'll just lay back … and enjoy what's left of the flight."

Maggie nudged the flight attendant, letting her know she wanted some private time.

In first class seat 1-A sat Margaret Erin O'Reilly. She reached up and turned off the reading lamp, pushed the quarter sized silver button on the inside of her armrest and laid back, closing her eyes. First class seat 1-A … now that sounded special, there was nothing too good for her and Clay.

Maggie rarely flew first class, and never on the Trib's money, but this trip was special and she was paying for this one. The letter, oh that special letter arriving direct from a time gone by made her entire life.

Wherever you are my "bestest" friend ... I know you had help in getting my letter delivered.

She'd spent the last four days reliving the past twenty-five years. With time on her side and one more stop left to close a long chapter in the book of her life, Maggie wanted to relish her gift and relive it all one more time.

I'm so grateful I've had someone like Clay in my life. I'm so saddened that his friend died on the streets after delivering my letter.

Pat felt so bad when he had to tell me that. A man just like Clay, a Marine, a human being dying under a bridge, nameless to the world. I know Clay said you were a bad person but ... well ... Moto ... I love you. I know you did this very well.

Maggie cried her way from O'Hare all the way to Cozumel and all night her first night in the luxury suite she rented to bury her past. She was overwhelmed with a mixture of tears of joy for knowing how much the man she loved had loved her as she nearly drowned in her tears, tears of sorrow knowing the incredible circumstances he'd endured with the killing going on all around him in the short time he was in the Vietnam War.

I feel so bad for Moto. Surviving the hell of Vietnam, having people not like him and then dying on the streets of Chicago and having no one to know you're gone. Life can be so tragic. I can't quit thinking about him.

Yet this incredible man somehow, someway, for some reason ... this incredible man brought this beautiful piece of our past to me, someone he never met and didn't know.

What a story? What a tribute to the human spirit that Clay and I talked about so very much. Oh God how I wish I could pay tribute to this great man and let the world know what he has done for me ... for us Clay. But who would care besides me? That is the tragedy of Vietnam.

Maggie had been traveling to Cozumel since before she could remember. She and Beverly had grown up spending winter holidays running on the white sandy beaches of Mexico. Mom and Dad O'Reilly loved the tradition of Christmas so the family often found themselves in exotic places. The girls always had anything they needed and most everything they ever wanted. Christmas was a time to open presents and jet off to the warm weather down south.

I love the beaches ... I had to get to the one place that represented peace to me. It's easy to be alone on a beach on Christmas and I needed to be alone. I needed to come to grips with my past and resolve everything before going to Beverly's. Her kids deserve a "merry" Christmas and not having Aunt Maggie depressed about a twenty-five-year old problem that won't go away.

Maggie couldn't remember if she'd ever been to her "special" place alone before. She and Beverly once found a secluded lagoon about an hour's walk from the hotel. They pretended it was their "special place" and would play for hours while the parents played tennis and were lost spending time with their own friends.

Christmas? It was a time to spend with your sister. That is until I met Clay. It was his special time of year ... Christmas Eve. At first I couldn't imagine he was serious about it ... but he was. It was so special to him; his favorite day of the year he often told me.

I loved that man. I wanted to spend my life with him. I realized in Cozumel, on our "special" beach, alone for nearly twenty-four hours ... he is still with me. He has been with me since I saw him off at the airport way back in 1967. He is here now flying first class. I love you Clayton Wesley Riggs. I will love you forever.

"This is your Captain speaking. We are about 30 minutes out of Indianapolis. I'm turning on the "fasten seat belt" signs and would ask that the flight Attendants to prepare the cabin for arrival."

Oh ... I don't want this to end. I am not sure if I'm ready for my last visit to the Well House! I don't know if I can ever give it up. I know I will always live my life with Clay close by, exactly as he's been for twenty-five years. I'm so sorry I didn't recognize it. Clay you are mine, and I won't let you go this time.

Maggie sat up, pushed the seat button again and brought her seat straight up, in the official, uncomfortable position. She reached up and turned on her overhead light.

I've got time. I've got to read his letter one more time. Then I have to read mine, my letter to him. I know he knows ... he knows how I feel but I needed to express it.

She reached under the seat in front of her, pulling the briefcase size purse from its safe position. She realized looking at the huge purse, that she hadn't changed much since her days at I.U. Smiling to herself knowing what Clay would say, she reached inside.

Clay would really laugh if he were sitting next to me now. He always made fun of me for the bags I carried back then ... this one's bigger. Oh how I wish he were here to see it.

Maggie carefully opened the brown, manila folio where she'd placed the most significant part of her past she'd ever recovered. Inside were both the letter Moto delivered to her just four days ago and the letter that sealed the truth of Clay's love for the young student he had met near the Well House at IU.

I have to savor these words one, more, time. I have to read every word one, more, time. Then, then I will keep my commitment to me. I will keep the commitment I made at my special place where all commitments must be kept. I will not open it again for one year ... and only once per year on Christmas Eve.

Maggie drank every word of his precious letter like she'd just spent the last week in a parched desert devoid of any moisture. She realized she'd spent the last twenty-five years suffering from a thirst for her true love. She savored every word like it was the last she'd ever read in her still young life.

I've become a better man because of you.

I want us to grow old together.

Your letters gave me the 'why' to endure any 'how.

Her mind collected sentences lined with gold and silver, words pieced together by a special man she'd never see again, a special man who touched her forever and gave the gift she held in her trembling hands.

I wanted so much to hold you in my arms and kiss you.

Maggie thought of the times they talked of the legend of the Well House where a girl would become a co-ed only when she would feel her true love's kiss on her lips at the stroke of midnight. A kiss they were never able to feel, enjoy or savor.

I want to be with you forever.

Forever?

Oh my ... forever? What is forever my dear Clay? What is forever? Is it what I feel right now? Is it you and I even though we're not really together? Is it what I feel glowing inside right now? Oh my!

Tears rolled down Maggie's cheeks like the monsoon rains her love endured for days on end. They were tears of hope for the love that came into her life from Hope, an unlikely little place for so much happiness. It was a little place where people still saw the good in one another and took care of their own.

We can never let our differences get in the way of the fact that we love each other.

Maggie sat staring out a window into the black of night. The pilot had just announced a slight delay in landing. He explained that heavy traffic in the air due to some weather diversions from O'Hare would delay their arrival by fifteen more minutes.

Oh good ... I can read my other letter. I need to read it now, before I get to the Well House.

She took the folio from the empty seat next to her, 1-B, glad that she was alone, after all it was Christmas Eve and who else would be traveling but a woman in love? As she removed the letter she had written in Mexico she thought of her imminent drive. The drive to Bloomington was a little over an hour. Perfect. She'd get there just before midnight and surely be alone.

Clayton's letter safe back inside her folio, she was ready to read her own words, the words in the copy she'd made of her letter … the one she'd written and sent out to sea in the Gulf of Mexico.

I can't believe I did this but something told me I had to let him know. I really thought about writing it and dropping it at the Wall in DC, like so many others but ... that represents death to me. I celebrate life. I celebrate Clayton Wesley Riggs.

On her last day in Cozumel, walking the beach alone, the same beach she'd walked and shared with Beverly her whole life, Maggie O'Reilly was touched with a feeling to let Clay know she understood.

She wasn't one to do 'crazy' or 'off the wall' things; after all she was an O'Reilly. But that day, the breeze, the warm breeze she felt … she knew what it meant.

I still can't believe I wrote this and dropped it out to sea. I can't believe it but I did and I am glad I did it. I could hear Mother, God rest her soul, telling me how foolish I am but I don't care. I know what I know.

December 24, 1992
Cozumel, Mexico

My Bestest Friend Clayton:

I love you more than life. I know you know where I am. I can feel your presence in the warm breeze that always accompanies my thoughts of you ... Your friend Moto ... and he is your friend ... died delivering your most precious letter to me.

I don't know where you are but I know you live. I don't know when I will see you but I know one day I will. I now know it is you who have comforted me all these years.

My Dear Clayton, we haven't been together for twenty-five years yet I know we've never been apart. What we both wanted we somehow got.

You remember Richard, the man my parents were sure I should marry? Well, when you didn't come home and time went on we dated and nearly married. I didn't know why but I went right up to the end and couldn't do it.

When your letter arrived, twenty-five years to the month later, I finally knew why something inside me wouldn't let me do it. I am already with someone ... you Clayton.

I came to Cozumel, my peaceful place and am leaving now for home. I'm stopping in Indianapolis so I can go to the Well House. It will be just you and me.

I'm driving down to make it official and let you know everything is okay. I will never "marry" Clay because I'm married to you and always have been. I am fine now. I know you love me.

I just wanted to go to "our" special place one more time. I wanted to stand at the drinking fountain and imagine the kiss we never had. I know you'll be there in spirit because I can feel it now.

So my dear, until we meet again in a place neither of us can imagine. Until we can get to the truth you so eloquently wrote of ... the truth that says we can never let our differences get in the way of the fact we love each other ... until then I do love and miss you my "bestest" friend ...

You take care and know this ...

I love you, forever.

Maggie

Maggie was jerked to the ground with the rest of the handful of Christmas Eve passengers. Reality landed as the tires screeched and the United Airlines 707 came back to earth at the Indianapolis International Airport. The plane was only half full and it emptied quicker than Maggie expected. She hurried to get her things together, careful not to crinkle the fresh copies of her message in a bottle.

As afraid of boats as I am and the people who run them down there I can't believe I took that charter this morning and dropped his message overboard.

Beverly wouldn't believe it either. I won't be able to share any of this with her, or anyone else for that matter. What Clay and I have is special. Maybe it's for the next life or for a time and place I don't yet understand?

The Well House ... I must get to the Well House.

45

December 24, 1992
Christmas Eve

Indianapolis International Airport

Maggie rushed off the plane and was surprised with the ease which she cleared customs. Maybe it was the Christmas spirit, she didn't know but wasn't complaining. She hurried to the rental car area and was surprised to find she was the lone renter at the Avis counter.

The agent, a man who looked like he didn't mind being there, was ready and made the process as painless as it could be. Bags in tow, car keys in hand, Maggie stepped outside and hit a wall of cold. It was like walking into a freezer. The temperature was nearing the single digits and it was Chicago cold. Maggie O'Reilly was on a mission. She was a Chicago girl and she wouldn't be denied this night regardless of what the obstacles became.

She pulled the Buick Regal out of the rental lot, following the signs and climbed onto I-465 heading south to her final stop on the way to closing a twenty five year gaping wound that wouldn't heal. Perhaps she had the cure in hand.

Oh my ... am I doing the right thing? What would Beverly say?

The traffic was light, most were now with loved ones, and the neighborhoods were lit with bright lights, the lights of Christmas and of love. Inside the festive houses, families enjoyed the season. Children were sure to be tucked away, waiting the arrival of Santa Claus and all the joy of tomorrow morning, Christmas Day, when Santa would do his magic. Maggie O'Reilly drove south to the place where it all began.

I have to do this ... for me ... for Clay ... for us. Is there an us? No one would believe there is. But I know different. This is different and differences won't get in the way of the fact we love each other. They won't. Clay said it and it wouldn't!

Maggie drove on I-465 and headed south on US 37 and as she did, her heart began climbing slowly into her throat.

This is it. I'm really doing this. I'm going back to Bloomington. It's been years. I'm going back to our place. I'm going back and close the wound that has haunted me for decades and leave, knowing he loved me; knowing that it really is time to put it behind me and move on. Beverly ... you're right.

With "Silent Night" playing on the rear speakers in the background, Maggie exited 37 and headed into Bloomington. Her daydreaming made the trip fly by as she soaked in the familiar feel of her old hometown. The I.U. Campus "was" Bloomington. But as big as it was and all the growth people talked about it wasn't visible tonight. The streets were vacant.

Christmas Eve in Bloomington was time to go home with your loved ones, not go for a walk and ferret out your past. Maggie didn't come to confront her past this joyous night; it was her future she sought so desperately to discover.

She pulled the Avis Buick up Indiana Avenue and parked in front of the Gables. Her heart pounded like she'd just run the hundred-yard dash. The trees on the west side stood naked, but for traces of snow that began to line the skinny limbs that were draped with white lights signifying the Christmas season.

Oh God give me strength. I have to do this and you haven't failed me yet. God be with me please.

Maggie opened her purse and pulled out her Marshall Fields' leather gloves Molly had given her as an early present. Somehow Molly anticipated everything.

Okay God ... this is it. Clay, here I come.

She opened the Buick door to a creak that echoed in the cold up and down the empty street. She was alone, scared, and happy no one was there to see her. Always safe, she looked both ways and crossed the street heading for the archway at the end of Kirkwood Avenue.

I can't believe I'm standing here. It's been like, forever.

She looked up Kirkwood and briefly thought of all the times she and Clay had walked amongst the throng of students pressing onto the narrow sidewalks and bulging out of all the action spots that called Kirkwood home.

Well, don't just stand here under the arch girl ... it's time Maggie O'Reilly. You need the courage of a Marine to do this ... God, again, be with me.

Maggie turned, looked up at the archway that held so much history for so many and took a step forward. The trees lining the walkway were like dark cut outs, silhouetted by a lightening sky.

Oh the times Clay ... the times and the talks ...

Maggie walked towards her target. The Well House at IU, the place where she and her forever love had dreamed and created a forever friendship; where she realized they both secretly believed they would kiss and where both silently hoped upon hope … they would one day marry.

This is it God. I am here. I have to do this. It's okay. No one's here and I have to put this behind me and you can help me God.

Maggie walked along the red brick path towards the original part of campus to the Well House. She stood, took a deep breath, like she could draw in twenty-five years of history in one long breath.

What time is it? Why does it matter? Oh it does ... I want to be here at midnight for Clay's favorite time of year. One last time and I can go on and live my life knowing it would all be worthwhile.

Maggie turned to the left and looked up at the Clock Tower. Squinting in the faint light of a late night, she could barely make out the hands of time hanging on its face.

I can't believe it's a quarter to twelve. It's still Christmas Eve Clay. Your favorite day and I am here at our favorite place, just the two of us.

Maggie turned and walked quickly down the path that led along the woods. Near midnight, walking without her favorite person at her side, the woods looked dark and foreboding. A trace of fear crept in to her as she walked, picking up her pace with a bead on her target.

Oh Clay is this what Vietnam felt like? Dark? Alone? Uncertain? I wish you were here to protect me. Oh ... you are, I know you are.

Maggie hurried up the small incline and reached her destination on the path. She stood in awe. There it was …

Oh my God, I did it. I'm here. Just hours ago I was on the beach, warm, safe and secure in my special place. Now here I am Clay ...

I'm at our special place. I'm here once again. I never thought it possible but here I am.

The journalist from the "Trib" stood still, cold wind dancing around her face as she soaked in the aura that glowed right before her eyes. The lights from the fifteen-foot poles bathed the unique, eight sided Well House in a pale light wash.

Ms. Madigan, Maggie O'Reilly walked slowly towards their special place with the woods to her right. She came up and stood with the Well House on her left. She stared in awe from behind the incredible structure built in 1908 by the grace of Theodore Rose, who gave it on behalf of Beta Theta Pi.

None of that mattered now.

I'm here Clay. I made it just like I said I would.

Maggie stood frozen, not from the early cold, so cold icy sounds cracked the night, but from the history of her vision.

There it is. There is the water fountain where I never got my kiss. I stand here and all I can do is imagine, imagine what it would have been like. I love you Clay. I love you.

She carefully stepped forward, not wanting to slip on the icy film now clinging to the cement sidewalks surrounding the Well House. One step and then another and Maggie made it inside the place where love rang true across the Hoosier campus for thousands of young couples seeking the same truth she sought tonight.

Maggie O'Reilly stood at the water fountain, her altar of forever love. She stood tall and straight like the Marine she longed to touch. She looked out and could see the sidewalk that ran down from the north.

Placing her hands on the cold stone of the fountain, she knelt, her knees resting on the frozen pavement inside the one place she longed to be.

God? I'm not very good at this but it's important.

Maggie's knees ached from the freezing cement as she knelt at the place she'd hope to kiss the man she knew she'd marry. The wind sent chills down the still petite, Clay would say, gorgeous body; the body of the sophisticated city girl he'd been moved to spend all his tomorrow's with until a family tradition of patriotism interrupted their spiritual union; the union that now stretched across a lifetime neither could anticipate.

God I came here to say thank you for letting me know Clay as a person and know that somehow he is okay. I know you sent that man, his friend, the one with that letter. I know you sent him to me after all these years of sorrow and wondering.

I don't know where Clay is. I know you do, and that is your mystery not mine. I just want you to know that I know you are there for each of us. I know you were with Clay and me through all these years and I know it is ours to have faith and not question.

Maggie stopped, listening, the cracking of the night cold picked up its chilling pace and the Lord would need to help her, the cold was winning, not like on the streets of Chicago … but winning by killing a special moment in time that one young lady had dreamed about forever.

God, I am not as good a person as I should be or could be and I don't deserve what you have given me but I love you for being there for me ... for us.

I know these things happen to us for a reason. I know the reasons will somehow be made known to us at some point in time. I just want to ask ... I may not be worthy ... but I must ask for your help.

Maggie stopped … startled by what felt like a warm breeze that spread across the back of her neck. She suddenly seemed to be wrapped in a blanket …

God ... I thank thee. Let my "bestest" friend know that I love him. He gave me the best life a woman can have by being the person he is. I don't know where. I don't know how. But I do know that one day dear God ... you will make it all better. I know that all is well as long as we trust in Thee.

Maggie sat, quiet, kneeling, relaxing, and leaning back to sit on her feet that she had curled up under her. Warm, as if she were sitting there with Clay right next to her in the middle of Indian summer.

The ice cracked shattering the night. It was ten minutes to midnight when the chimes would ring in the clock tower. It was mere moments before Christmas Day, and what better present than the warmth of someone or something the educated girl from the city couldn't explain and must certainly be a gift from the God she was now calling on.

She knelt quietly, taking in the spirit of one special moment that Maggie hoped would usher in a new era of her life. Relaxed, heart no longer racing like a runaway engine, Maggie was about to open her eyes when she heard a sound.

What is it? Ice cracking? What? It's moving.

The noise invaded the serene of Christmas Eve night surprising her. Yet what surprised her more was the calm that arose inside of her. The warmth came back, surrounding her, wrapping her like a mother with her newborn child, protecting them from the evils of a world she couldn't explain.

The sound was clearly someone walking, more than one. Maggie opened her eyes; three figures were silhouetted in the light of the building security lights showering them from behind. The three figures were walking towards the Well House, heading towards her down the sidewalk from the north.

Still on her knees, her eyes just above the edge of the water fountain, Maggie peered at the approaching unknown figures.

What do I do? What are they doing here? How do I get out of here without a scene?

About ten yards in front of the Well House, the sidewalk split with one lane heading straight in towards Maggie, the other leading off to Maggie's left to the circle of benches, that in warmer weather were filled with the sights and sounds of couples in love.

Do I get up? Do I try to sneak out the back and run to my car? The ice ... I can't run. Oh God?

Maggie watched as the three lone figures in the night stopped, they appeared to be talking, looking ...

Are they wearing uniforms? Police. Yes, maybe they're police. Two of the three have hats and are very rigid. One seems to walk different than the others and seems to have a limp.

The hats walked off to the left, towards the benches reserved for those special times on a warm Indiana night. The lone figure, now appearing slim and unsure, a tall shadow really, walked haltingly towards her, displaying a pronounced limp, moving carefully on the ice towards the Well House and Maggie O'Reilly.

What do I do? They'll think ...

Maggie felt a sudden calm, a wisp of warmth, a strange longing, and a fleeting glimpse of times gone by as the dark figure walked her way. She quietly stood, bathed in the light of the Well House and the now star filled night of Christmas Eve. The skies had cleared and the entire area had a silvery glow.

Why do I feel the way I do? Why am I so calm, warm and tingly? Why am I not scared with a strange figure approaching in the night? This is not like me at all to be brave at a time like this.

The hands of the clock tower inched their way, carefully creeping to the hour of midnight when the clock would strike, ushering in the day we know as Christmas. Maggie stood, frozen in a world where nothing seemed real. Snowflakes fell from the heavens like lacy curtains, yet they seemed to be falling from a crystal clear sky.

Is this a dream? Am I in a fairy tale? Am I imagining all of this? Why do I feel so warm and so full of peace? I do not know. When I awake maybe I am really still in Cozumel? Or maybe I didn't stop here and am dreaming in my apartment in Chicago? That must be it. Oh God is that it? I am dreaming ... right?

Within seconds the chimes on the Clock Tower would ring loudly proclaiming to the world that yet another day had ended and a precious new one was now to begin. On this day the world celebrated the birth of a Savior, God's only Son.

Like Odysseus home from the Trojan Wars, the lone figure in the night, a warrior home from battle, walked slowly forward and stepped into the Well House where Maggie O'Reilly stood. Her mind was instantly racing back to the dream she experienced at "The Wall." The dream where she stood at a place where spirits meet, a place where we meet God and know that God is Love, Love is Truth and Truth goes on forever.

The two figures stood tall, peacefully peering across time and a stand of stone known in the world as the fountain, neither knowing if they were earthly beings on a spiritual journey or spiritual beings standing on earth.

Oh my God ... please help me know what to do, I am lost in time.

Their eyes met and she could see in the dim light of the Well House and knew that it was he, her knight in shining armor, her Sir Walter Raleigh, her Clayton returning from the dead to stand alone and alive where they always dreamed they would be.

In one singular moment, Maggie's life appeared before her eyes as one eternal round. She was lifted on the wings of time to one special October day, a day long ago when the autumn leaves melted like crayons in the hot sun, blending into a Technicolor carousel of delight that warmed her heart like the day she met the one person who would forever change her life.

She stood, suspended between time and eternity, her eyes overflowing with years of love, as tears washed down her now rosy cheeks, flowing with hope from beautiful eyes, eyes ripe with anticipation.

Maggie brimmed with pure inspiration that came from a source she knew only as God. She slowly stretched her delicate hands across the fountain, the symbol of love lost and gained, hoping upon hope she would be touched in return by the hands of a lone figure in the night, hands at one time, she knew so well.

The silence that had spanned eternity was broken seconds before the day would be changed by the sound so many waited for on this special night. It was a night where the sound of the chimes of the Clock Tower rang true.

"Clayton?" Maggie spoke with hushed words, words of faith and hope, words filled with a quiet love that linked generations, praying to her God as she had never prayed before that this dream would not end.

Oh God what am I doing?

Maggie's words had barely stepped from her lips when the hands of the Clock Tower came together at the exact stroke of midnight as they have faithfully done for decades. The chimes spoke their melodious tones and rang out declaring peace in a troubled world. Christmas Day on the campus of Indiana University had now begun as it had for many a day but this day would be like no other.

"Merry Christmas, Maggie Erin O'Reilly."

Hands that had not met in two and one half decades touched a mere foot above the fountain of their dreams. Two figures in the night, standing in the Well House of their hopes and desires, leaned forward as if they had each received a gentle nudge, a nudge from the God who sustained them through the ages, and their lips met for the first time.

Love radiated through their bodies, bodies joined in an eternal circle of love after a lifetime of separation. Their mouths parted and in that first kiss they both knew that their love was complete and their friendship and love were sealed forever. Their pain and loneliness was washed away by the melody of chimes Bloomington knew so well.

The stars shone brighter that night, the air was sweeter, and a warm breeze gently touched the branches of the trees around the Well House. The branches, like violins, played a long forgotten melody, a melody of love, and a melody of happiness, of hope and of joy, a “Stardust Melody.”

46

December 25, 1992
Christmas Morning – WUSH TV
Indianapolis, IN

"Good Morning Indiana and Merry Christmas!"

The voice that Indiana was waking up to was that of Jen Lorenz, the Anchor of the local WUSH Morning News.

"And a Merry Christmas it is … at least for one former Marine … and we hear perhaps his long lost lady."

The second voice was that of Morning News Co-Anchor, Zach Benedum.

"The **Breaking News** of this Christmas Day is guaranteed to crack the hearts of even the most hardened 'bah humbug' types out there."

"Zack is referring to the biggest news of the year and it's right here in Indianapolis. We don't have many details but here's what we do have. The White House announced in a press conference just this morning that a POW has been recovered and returned from the Vietnam War! That's right … a prisoner of war has been returned!"

Jen Lorenz, usually professional and subdued was ecstatic like the rest of America. She couldn't control her enthusiasm this Christmas Day.

"All we know at this point Indiana is … Merry Christmas he's a Hoosier!"

Benedum, an IU grad himself, couldn't resist pumping up the Hoosier audience and anyone else that might be listening.

"The man recovered is identified as Clayton Wesley Riggs, a Marine from Hope, Indiana who was reportedly killed in a battle at Con Thien twenty-five years ago today!"

The two Anchors were grinning ear to ear as if they had made the recovery themselves. Lorenz started to fill in the holes in the story with the information available as the stations phones began ringing off the hook.

"What we know at this point is that he was discovered in a small village in Laos by a U.S. team searching for MIA's. People who didn't know the war was over and just kept him as a prisoner were apparently holding Riggs.

One report we have is saying that he was noticed by a member of the U.S. search team who himself was a former Marine and Vietnam Veteran. Early reports are saying his name is Carlos Vance."

Benedum broke in to make a point of clarity for many skeptic listeners.

"Before you say, 'Hey, Zack that can't be true' … don't forget the Japanese guy who came out of the jungle after World War II and it was 40 years later. Riggs has only been there twenty-five years. Welcome home Clayton!"

Lorenz picked up, clearly elated with the report.

"They're reporting that he's been in US hands for three months, presumably under going debriefing and the expected physical tests after two and a half decades in the jungle. It's reported he's in remarkable condition considering all he's been through.

But Hoosiers, get this … his first request last night on the way to the White House and freedom … to stop by Indiana University, his alma mater and visit the Well House."

It is reported that two U. S. Marine escorts 'quietly' took him to Bloomington around midnight and let him spend time at his "special" place, the Well House at IU."

Lorenz turned to her co-host, Zack Benedum for the exciting end of this remarkable story. It was a story that would resonate with every Hoosier north to south and east to west, and create a legend for the ages that would forever have its place at IU.

Benedum smiled and began to close the Morning News.

"There is one, as yet, unconfirmed report of a lady being at the Well House at the same time as our returning POW. The White House has not responded to this report. We hope to have more on that as the day goes on."

"For WUSH – TV and my co-host Jen Lorenz, this is Zack Benedum and we … well … as I end this broadcast I have to say … Hoosiers, is if you don't believe in Santa Claus after hearing this story … shame on you, there's no hope."

Merry Christmas Indiana and Merry Christmas Clayton Wesley Riggs … we look forward to being there when the young man from Hope, who now certainly gives us all hope, returns to our great state and his great town to the hero's welcome he deserves.

Merry Christmas and Good Morning!"

Epilogue

April 30, 1993
Hope, Indiana

"Riggs Homestead"

Dear Beverly,

It is near midnight on a day eighteen years ago when Saigon fell to the communists. I can't tell you how my life has changed since the "miracle" of Christmas Eve. It is all so unbelievable and neither of us would ever imagine life after the war and all.

Clay is doing well, all things considered, and has not lost his sense of humor; bless him, even if his laughter is more rare than it could be. So, of course, I indulge him and tease him, too, whenever I get the chance. He's getting used to it.

I informed him that an average person gets about fifteen laughs a day, and we have to fill his quota from the years when he didn't get any. He looked at me with a soft smile and said that means, "I'm never going to cry again." It almost broke my heart. So he's making progress in this area—gaining weight too along with laugh quotas.

Clay says very little about his experience in Vietnam, though he did talk about the varieties of fowl those farmers keep. It seems in the last few years anyway he was working on the land there as well, and though I imagine much worse, I try not to think about it. That was then, and this is now, as they say. Onward and upward!

Clay has deep scars along his arms and back and I traced them with my fingers once, hoping he might open up and talk about it. I think he needs to talk to someone, but he refuses to go to the Veteran's Administration to meet up with other vets or apply for services. He says little.

Beth reminded him it was his right, and he should take what is due to him. But after finding out how poorly the vets are treated he was discouraged all over again. He knows all about the homeless on the streets of Chicago and everywhere else and the statistics on how many of these people served their country in the war and how little the government seems to care. Their benefits are being taken away from them as every year passes, by the very guys who are waving all the flags. Disgraceful.

I did learn that he was held in Laos all of his captivity. He was moved about the mountains on different occasions but was mostly held in one area or community. He said in the early years the conditions were difficult but I get no details.

He did say that when the U.S. Search Team came in to the village the first time they hurried him into hiding and made sure he stayed quiet. He said that after they left was a time when his spirits were most challenged in all those years.

When they returned a couple weeks later the village Chief was gone and the others didn't think to usher him out and make him hide. So he stayed in plain site and worked in the garden when one of the Americans came over and challenged him. He was afraid but finally broke into tears and they knew.

I don't know much more, he keeps me with bits and pieces and you know me, I methodically go when he is asleep and write notes, a little map of my own to piece together our decades apart.

The one strange part at this stage is that one of the Americans was apparently a former Marine Officer that he knew in Vietnam. As far as Clay has felt comfortable sharing, I guess the poor fellow had a breakdown and Clay nearly does too when he feels to talk about it, which is rare.

When we go to pick up movies to watch in evenings he avoids war stories, along with the violent ones. We do a lot of comedies, documentaries, biographies, and histories that deal with something other than humans' inhumanity to humans. It leaves little to watch at times. TV Sitcoms are okay but he doesn't like the tube much for the ads and depressing news and its general noise. Almost like too much too soon.

He is no longer innocent, but he still has a great deal of compassion and a purity of sorts deep inside that will never go away. We listen to a lot of music, the whole range. I have been serving as official history teacher, trying to catch him up on what has happened since he left. There is so much it's hard to do.

There's nothing like taking a quarter century sweep of historical events to make you examine your own life and national culture, let alone the state of the world. I'm getting reeducated along with him.

When I told him of the assassinations of Robert Kennedy, Martin Luther King and John Lennon tears filled his eyes and he simply said, "when will the killing stop and the living begin?"

At the Well House, he asked about the General and his posterity and I told him about the new General in town, Robert Montgomery Knight and the Hoosiers winning three national championships. He was s-o-o-o proud.

We talk little of current politics, and I don't think he's registered to vote (we'll get to that later in the season). When he saw an old clip of Dukakis running around in the jeep wearing an army helmet he just about got sick, and who can blame him for that.

He's encouraging me to write more poetry, and I regularly leave little love poems under his pillow. He's starting to write them back, too. Very heady stuff, writing love notes to someone you live with but not sleep with. Not yet. But neither of us is in a hurry.

As you know, romance is strongest in your youth it seems, and we flirt like teenagers. It's fun. For my birthday he made me a great card with a note about how hot I am for being a January baby, calling me his own personal space heater.

And for Valentine's Day he took me back to 'our' place ... the Well House. We weren't able to have the picnic we so enjoy but he did surprise me more than you can imagine with ... you guessed it, a diamond ring. Talk about sweet!

When he put it on my finger he apologized for only getting one—since he once put five on my hand years back at a jewelry store in Bloomington. I wear it with pride and am anxious for our future.

Twenty-five years ago! I can't believe it? Clayton chose our anniversary for our wedding date, the day when we first met at the Well House. So you must put October 17th on your calendar! We'll be making arrangements for the ceremony and reception soon. You MUST make sure Ben and the kids come. Make sure you book early. The hotels fill up fast in leaf season, and they'll be at their peak.

We do take one day at a time. After being away for so many years, returning to his true love isn't without its challenges. We are the same but so many other things have changed.

Our relationship has not changed much at all. Some dreams we might have had when we were kids are out of reach, but these are surprisingly few. In the rhythms of our daily life, as in many things, we are very compatible, for we both love the quiet of the countryside and our simple lifestyle.

My heart still pounds like crazy whenever I even as much as think of him, I'm so in love. I never stopped loving him, but this is different. And I don't mean to say I told you so (even though you know I can't resist) but I was right, wasn't I? (As was old Grandmother.) He *was there all along waiting to come home to me. I just knew it.*

He told me that thinking of his home and farm and Bloomington and me and his family is what kept him sane. He said he always kept Hope in his heart, and faith in his actions. He told me my letters kept his faith alive and because of them he was able to survive the early years that were the most difficult.

Well, it's getting late now. I will write when I can but remember I love you and the family. I am happy Sis ... in my dreams this was not possible but God has brought the love of my life home.

We have many difficult times ahead as you can imagine. Clay spends most of his time on the farm in an effort to get in touch with his past and as he says, "then I'll decide about my future." I am okay with that, you know. I love him and I will love him forever.

We will see you in October. I can't wait to show you the Well House, the magic spot that brought Clayton and me together and kept us bound by a golden thread that war and death and distance and decades could not deny or break. I can only thank hope and heaven for that. Along with a touch of magic and luck of the Irish, or is it simply fate and the power of love with a little "Stardust" mixed in?

Big Sis ... I am getting married!

See you on my special day!

Your Maggie

About The Authors

Mark Van Voorhis and Ed Kugler have been friends for nearly three decades. They came together to write a blockbuster of a book. Ed and Mark are friends with a difference. Ed is a former Marine sniper and Mark is a romantic and a present day Walter Mitty. Together they have created a dynamite read.

Ed is the author of four previous books, a speaker and consultant. He helps people and organizations to change and reach their goals. He and his wife Gloria have been married for thirty-five years. They have three children and two grandchildren.

Mark is a graduate of Indiana University with an undergraduate degree in history and a Masters degree in Secondary Education. He and his wife Joannie have been married for thirty-four years and are the parents of six children and six grandchildren.

Readers can contact the Authors by e-mail with comments at mfvanvoorhis@hotmail.com.

Printed in the United States
35529LVS00009B/1-18